T5-AVO-797

DISCARDED BY

MACPHÁIDÍN LIBRARY

CUSHING-MARTIN LIBRARY
STONEHILL COLLEGE
NORTH EASTON, MASSACHUSETTS 02357

PUBLIC OPINION AND NATIONAL SECURITY IN WESTERN EUROPE

CORNELL STUDIES IN SECURITY AFFAIRS
edited by Robert J. Art and Robert Jervis

Public Opinion and National Security in Western Europe

RICHARD C. EICHENBERG

Cornell University Press

ITHACA

Copyright 1989 by Richard C. Eichenberg

This book was written under the auspices of the Center for International Affairs, Harvard University.

All rights reserved. Except for brief quotations in review, this book, or parts thereof, must not be reproduced in any form without permission in writing from the publisher.

For information, address Cornell University Press
124 Roberts Place
Ithaca, NY 14850

First published 1989 by Cornell University Press.

International Standard Book Number 0–8014–2237–X

Library of Congress Cataloging-in-Publication Data
Eichenberg, Richard C., 1952–
        Public opinion and national security in Western Europe / Richard
C. Eichenberg.
            p. cm. — (Cornell studies in security affairs)
        Bibliography p.
        Includes index.
        ISBN 0–8014–2237–X: $29.95
        1. Europe—National security—Public opinion.   2. Public opinion—
Europe.   3. North Atlantic Treaty Organization—Public opinion.
I. Title. II. Series
UM846.E33 1989
855′ .03304—dc19   88–38906
                                                                     CIP

In memory of
Professor James Baker Donnelly
1929–87

Contents

Contents

List of Tables

List of Figures

Acknowledgements

First things first: without the advice and support of Deborah Shelby Eichenberg, I could not have completed this book. Although the book took four years to research and write, she never asked when (or if) it would be finished. For that, as well as for innumerable words of encouragement, I am very grateful.

The ideas in this book reflect my long collaboration with two friends and colleagues, William K. Domke and Catherine McArdle Kelleher. My research on public opinion and security grew out of our collaborative project on the political economy of defense spending, and in countless meetings and writing sessions they stimulated me to think hard about the issues described here. In addition, they joined in my hunt for every available poll, and they shared research accommodations on two continents. I owe them a great debt, both for their help and for their friendship.

The research and writing of this book was supported by two institutions that have done much to further the study of the domestic politics of European security: the Ford Foundation and the Center for International Affairs at Harvard University. I began writing the manuscript during my year in the Center as a Ford Postdoctoral Fellow in European Society and Western Security. Early versions of several chapters were discussed in the Lunch Group of the Ford Fellows and in the Center's National Security Study Group. The staff of the Center, led by Chet Haskell, Janice Rand, and Mike Tiorano, were unfailingly helpful and cheerful. During my stay in the Center and through my subsequent association with the Ford Program, I enjoyed the counsel of several cohorts of Ford Fellows. I am especially grateful to Alice Cooper, Jeffrey Herf, and Jane Stromseth for long discussions and much advice on the subject of the book. I also owe thanks to the Center's Director, Professor Samuel Huntington, and to Professor Robert Putnam of Harvard, for their support of my research and for making the Center a stimulating and productive environment.

It took three years to accumulate the public opinion data for this book. I could not have succeeded without the help of a number of institutions and individuals. Among those who provided data and gave permission to use it here, I am particularly thankful to: Robert Wybrow and the British Gallup Poll (Social Surveys Ltd); Jan Stapel and the Netherlands Institute for Public Opinion (NIPO); Connie de Boer and the POLLS Archive at the University of Amsterdam; Kenneth Adler and the Office of Research, United States Information Agency; the Press and Information Offices of the Dutch and West German Ministries of Defense; the Inter-University Consortium for Political and Social Research; the US National Archives; and the Steinmetz Archives, Amsterdam. Colleagues who were kind enough to share data from their own research include Ivor Crewe, Oksana Dackiw, Russell Dalton, Wolf-Dieter Eberwein, Philip Everts, John Fenske, Hans Rattinger, Tom Rochon, Gebhard Schweigler, Heinrich Siegmann, and Steve Szabo. Of course, none of these institutions or individuals bear any responsibility for the analyses or interpretations presented here.

I owe a special debt of thanks to Robert Art, who read the entire manuscript and provided detailed suggestions for improving it. My thanks also go to several colleagues who read drafts of chapters and offered helpful suggestions: Paul Allen Beck, Alice Cooper, Russell Dalton, Mary Hampton, Barry Hughes, John Jenke, Paulette Kurzer, Robert Shapiro, Jane Stromseth, Steve Szabo, and Gregory Treverton.

I was fortunate to receive the comments and criticisms of several scholarly groups during the drafting of the manuscript. The initial ideas for Chapter 3 were first discussed in the Visitors' Seminar of the Center for Science and International Affairs at Harvard's John F. Kennedy School of Government. An earlier version of Chapter 4 was presented in the George D. Aiken Lecture Series at the University of Vermont. My overall conclusions benefited from discussion with students and faculty at a colloquium of the School of Public Affairs, University of Maryland.

The friends and colleagues listed above have labored mightily to minimize my errors. For that I am grateful, but I alone am responsible for any flaws that remain in the final product.

The book is dedicated to Professor James Baker Donnelly, who passed away in 1987 after twenty years of teaching at Washington and Jefferson College. Professor Donnelly was an inspiring teacher, a mischievously persistent editor, and a joyous wit. I suspect he would have been proud of this book by a former student, although he would certainly have read it with blue pencil in hand. I will miss that, for were it not for his influence, I could not have written it at all.

List of Abbreviations

ABM	Anti-ballistic missile
CDA	Christian Democratic Appeal (Netherlands)
CDU	Christian Democratic Union (West Germany)
CSU	Christian Socialist Union (West Germany)
D'66	Democrats '66 (Netherlands)
FDP	Free Democratic Party (West Germany)
IKV	Inter-Church Council (Netherlands)
INF	Intermediate-range nuclear forces
NATO	North Atlantic Treaty Organization
NFU	No first use
NIPO	Netherlands Institute for Public Opinion
PCF	Communist Party of France
PvdA	Labour Party (Netherlands)
RPR	Rally for the Republic/Gaullist Party (France)
SALT	Strategic Arms Limitation Talks
SDI	Strategic Defense Initiative
SDP	Social Democratic Party (Britain)
SPD	Social Democratic Party (West Germany)
UDF	Union for French Democracy
USIA	United States Information Agency
VVD	Liberal Party (Netherlands)
WTO	Warsaw Treaty Organization

1 Introduction

The security challenges of the 1980s caused a fundamental change in the scholarly study of defense politics. Because of the domestic uproar that troubled all Western societies during the decade, the study of public opinion became an important part of the study of national security.

This is nowhere more evident than in the study of European security. *Security specialists* routinely base their arguments on the presumed state of public opinion. For example, most studies of NATO's conventional force posture begin with the assumption that public opinion will not tolerate the additional spending that many feel is needed to improve conventional forces. In addition, the assumption that European public opinion now demands "arms control at any price" has become almost self-evident in the recent literature.

A similar preoccupation with public opinion characterizes the work of *political theorists*, who find the politics of European security a particularly useful testing ground for their ideas. For example, theorists of generational change see their ideas about the "new politics" of the post-industrial age confirmed in domestic debates over security issues. Students of party systems see the public's rebellion as the result of the failure of political parties to integrate the public's concerns about national security.

Finally, specialists in *public opinion analysis*, including professional pollsters, have also become more interested in issues of national security. For them, public opinion surveys on such issues as nuclear weapons, NATO, or defense spending are interesting because they represent a laboratory for the broader study of opinion dynamics. Not only can one trace opinions on specific issues of interest, one can also treat more general themes, such as the impact of technology or the fear of war on the mood of the public. The controversial nature of security issues makes them all the more appealing to the pollsters.

These three groups work largely in isolation. This book originated in my feeling that each could profit from the work of the others. This is particularly true for political theorists and for experts in public opinion analysis, for their work is often uninformed by the work of specialists in European security. For security specialists, it is not all that novel to discover that the public is troubled by NATO's policy of flexible response – it is an issue that has plagued the Alliance since at

1

least 1962. Nor is it necessarily surprising that the public sometimes seems confused and inconsistent – this is a tradition among the governments of the Alliance. This is not to say that the polls are not useful. Rather, I am suggesting that a fuller understanding of public opinion can be gained by studying both the substance of the issues faced by the Alliance and the compromises that NATO has employed in the past to manage these issues.

The opposite is true for security specialists. If they are to study public sentiment with profit, they must pay closer attention to the methodology of public opinion analysis. Close study of question wording, the size of percentages, and the historical evolution of opinions are essential. In addition, many of the polls cited in recent years are available for earlier historical periods. They are rarely applied. As a result, continuity is sometimes characterized as revolutionary change, and real change is not noticed at all.

Finally, both security specialists and opinion experts can profit from closer study of basic works of international and comparative theory. The best example arises from the recent concern for the "successor generation" – the fear that young people in Europe are turning away from the Alliance and its policies. Recent scholarship on generational change does predict such an evolution. None the less, the theory is more nuanced and tentative than is currently recognized in discussions of generational change within NATO. There are, for example, important qualifications to the theory that are based on such factors as the persistence of traditional, ideological polarization and differences among party systems. The potential impact of generational change (as well as other political forces) can only be understood in relation to these factors.

In this book, I attempt to draw on the strengths of each of these approaches. The result was a tall order for me, but it represents a challenge for the reader as well. Careful attention to the techniques of public opinion analysis requires the presentation of full – sometimes multiple – question wordings. I have therefore set out numerous tables of opinion data so that the reader can make independent judgments. However, the data alone do not tell the full story. The issues discussed in this book have histories of their own, and the interpretation of opinion polls on these issues requires attention both to the substance of security choices and to NATO's experience in dealing with them. Although security specialists may find it repetitive, this history is essential to others who would interpret the polls.

The organization of the book reflects my desire to integrate the substance of security issues with careful attention to the methodology of opinion analysis. Chapter 2 provides an overview of methodological issues in opinion analysis and a brief review of theories that might explain historical change and domestic polarization in public opinion. In Chapter 3, I set the larger context of security opinions by reviewing debates about the extent and consequences of change in the East–West military balance. I then analyze the evolution of public perceptions of the military balance and the confidence of Europeans in Western deterrence and defense capabilities. Chapter 4 builds on this analysis by examining public attitudes on such fundamental questions as the utility of force, deterrence, and the fear of war. This chapter also includes a review of public opinions on arms control issues and an assessment of the putative lessons of NATO's 1979 INF decision for current and future issues in European arms control. Chapter 5 analyzes the level of public support for NATO within the three "pillars" of security, economic, and political interests that support the Alliance. Chapter 6 explores the extent to which the public is willing to pay the price of defense by examining the level of popular support for defense spending. Finally, in Chapter 7 I explore a number of larger issues that arise from the analysis. After summarizing the degree of change and continuity in European opinions (and the reasons for both), I explore the extent to which the opinions of European publics differ from those of their leaders and from American public opinion. I also develop comparative hypotheses that relate the polarization and impact of public opinion to the nature of party systems, national traditions, and other factors.

The comparative nature of the book is worth emphasizing. Although many of our ideas about the evolution of public opinion are inherently comparative (involving differences in national interests as well as variations in domestic institutions), there are at present few comparative studies of the subject. Those that do exist are in the literature of comparative politics and are rarely cited by students of security or students of public opinion. In addition to drawing on the hypotheses and data in these works, I chose the countries for this study to provide some variation in both international outlook and in domestic institutions. The importance of France, Britain, and West Germany as the "big three" of European NATO members is obvious. In addition, as Chapter 7 demonstrates, they show interesting differences in party systems and in the degree of social change in the post-war period. The Netherlands is interesting for these same reasons, but I included the Dutch in this study for an additional reason: it was in the Netherlands that popular concern about security policy first became evident (during the neutron bomb controversy of 1977), and it is one of the most "populist" political systems of Western Europe.

The book presents materials not yet available in any single source. For example, for each of the issues described above, I am interested in describing the degree of change and continuity in opinions over time. Thus, each chapter begins with a description and analysis of historical polls retrieved from hundreds of governmental, commercial, and scholarly surveys conducted over the past thirty years. The result is an historical comparison that has heretofore eluded researchers on security opinions. Secondly, for each set of issues, I retrieved and analyzed more recent surveys that are available from data archives. Thus, each chapter also includes a detailed analysis of opinions within important sub-sectors of the population. Again, the result is a considerable improvement on existing research. Although most theories of opinion change and cleavage focus on particular societal groups (such as the young educated or young adherents of the Left), detailed analyses of these groups is surprisingly scarce in the existing literature. As we shall see, this gap has hindered progress in understanding the roots of European opinions, for detailed analysis of archived data shows that our dominant hypotheses require revision and integration.

These observations reveal a paradox in the recent surge of attention to public opinion on security issues. When the public's concerns became evident during the 1980s, the materials that would allow a thorough study of their roots were simply unavailable. To be sure, some recent surveys were available from survey archives, but even these were not without difficulties, for they demanded time and resources to retrieve, process, and analyze. In addition, the location of numerous surveys in American and European archives had not been documented. The surveys of the United States Information Agency (USIA), a valuable source, had only recently been deposited in the National Archives, and the condition of the data was anything but "ready". Further, most of the historical materials existed on paper only, in the reports and files of government agencies and commercial firms and in scholarly works on both sides of the Atlantic. Except for the earlier reports of the USIA, little of this material was published. Moreover, there was no comprehensive guide to the surveys of a single country, let alone to surveys in several countries. Put simply, the eruption of public concern about issues of national security found scholars unprepared.

For this reason, I have gone to great lengths to document the data collected for this book. The tables contain complete question wording, and I have provided as much detail as possible in the presentation of the data themselves. In addition, Appendix 2 contains a description of the types of data that are available and where they can be obtained. Finally, the Bibliography provides an exhaustive list of opinion surveys available from governmental agencies and survey archives in Europe and the United States.

I think the results of this effort confirm the utility of a comparative, historical approach. Some of the conclusions of the study stand out, and they are worth mentioning at the outset. One significant finding is that both change and continuity characterize the evolution of opinions, and the reasons for this are important. Some opinions are largely unrelated to security considerations. For example, opinions of defense spending react to economic and budget conditions rather than to wider debates about security, strategy and arms control. A second example concerns the confidence of Europeans in their security, which changed surprisingly little as a result of changing perceptions of the military balance. The reason, it seems, is that confidence in security derives more from the behavior, leadership and institutions of alliance partners than from calculations of the military balance. A final example demonstrates the utility of integrating broader theory with analyzes of public opinion. Opinions of the NATO Alliance are extremely stable – and highly supportive. The attraction of alternatives, such as neutralism or a European option, is low when compared to the current structure of the Alliance. This suggests that public opinion – like Alliance governments – are aware of the constraints imposed by the East–West power structure and by the difficulties of national interest and historical suspicion that would accompany attempts to pursue alternative arrangements. Just as students of alliances see little prospect of a dramatic departure from present arrangements, public opinion sees alternatives to NATO as infeasible, unpopular, or both.

The analysis also suggests that we need to revise our understanding of the underlying reasons for domestic polarization in security opinions. For example, the literature of the 1980s first advanced and then discarded the "successor generation" thesis as an explanation of domestic polarization. Yet my analyses show that, when attention is focused on the combined influence of generational experience and level of education, the "successor generation" is indeed unique in its skepticism of NATO's traditional policies. None the less, this does not suggest that security politics have been completely transformed, for there is also clear evidence of the persistence of traditional ideological quarrels on issues of national security. As is usual when research progresses, the data show that no single factor explains polarization on security issues. Instead, European opinion resembles a "glacier" process in which the "new" politics of generational change overlay continuing polarization in the "old" politics of ideology and partisanship.

Finally, the data presented in this book challenge two popular notions about the politics of European security. One is that the public is out of tune with its leaders – that governments are increasingly pressured from below to modify traditional approaches. As I show in the final chapter, there is little evidence for this view. With the qualified exception of the nuclear issue, public and élite opinion are largely in agreement, and one might even argue that public opinion has developed *in reaction to* leadership opinion. The second challenge to the conventional wisdom arises from a comparison of American and European opinion. Especially in the early 1980s, it was widely supposed that NATO would come under increasing strain as American opinion moved toward a more "hardline" stance while European publics hesitated. Yet the data show that at least by the mid-1980s, American opinion was very similar to European opinion. As I conclude in Chapter 7, opinion data from both sides of the Atlantic indicate that consensus on security issues will be found in centrist policies that combine – and compromise – the fears and preferences of competing generations and political parties. This conclusion is hardly dramatic, for it suggests that the politics of security have changed less than we think. None the less, it represents a significant caution to the appealing notion that the dramatic events of the day signal a revolutionary departure.

2 Crisis or Consensus? Public Opinion and National Security in Western Europe

When the NATO Alliance celebrated its thirtieth anniversary in 1979, few would have predicted that the very existence of the Alliance would soon be in doubt. Most commentaries stressed the theme of continuity in the Alliance, a continuity that rested on a firm basis of common interest in security, economic, and political affairs. In addition, the mutual interests of the Western nations were reinforced by a stable East–West power structure that rendered alternative security arrangements infeasible, unpopular or both.[1]

Yet ironically, the year 1979 also saw the beginning of a "crisis" in the Alliance. NATO's decision in December 1979 to modernize its intermediate nuclear forces (INF) caused the most visible controversy, but it was by no means the only one. As recession deepened in 1980 and 1981, trade and monetary disagreements aggravated the chronic problem of defense burden-sharing. American policies outside the NATO area were widely criticized in Western Europe. For their part, Americans found much to criticize in European views on arms control and on the broader issue of how to deal with Soviet actions in Eastern Europe and elsewhere. As early as 1981, many observers had concluded that NATO was in a fundamental crisis, and some analysts doubted the viability – and even the utility – of the Alliance.[2]

To be sure, many continued to believe that common interest and external constraint would see the Alliance through. In addition, by 1984 the combined effects of economic recovery, a more moderate tone in Washington, and, ironically, the fact of INF deployment itself, brought a calming of transatlantic disputes. In Europe, the electoral success of pro-deployment, Center-Right governments brought recognition of a substantial reservoir of popular support for the Alliance and its policies. Even before the signing of the "double-zero" arms treaty in late 1987, the "crisis" of the early 1980s seemed to have passed.

None the less, assessments of NATO's viability continue to differ. Indeed, one feature of the quieter phase in the Alliance has been the proliferation of reform proposals designed to head off the next crisis in NATO. But regardless of the degree of optimism about NATO's life expectancy, it is clear that the growing importance of public opinion marks a new stage in the history of the Alliance. Of course, the role of the public was most significant in popular protest against the INF deployment, but it had broader implications, depending on the country or the issue at hand. In West Germany, opposition to INF was soon tied to the larger questions of the Federal Republic's national identity and allegiance to the West ("neutralism") and to Germans' acceptance of – and even affection for – their American partners ("anti-Americanism"). Broader analyses of European politics ranged from near panic-stricken charges of "pacifism" to the calmer – if no less troubled – view that fundamental domestic and international changes had undermined the consensus that formerly supported Alliance policies on defense spending, arms control, and partnership with the United States.

Indeed, as NATO's crisis deepened during the early 1980s, scholars began arguing that domestic consensus was now the primary task of the Alliance. Lawrence Freedman, for example, observed that "whether a strategic doctrine is acceptable to the people for whom it has been developed is as important in an alliance of democratic societies as that doctrine's ability to impress the enemy".[3] The politicians seemed to agree. Francis Pym, then Minister of Defence in Britain, summarized the situation in 1982 by noting that governments of the West were in danger "of failing the task, critically important to the security of the Atlantic Alliance, of retaining broadly based popular support for their defense policies. . . . Without question we *can* maintain the peace. But we can do so only if we can win the hearts and minds of our peoples, earn their acceptance, and draw on their fortitude."[4]

THE PARADOX OF CONSENSUS AND CRISIS

If there was growing acceptance of the view that the public's role in security policy had become critical, it soon became clear that public opinion could not be easily determined and certainly not simply characterized. Whereas many had feared growing neutralism, opinion polls showed strong adherence to the Alliance – in most cases stronger than in previous years – and attachment to NATO was strongest in precisely those countries that had raised the most concern (West Germany). Whereas large and intense protests suggested widespread anti-nuclear sentiment and even pacifism, many polls showed continued acceptance of NATO's policy of nuclear deterrence, even in the Netherlands, the country with the most intense and emotional peace movements. Further, although growing anti-Americanism was often cited, opinion surveys showed that Europeans really did like Americans and considered them very good friends indeed. Finally, to confuse matters completely, many polls showed that support for defense policies was *weakest* in the country where it was least expected. In France, for example, peace movements were quite weak, and the government and intellectual élite had been moving steadily toward a hardline stand on nuclear and other East–West issues. Observers spoke increasingly of the French "consensus" on these issues. Yet the polls showed that the support of the French public for increased defense spending was lower than in any country of the Alliance, and as we shall see in subsequent chapters, the polarization of French public opinion is very pronounced.

In short, the generalizations of the early 1980s had dissolved in a confusing series of contradictions. Perhaps this was to be expected. In the first place, simplifying labels such as "pacifism" or "neutralism" were largely ahistorical, however appealing they might have been as attempts to understand events that were unfolding rapidly. They ignored the fact that the Alliance had experienced considerable disputes on nuclear (and other) issues, disputes that had somehow been resolved without the loss of domestic support for the Alliance and its policies. Further, in the early 1980s, interpretation of public opinion polls was fragmentary and selective, thus violating the first rule of public opinion analysis: to be careful with isolated questions or singular question phrasing that might confuse a short-term fluctuation with a trend or misread what "opinions" really are or how deeply they are felt. For example, it should come as little surprise to find (as we do in Chapter 4) that public acceptance of nuclear weapons is stronger when NATO commitments or Soviet deployments are mentioned in the question, or that support for the INF deployment was higher when the arms control track of the 1979 decision was mentioned in the survey. Although some questions did reveal the public's nervousness about nuclear weapons, a comparison of a number of different wordings suggested that this nervousness was hardly pacifist or even uniformly "anti-nuclear".

A second problem with analyses of public opinion during this period was the reliance on data published in contemporary government polls and news sources. There were two results. First, it was difficult to sort out the degree of change and continuity in public opinion, for governments and newspapers tend to commission surveys on only the most recent issues and events. They rarely repeat a question over a number of years. Although there are historical polls in the files of government agencies and in survey archives, these had not been retrieved and collated when NATO's "crisis" focused attention on the sentiments of the public. The second problem was that these secondary sources rarely offer the detailed breakdown of opinions that is necessary to uncover the structure of public opinions. It is true that surveys are often reported according to the age, educational level, or other characteristics of the respondents. However, as I argue below, most hypotheses about public opinion and national security are based on the *combined* effects of these factors. The study of these combinations requires the analyst to retrieve the surveys from the archives and compute the combined breakdowns. Until recently, there was almost no attention to this task.[5]

An additional problem was that the preoccupation with pacifist and neutralist movements – certainly present and highly visible – none the less distracted attention from the possibility that concern was not confined to the minorities who organized and participated in protest demonstrations. As Michael Howard argued in early 1983, the doubts expressed by the peace movements differed in intensity but not in kind from the increasing worries of citizens, strategists, and governments.[6] If a future consensus on security policy is to be found, it must address the fears and concerns of this broader group.

At a minimum, the apparent contradictions of recent opinion surveys and survey analysis indicate a need for a comprehensive examination of public opinion on security issues. This book is an attempt to fill that need. The pages to follow are based on hundreds of public opinion surveys conducted in Great Britain, France, West Germany, and the Netherlands on such issues as nuclear weapons, the military balance, the utility of NATO, images of the United States, and support for the defense budget. While I do present some surveys commissioned by newspapers or commercial polling agencies, most of the analysis is based on historical surveys retrieved from government agencies and from survey archives. Some surveys are limited to recent years, while others extend as far back as the 1950s. In many cases, multiple polls are available for each security issue.

Taken together, the surveys examined here address three central questions about public opinion in the NATO Alliance. First, how much has public opinion changed and how much has it remained stable? Secondly, is there a general pattern within the overall "public" that can be explained by the age, level of education, or political affiliation of citizens? Thirdly, what *explains* change and continuity and the underlying pattern of opinions on different issues?

THE ORGANIZING FRAMEWORK

To address these questions coherently requires some framework by which to organize the wealth of available opinion surveys. Although there are a large number of surveys covering different historical periods and security issues, to examine these polls *ad seriatim* would doubtless lead to the same contradictions noted above. To treat opinions on each and every issue as equally important to the Alliance's legitimacy would be to ignore NATO's considerable history of ambiguity and compromise and thus to risk exaggerating differences that do exist. Moreover, without some historical or theoretical background, we lack a standard against which to judge the survey responses. How much has support for NATO declined? Why should support for the Alliance fluctuate? How do citizens reconcile negative views of the INF deployment with support for the Alliance and for partnership with the United States? Flynn and Rattinger aptly summarized the task of theoretical organization in the conclusion to their own review of public opinion on national security: "In a study like this, one is dealing with hundreds of thousands of tiny pieces of information. . . . The problem for the researcher as well as the political decision maker is to make sense out of such a multitude of individual observations."[7]

I bring order to the interpretation of the survey results in two ways. First, rather than simply wade through the polls, I have grouped the material into four broad issue areas. As noted in the Introduction, the analysis begins with the subject of perceptions of the military balance and confidence in deterrence. Subsequent chapters deal with nuclear strategy and arms control, the NATO Alliance, defense spending, and the relationship between élite and public opinions. Of course, these sets of issues do not represent discrete, isolated choices – for governments or for the public. Support for defense spending is presumably dependent on perceptions of the military balance, just as attitudes towards the NATO Alliance are dependent on confidence in the United States. Thus, where it is possible to use surveys that are available from archives, I also explore the interrelation of defense policy opinions.

The second organizational question is that of historical and theoretical expectations. Should opinions change? Why? Why should different societal groups see security problems differently? Recent attention to European public opinion has relaxed fears of a generalized pacifist or neutralist orientation, but less progress has been made in identifying which social, political, economic or strategic factors are most important to opinion change over time and to domestic cleavage at any one point in time. To frame these questions, I employ three sets of theoretical arguments of relevance to change and cleavage in opinions of defense policies.

The Utility of Force

Popular concern and protest about security is usually seen as a sudden development of the early 1980s. Yet the erosion of domestic consensus on security policy might have been predicted from the writings of important international relations theorists of the 1970s. These works are described in detail in Chapter 3. Here it is important to describe three changes that were emphasized in the theoretical literature because they are fundamental to public perceptions of security problems. The first was the effect of the Vietnam War on perceptions of the utility of military force as an instrument of foreign policy. The "lessons" of Vietnam are still a subject of debate, but that is precisely the point. Indeed, the loss of consensus on the utility of force may be the primary legacy of the war. Moreover, a severe constraint on governmental action is the recognition that the use of force may not command domestic support unless the objectives are clear and the interests vital. In short, the effect of the Vietnam War was not so much to shift the consensus away from military force as an instrument of policy as it was to make public support for the use of force more problematical.

The second change was the emergence of strategic nuclear parity between the United States and the Soviet Union. Codified in the SALT I Agreements in 1972, the emergence of parity had the effect of reinforcing doubts about the utility of force. Parity in the assured destruction capabilities of the superpowers introduced caution into the calculations of the superpowers and the smaller "middle powers" of Europe, for the escalation of even minor conflicts risked total annihilation. Moreover, if stalemate had been reached at the strategic level, of what utility were additions to other forces, the use of which was in doubt in any event? Although mutually assured destruction was an uncomfortable method of stabilizing international relations, it did suggest the logic of arms reductions and the potential futility of adding to existing arsenals. In 1972, Henry Kissinger said in support of the SALT I Agreements that the United States and the Soviet Union had developed a "certain commonality of outlook . . . now that both we and the Soviet Union have begun to find that each increment of power does not necessarily represent an increment of usable political strength".[8]

Finally, during the 1970s, issues other than military security began to dominate the agenda of international politics. Economic difficulties were primary among these "new issues" of the 1970s, but other problems, such as pollution, migration, and ocean development, also became salient. Robert Keohane and Joseph Nye were most prominent among students of international relations in observing that the emergence of these issues could further reduce the relative utility of force, for a singular feature of such issues was that they could not be solved by military means. Although Keohane and Nye did not argue that military force had lost all utility – in fact, they pointed out that for some countries or issues the opposite might be the case – they did suggest that pressing new problems would demand relatively more resources and attention.[9] Government officials seemed to agree. Again, Kissinger was among the most direct: "The problems of energy, resources, environment, population, the use of spaces and seas now rank with questions of military security, ideology and territorial rivalry which have traditionally made up the diplomatic agenda."[10]

Political developments soon indicated that these theorists had hit the mark. American governments became increasingly concerned about the political effects of strategic parity and mutually assured destruction, especially on the confidence (and allegiance) of the European allies. Later in the decade, observers on both sides of the Atlantic emphasized the change in the strategic balance as a cause of both declining alliance cohesion and of the decay in the domestic security consensus.

I shall examine public opinion relating to these issues in Chapter 3. Here it is sufficient to observe that change in the strategic balance and in the issues of concern in international politics were probably not lost on public opinion. Politicians themselves spoke of the decline in the "marginal increments of political strength" to be derived from military power. The arms control initiatives of the 1970s were well publicized, and the economic and social dislocations of the decade hardly needed reinforcement. In such an environment, should it be surprising were popular attitudes to shift toward the view that more military force was not necessarily better?

The Successor Generation

As public involvement in security debates has grown, attention has shifted from the question of how many people hold particular views to the question of who holds them. In both Europe and the United States, much attention has been focused on the young – the so-called successor generation. In the article cited earlier, Defence Minister Pym pointed to the changed perceptions of the young to explain the erosion of consensus on security policy: "It is becoming hard for rising generations in the West to accept that the security of the affluent societies in which they live needs to be defended. . . . The educated and sophisticated young people of today are less likely to accept without question a description of world affairs that attributes to the East–West balance a primary and fundamental importance."[11]

Generational change has been the focus of considerable scholarly work. Ronald Inglehart's theory of a "silent revolution" is the best known. Inglehart argues that a gradual but profound transformation is underway in advanced, industrial societies. A crucial factor in this transformation is the differing experiences of successive generations. Those generations that grew to maturity after the Second World War were much more secure economically and militarily. They did not know either extreme material deprivation or the bitterness of war experienced by their elders. As a result, the younger generations are less likely to emphasize the older, "materialist" values that placed primary importance on economic concerns and national security.[12]

The political significance of the "successor generation" is magnified because of the much higher educational levels that resulted from the post-war expansion of European universities. That expansion was truly prodigious. In 1960, an average of only 7 per cent of 20–24 -year olds attended university in the four countries under study here. By 1975, the percentage had grown to an average of 17 per cent.[13] The growth of the universities has a special significance for students of generational change; it represents a tremendous increase in the proportion of the population with the sophistication and motivation to participate in politics. Moreover, the turbulent political events on the university campuses of the 1960s were evidence of a change in attitude and political style that could reinforce – perhaps magnify – the process of generational value change underway in society at large. Finally, the political significance of the educated members of the successor generation is heightened by the fact that "tomorrow's leaders" will presumably be drawn from this pool of society's best talent.

Once again it is Inglehart who has most explicitly linked the growth of higher education to generational political change. For him, both the affluence and attitudes of the university educated are important. Despite the fact that European higher education is generally free, presumably the motivation to study and the ability to finance several years of living expenses are higher among the (now enlarged) middle and upper classes – precisely those classes in which value change would be most pronounced. Moreover, the cognitive effect of education is equally important. Not only does education expose students to a new, more cosmopolitan set of ideas. The educational process itself encourages new ways of looking at the world:

> The more educated have developed certain skills – above all, skills in dealing with abstractions. These skills might enable them to cope more readily with new ideas and remote objects. The new and distant might seem less threatening, which could contribute to a relatively open and cosmopolitan world view.[14]

While Inglehart emphasizes the social background of students and the cognitive effects of the educational process itself, others point to socialization effects: the political experience of those who attended university in the 1960s and early 1970s. Students born between 1945 and 1950 entered university during the mid to late 1960s and experienced the near pervasive student revolts of the period. As Seyom Brown has noted, student protest was directed not just against the United States and the war in Vietnam, but encompassed more fundamental issues of social and economic organization. Further, the 1960s also saw the growth of critical analyses directed not just against the putative weaknesses of capitalism and the excesses of economic growth, but also against prevailing theories of deterrence, arms races, and the postwar alliance system.[15] The 1970s did bring calmer times to European campuses, and some student activists later turned to work within established institutions, but it is precisely the succession of this more skeptical generation to leadership positions that preoccupies many observers of European politics.

Surprisingly, few observers have pointed to the fact that the university educated should also be better informed about the ambiguities of defense policy that preoccupied both strategists and policymakers during the 1970s. One could hardly claim that defense studies have been a major part of European university curriculums, or even that the university generation of the 1960s and 1970s now devote inordinate attention to defense issues. Still, the level of information on such matters as the strategic balance, East–West relations, arms control, and weapons costs is comparatively higher among the more educated. To the extent that security problems and politics have become more contentious in official and expert circles, one would expect these debates to be perceived first among the better educated of the "attentive public".

Whether young graduates are therefore more hostile to defense policies is a separate question. After all, the older, educated "attentive publics" are presumably aware of policy debates as well, and they too experienced the "cognitive" effects of higher education. Moreover, the theory of generational change is itself subject to competing explanations.[16] Primary among these alternative explanations is the possibility of *life-cycle* effects. In the life-cycle interpretation, distinctive views among the young are simply the result of the temporary ideals and tensions that characterize youthful citizens. In Beck's words:

> Young adulthood . . . is a time for challenging established practices and norms, as the young struggle to develop their own identities. From time immemorial, the young have staffed the armies of protest and revolutionary movements. . . . After the early years of adulthood, most [Americans] settle into marriage, a family, a career, home ownership, or other responsibilities. . . . Middle-aged adults are less inclined to challenge established ways.[17]

Although the young may exhibit critical views on defense and other policy issues, these views will moderate as the young become more established in their identities, careers, and families.

However convincing the *life-cycle* thesis, there is growing evidence that generational change has in fact taken place over the last two decades. In the most comprehensive study, Inglehart shows that, despite fluctuations during the economic troubles of the 1970s, the values of the young continued to be distinct from those of their elders. Other studies have also demonstrated that generational change is not totally removed during the life-cycle.[18]

Perhaps Jennings is closest to the true nature of generational change in his study of American youth. Jennings has traced the same sample of respondents from the high-school class of 1965, precisely the generation that was exposed to protest movements of the Vietnam era. In his latest re-study of this cohort, Jennings finds that, although all Americans have become more conservative in their views since 1965, those who had identified themselves as protesters in the generation of 1965 none the less remain distinct (and less conservative). In summary, there had been aging effects, but the residue of generational change remained as well.[19]

Thus, there is evidence that generational change has affected Western societies over the last two decades, although a combination of generational change and aging effects cannot be ruled out. To the extent that generational differences in security attitudes are discovered in contemporary surveys, it is probably best to be cautious about predicting how long and to what extent they will persist. None the less, for policy purposes, eventual moderation in the attitudes of today's youth is probably beside the point. Governments will find little solace in the observation that generational conflict may subside in the future, for NATO faces its security challenges now. And the attention of NATO governments to the concerns and beliefs of young people is testimony to the appeal of generational change as the primary explanation for change and division in public opinion.

Familiar Faces: Political Parties and Political Beliefs

If the successor generation thesis is widely accepted in official circles, it has recently come under closer scrutiny by scholars. One reason is that the rush of scholarship designed to uncover the sources of public alienation have found inconsistent evidence of age differences in public opinion. Certainly there are some surveys in which age differences exist, but they are not uniform across issues, time periods, or countries. In one study, there were clear age differences on such issues as the Soviet threat and détente, but on the nuclear issue *older* respondents were the most critical. Similar inconsistencies show up in other studies.[20] Moreover, in their examination of surveys from the early 1980s, Flynn and Rattinger found that generational differences were much overshadowed by the polarization of security opinions along the traditional Left–Right continuum of political parties.[21]

This pattern was confirmed in a study by Inglehart, who finds that European attitudes towards defense spending are closely related to the traditional Left–Right ideological continuum most commonly associated with the old, material political cleavages. He hypothesizes that defense issues were transformed by the Vietnam War into an issue of "social change" governed by familiar ideological notions of progress and status maintenance, just as traditional economic concerns are governed by the "change–status quo" framework.[22]

Because of the impact of the Vietnam War, this interpretation is plausible. However, it ignores the fact that Europe has a long tradition of ideological conflict on security issues. Michael Howard has traced the considerable historical continuity to critiques of military force, first among enlightenment liberals who saw war as the result of the narrow self-interest of feudal and aristocratic élites, later among socialists who saw war as the product of the greed of industry (especially the arms industry) and the expansionist tendencies of capitalist societies. As Howard and others have shown, this critique of military force has characterized idealist thinking from the ideas of Erasmus to the arguments of the peace movements of recent years.[23]

The idealist critique is well known, but a review of its basic tenets provides a useful background to contemporary debates.[24] The primary argument is clear: military force is the problem rather than the solution. Whereas conservatives see a balance of power as the key to security in an imperfect world, the liberal idealists see force, if not as the cause of war, then certainly as an imperfect instrument that exacerbates the underlying conflicts that give rise to war. The corollary is therefore that peace can be secured only through negotiation, the regulation of underlying conflicts, or through the "integration" of societies through trade and interdependence. Finally, there is the domestic component of the idealist critique. In the nineteenth century, the Left had a clear self-interest in limiting the influence of the military, for in most European countries a conservative military élite stood in the way of democraticization. More recently, the defense budget has been seen as a drain on the program of social reform pursued by the Left.

These ideological differences were not erased by the tensions of the Cold War. Indeed, despite the crisis atmosphere that accompanied the creation of NATO in 1949, parties of Left and Right continued to differ on such issues as the nature of the Soviet threat, the need for NATO, the acceptability of nuclear weapons, and the issue of how much to spend for defense.[25] The "centrist consensus" that emerged in the early 1960s may have submerged these early differences. None the less, they became prominent once again during the late 1960s and early 1970s, when there was growing debate about East–West relations, détente, and the increasingly pressing question of what and how much should be sacrificed to finance national defense. As described in more detail in Chapter 7 below, there were strenuous debates about détente and defense spending in most European countries during this period. More recently, European parties have increasingly emphasized their role as organizer and representative of views on defense issues. In summary, it may be that the difficult choices of the 1980s have merely reawakened partisan and ideological approaches to defense policy that were dormant during the "consensus" of the early 1960s and the relative international calm of the détente period. Far from representing a "new" clash of young and old, defense policy debates may simply be a resurrection of the familiar historical conflict between Left and Right.

THREE VIEWS IN COMPETITION?

The foregoing perspectives on public opinion provide the theoretical organization of this book. Whether the issue is the public's perception of the military balance, their views of strategy and nuclear weapons, attitudes towards NATO, or opinions of the defense budget, I examine the extent to which opinions are influenced by changing views of the international situation, by generational differences, or by partisan affiliation.

These theoretical perspectives are not unrelated. For example, it is likely that perceptions of change in international politics will be most pronounced among the younger generation, for it is this group that experienced Vietnam, détente and arms control during the crucial period of adult socialization. Further, as the young generation of Europeans are proportionately the best educated, we would expect them to be more highly sensitized to debates over such issues as the utility of force and the costs and benefits of arms control. Similarly, since it has often been argued that younger, educated Europeans identify increasingly with parties of the Left, it could be that the ideological polarization of defense politics is a generational rather than a "traditional" phenomenon.

These relationships are difficult to sort out with finality. However, using survey analysis, it is possible to confront simple "bivariate" arguments with the facts. If the effects of change in global politics have influenced more than just the younger generation who did not experience the bitterness of the Cold War, this should be evident by comparing the attitudes of younger and older Europeans. Similarly, if the growing polarization of defense politics results from the disproportionate identification of the young with the Left, we should be able to see this phenomenon by comparing the defense views and party commitments of younger and older Europeans.

These brief examples make clear that no theoretical argument is immune to rival interpretations. For example, although the successor generation has not experienced a World War or Cold War, should this make them more or less critical of defense policies? Is it not equally possible that the older generation would be more anti-militarist precisely *because* they have experienced the horrors of war? Further, the older generations are the largest beneficiaries of the public budget, hardly a position that would increase acceptance of defense spending at a time of budgetary retrenchment. One could multiply these doubts about the plausibility of any particular argument: the utility of force (at least for Britain and France) has proven not to be outworn; the parties in France seem to have moved *closer* to a consensus on nuclear issues than they have been in the past; and the parties of both Left *and* Right in West Germany stand fully behind the *Ostpolitik* begun by Chancellor Willy Brandt in 1969.

This is precisely the point. Although the increasing importance of public opinion to defense policy has brought a search for a single pattern that underlies the public's views on defense, it is likely that no one theory will explain all attitudes on all defense issues. In fact, if the experience of the past several years is any guide, different opinion patterns may characterize different issues, and opinions are likely to differ among the countries of the Alliance. None the less, by organizing the study both substantively and theoretically, we will at least have a set of categories for assessing the generality of change and polarization on different defense policy issues. The utility of theoretical organization may well be to introduce complexity to replace the confident simplifications of the past. Given the haste with which "single-factor" theories have been accepted by governments, such a finding would be of more than academic interest.

THE POLLS: VICES AND VIRTUES

If theoretical organization is necessary to a coherent assessment of change and cleavage in public opinion, in the final analysis it is the accuracy and quality of public opinion surveys on which the study must rest. Here there are two separate issues: the technical quality of public opinion surveys and the problems of interpreting them.

The technical qualities of good surveys are well understood.[26] Certainly the most important are sample design and the size of the sample. Representative national samples are preferable to less representative methods, such as simple quota samples, because the former provide a greater chance that all members of the population might be sampled. Larger samples are preferable because sampling error will be minimized, although there is a threshold in sample size beyond which reduction of error becomes quite costly. Finally, surveys based on "in-the-home" interviews are preferable to telephone surveys because the interviewer can establish personal contact, and the method avoids undersampling of social groups who are less likely to have telephones.

From the standpoint of survey quality, we are in a good position to make accurate statements about European public opinion on defense issues, for the material available is with few exceptions based on national representative samples of sufficient size to achieve the 3 per cent error rate considered optimal by survey researchers. One experienced analyst has noted that European surveys may be somewhat better than some American surveys because the availability of complete national voter registration lists allow for very good probability sampling to insure the representativeness of the results.[27] In such a situation, the most pressing task of interpretation is careful attention to the size of the overall sample and to the size of the sub-samples (such as age or education groups). Almost all of the surveys in this book are based on samples of about 1000 respondents, allowing for confidence within about 3 per cent of the "true" distribution of public opinions. In addition, Appendix Table 1 contains a guide to the statistical significance of differences between sub-samples.

Of course, sampling is probably the least controversial aspect of opinion surveys. To the extent that the sample is representative and sufficiently large to ensure confidence that the percentages are reflective of national opinions, the issue becomes "how good are the survey questions themselves?" Here the issue of question wording is paramount, and there are two parts to the problem. First, any study of *historical change* in public opinion requires that the same question be posed over a number of years. Unfortunately, this is rarely done, even by government agencies responsible for monitoring change in opinion. Instead, the analyst must deal with frequent variations on similar questions, confounding the task of distinguishing real change in opinions from change in question wording. For this reason, I have reproduced complete question wording when historical change is discussed in this book. Further, in those cases where multiple wordings are available for overlapping periods of time, I compare the results for different questions in an attempt to disentangle real change in opinions from the effect of variation in question wording.

A more difficult problem arises when there is variation in question wording on a particular issue during a short timespan. As several prominent news reports indicate, it is possible to find drastically different levels of support and denial on defense issues even within the space of several months. In West Germany, for example, support for the INF deployment during the summer of 1983 seemed to vary by as much as 50 percentage points, depending on the time of the survey and variation in the question asked. In Great Britain, support for defense spending in 1983 varied greatly with question wording.[28]

There are at least three interpretations of such shifts. The first, quite simply, is that opinions really have changed as a result of changing assessments of the military situation or in response to governments' pronouncements on the issue. Secondly, some observers argue that, since the public's level of expertise and interest in security affairs is low, opinions on defense issues are prone to rapid change and even inconsistency regardless of events or policy pronouncements. Finally, we must recognize that variations in question wording often represent genuinely different aspects of security choices and therefore produce genuinely different responses. This is understandable – and even laudable – in an area where sophistication and nuance are considered hallmarks of good policy.

Each of these interpretations will compete for attention in the chapters to follow. Although final answers are rarely possible, the need to disentangle question effects and real opinion change does emphasize an important point about public opinion analysis: many difficulties arise as much from *interpretation* of the survey questions as from technical problems with the surveys themselves. Further, interpretation of change in opinions requires not only accurate percentages from sound survey techniques; it also requires an understanding of the context of events and the complexities inherent in the defense issues under debate.

The task of interpretation is easiest when variations in wording reflect controversial choices in defense debates or when responses to an identical question produce dramatic short-term shifts. To use an example cited earlier, it is both interesting and useful to know that public opinion is more tolerant of nuclear weapons when Soviet deployments are added to the survey question, for it suggests that a generally negative attitude towards nuclear weapons can be offset when the practicalities of the military situation are raised. Similarly, changes in response to an identical question over a short period of time are revealing when they occur parallel to major changes in the policy environment. In subsequent chapters of this book, I shall examine such a change in opinions of the defense budget during the 1981 recession and in attitudes towards INF before and after President Reagan's arms control initiatives.

Interpretation of the polls is much more difficult when opinion change is less than dramatic or when the percentages are ambiguous in their meaning. In many cases, the public opinion glass is half-empty or half-full, depending on the perspective. For example, we shall see in Chapter 6 that European attitudes towards defense spending, when tested in the familiar "increase", "decrease", or "keep the same" question, are concentrated in the "keep the same" response. Although this finding is very consistent, interpretations of the data range from the optimistic to the apocalyptic. In a study of French opinion, Michael Harrison observes that "real-defense expenditures rose consistently in France during the 1970s. . . . French public opinion supports such a policy, for 50% of the public want the level of defense to remain the same, whereas only a few want it to decrease . . . or increase." Finding a very similar distribution of attitudes in other European countries, Adler and Wertman see the glass at least half-empty: "for, contrary to the agreement made in NATO by their governments, six in ten in Britain and about seven in ten in West Germany, Norway, the Netherlands, Italy, and Belgium favor either keeping defense expenditures at present levels or reducing them". Finally, Feld and Wildgen studied exactly the same polls as Harrison and Adler and Wertman, yet they concluded that the glass was all but dry: "[the survey] . . . is suggestive of what commentators have in mind when they discuss Finlandization. . . . The lack of substantial support for increased defense spending in West Germany is a manifestation of a strong pacifist and neutralist attitude among many Germans, especially the youth."[29] Although opinions of defense spending in France and West Germany are close to identical, different analysts see toleration of high defense spending in one country and pacifism in the second.

A useful interpretation of these patterns must relate public opinions to government policy. As it turns out, European public opinion during the 1970s (and even earlier) nearly always favored the "keep same" response. This suggests that governments in the past have had some leeway with defense spending – with few exceptions, European governments increased defense budgets by about 3 per cent annually. Even when the glass appears both half-empty and half-full, interpretation of the impact of public opinion can be made clearer by combining analysis of the surveys themselves with the background and outcome of past policy choice.

This is not to say that there are no bad public opinion surveys. In fact, the recent surge of interest in the public's attitudes towards Western defense has brought some poor surveys in its wake. Some questions contain background or "lead-ins" that are controversial or inaccurate. For example, the United States Information Agency (USIA) included a question on European surveys in 1981 and 1982 that began by stating: "Well, as you may know, the Russians have about 450 nuclear warheads on new medium-range nuclear missiles – the SS-20s – aimed at Western Europe, while NATO has no such missiles aimed at the Soviet Union."[30]

As a test of general sensitivity to Soviet capabilities, this question has definite utility, but for both scholarly and policy purposes it is inadequate. The statement that "NATO has no such missiles" is one that was much debated during the INF episode. If one is interested in a reading of attitudes toward INF deployment as they formed and changed during this debate, this question must be supplemented by additional questions that probe for differing interpretations of the INF balance.

More subtle and amusing difficulties have arisen from the interest in neutralism. In West Germany, a 1981 poll repeated earlier surveys asking if the Federal Republic should remain allied with the United States or become neutral, "for example, like Switzerland". Once again, the question has some utility, for the model of armed neutrality practiced by Switzerland does have hypothetical meaning – however remote – for the Federal Republic. But there are two weaknesses. The hypothetical nature of the question is the first, especially in a country for which external constraints have been much more significant than for other countries. Equally important, the question may evoke positive images that are irrelevant to the Swiss military posture. Anyone who has vacationed in Switzerland is aware of its scenic and culinary virtues. In fact, when a range of less idyllic alternatives are posed to West Germans, neutrality is much less favored than it is in this question.[31]

The same is true of other West Europeans, especially when surveys allow comparison of peoples' view of the *difficulties* of alliance with their assessment of *alternatives* to NATO. In April 1980, for example, the *Washington Post* published a European poll asking if "our governments should back the US against the Soviets more than it has until now . . . or do everything possible to stay out of arguments between the US and the Soviet Union". The headline summarized the findings: "West Germans, British Want to See Limits on Support for US". Yet in the same survey, over 60 per cent of these British and German respondents expressed the view that US military support was essential to their security. In a separate US government poll conducted in the same month, overwhelming pluralities expressed a preference for remaining in NATO over alternatives ranging from accommodation with the Soviet Union to the creation of a European defense effort. Although these and other polls do reveal disenchantment with American policies, they also show that Europeans do not at present consider neutralism a viable alternative to the NATO alliance.[32]

One is tempted to generalize these examples with a warning to avoid survey questions that juxtapose positive and negative images in the abstract. A colleague has termed this the problem of "good things and bad things" in opinion surveys.[33] Considered in isolation, there are many security choices that evoke almost automatic acceptance or rejection. Most would agree that nuclear weapons themselves are distasteful; that efforts to relax international tensions are noble and worthy of support; or that arms control is preferable to a buildup of military force if it will provide equivalent security. None the less, it is the dilemma of security policy that achievement of these objectives cannot always occur in equal measure. Security policy, and thus opinions about security, is more a matter of balance – tradeoffs of the good and the bad.

Despite this simple fact, a number of surveys offer the good or the bad without mention of constraints or tradeoffs. In West Germany, respondents were asked in 1980: "should Germany continue the policy of détente in the future, or don't you think it makes sense to continue?"[34] Now there is no question that West Germans think that détente, in general, is a good thing (no political or social group showed less than 60 per cent in favor of a continuation of détente). None the less, other questions indicate that West Germans also show considerable ambivalence about Soviet intentions, and there is even support for compromising or foregoing détente in some circumstances (two months after the above survey, 63 per cent of West

Germans supported the boycott of the Moscow Olympics, and 50 to 60 per cent have consistently shown mistrust of Soviet intentions in détente and arms control).[35] Few students of West German public opinion or foreign policy would deny that détente is an important goal for the Federal Republic, but isolated polls which ask hypothetically if détente "should continue" are likely to elide the question of when and under what circumstances détente will take a lesser priority to other courses of action.

Finally, even the most penetrating opinion surveys are of little value when interpretation is faulty or when incomplete results are presented. For example, in their analysis of a 1980 European survey, Feld and Wildgen reproduce figures showing that, in their predictions of the "most powerful nation in five years time", 20 to 30 per cent of West Europeans chose nations *other than* the United States or the Soviet Union. The authors conclude: "This may be one of those instances where the wish spawns the idea. There is a kind of pious hopefulness in this view, either for the emergence of a more congenial country as a third power or a neutralizing force constituted by the whole of Western Europe."[36] Feld and Wildgen do not reproduce a detailed breakdown of *which* third country or bloc was chosen by survey respondents as likely to be most powerful in five years. When these figures are retrieved, it turns out that in no country is the "whole of Western Europe" (the European Community) chosen by more than 2 per cent. Not surprisingly, the largest number of Europeans see the People's Republic of China as the emerging competitor to the superpowers.[37] The PRC's power may or may not be congenial to European interests, but certainly estimates of China's future power do not require "pious hopefulness" – common sense will do.

Of course, debate over the meaning of survey results can arise for reasons other than faulty presentation. Kaltefleiter, for example, traces West German perceptions of the NATO–Warsaw Pact military balance as part of a broader analysis of West German surveys on defense issues. Since West Germans increasingly see the Warsaw Pact as more powerful, Kaltefleiter concludes that the West German defense consensus is breaking down – a conclusion he sees buttressed by other poll results.[38]

Kaltefleiter's interpretation is not an unusual one. It is consistent with many recent commentaries on the political impact of change in the East–West military balance. None the less, by using the survey on perceptions of power as a measure of consensus, he implicitly assumes one of two things: that consensus in the past was based on

NATO superiority – a reasonable but debatable point; or that West Germans would *prefer* NATO superiority. At a minimum, by relating perceptions of power to the general consensus on defense issues, Kaltefleiter is assuming that support for the Alliance is a function of perceptions of the military balance.

None of these assumptions is unreasonable. Indeed, as I note in the next chapter, many recent analyses of the Alliance begin by arguing that changes in the military balance underlie the strains of the recent past. The point is that this survey alone provides little basis for the conclusion. In fact, in the same survey question cited by Kaltefleiter, the plurality (47 per cent) of respondents see *equality* in the European military balance, and other polls show that by overwhelming margins, West Germans (and other Europeans) *prefer* this state of affairs. Moreover, changing perceptions of the military balance have had little impact on the public's confidence in the Alliance's ability to deter and defend in Central Europe (although it has never been extraordinarily high). In fact, despite some dramatic shifts in perceptions of American and NATO power, confidence in security has changed only little.[39]

Perhaps the confidence of survey respondents should be read as ignorance or wishful thinking, but one could argue that such a stance is hardly novel in the history of the Alliance. In any event, differences in interpretation are not due to inaccurate or faulty polling – the questions are relatively "clean" and straightforward. Rather, reasonable differences of interpretation arise from differing views among analysts of the political significance of the military balance and how much this has changed. More and better polls will not resolve such differences.

These examples of abstract or misleading questions, faulty presentation, and competing interpretations reinforce the argument made earlier. The use of single surveys to characterize "public opinion" can produce highly inappropriate conclusions. None the less, the vice can also be turned to virtue, for a comprehensive review of many questions using a variety of question wordings may reveal the sensitivity of public opinion to the different factors that affect national security choices. As Hans Rattinger perceptively observes, the numerous surveys conducted during and after the INF debate have yielded a sort of "natural experiment".[40] If opinions are systematically different when different choices and tradeoffs are included in survey questions, we can begin to sort out the variety and significance of the factors that affect public perceptions of national security issues.

Moreover, by examining change in a variety of opinions as events and political debates unfold, we can begin to address the most difficult question of all: who is leading whom?

ELITE CONFLICT AND PUBLIC OPINION

There is paradox in the fact that statesmen and journalists have defined the problem of domestic consensus in a bottom up, "plebiscitory" model in which governments are increasingly pressured by public opinion to modify existing policies. Until quite recently, the research of political scientists pointed to the opposite conclusion. Although most studies were based on American public opinion, these and a few comparative studies suggested that public opinion *followed* rather than led government statements and policies. Further, there was good evidence to indicate why this should be the case. Most of the general public have a low interest in security matters, so that their attention and interest is usually stimulated by official statements and action. And since few citizens have a detailed familiarity with security policy issues, when debates arise they look to the government or to other knowledgeable observers (in the parties, media, or interest groups) for guidance on the issues.[41]

Of course, there is nothing in such studies to indicate that the public, once mobilized, would always *agree* with official policy, but these studies do suggest that increasing debate and discussion – and perhaps change in public opinion – have their origins in élite debates rather than in opinions that originated with the public at large and were pressed on unwilling governments. Some of the theoretical ideas reviewed above would also suggest that public opinion is a reaction to élite debate. The changes in international politics emphasized by the "power and interdependence" school were often expressed in the statements of government spokesmen – I have cited Kissinger as a prime example. Further, debates about the utility of force and the significance of strategic parity were carried out both in governmental statements and in important scholarly and popular journals. It seems understandable that public opinion might react to the intensity and fractiousness of these debates, if not wholly to agree with any side.

A similar process might be seen in the role of political parties. While the 1960s were a period of relative consensus among the parties, the late 1960s and early 1970s brought increasing polarization on such issues as détente, the relative weight to be placed on arms control and arms modernization, and the extent and manner in which nations of the Alliance should respond to Soviet actions in Europe and elsewhere. Since the public generally is not informed in detail about such issues, it seems plausible that opinions were shaped by the institutions in which guidance on the issues could be found. As I argued above, there was a tradition of ideological conflict that provided such cues.

Finally, the view that élite fragmentation leads to public polarization has gained growing acceptance among leading students of domestic politics in the Atlantic Alliance. For example, Stephen Szabo has argued that in West Germany, divisions in public opinion reflect a breakdown in the élite consensus, and he traces the decline of consensus among élites to the successor generation of younger élites whose experience and education have differentiated them from their older colleagues.[42] Similarly, Gregory Flynn summarized the results of a number of European surveys by observing that:

> The origins of increased questioning of Western defense and especially nuclear policies comes not from the public at large, but from highly educated, politically attuned, well-organized, and emotionally engaged individuals. Rather than democratization, the phenomenon thus has more to do with an evolution of Western "élites". . . . Experts and political élites alike have been uncertain about both the significance of, and the appropriate policy response to these [economic, political and strategic] developments.[43]

All of this suggests that the popular picture of NATO governments held hostage by public opinion may be incorrect at worst or misleading at best. Rather than a "bottom-up" process of "élite challenging" opinion, we may be witnessing a "top-down" process of élite fragmentation in which increasing dissensus is communicated to, and reflected in, public opinion. Far from being a driving factor in the politics of defense in NATO, change in public opinion may simply be an additional manifestation of conflicting perspectives among élites.

Certainly the polls would support a "top-down" interpretation. For example, just *before* the INF controversy, a survey for the West German Ministry of Defense showed that only 10 per cent of the public had heard of flexible response, and only 14 per cent could identify the amount of money spent for defense. In the Netherlands, one of the more "populist" political systems in Western Europe, only 23 per cent of the population claimed in 1977 to pay much attention to defense matters. Even *after* the intense defense debates of the past few years, security issues remain relatively less important to Europeans than "bread and butter" issues such as inflation, unemployment and public spending.[44]

But if there is growing evidence that élite and expert debates stimulate change in public opinion, the comments of Szabo and Flynn suggest that we do not yet understand the precise nature of the breakdown in consensus. Flynn's observation suggests that the origins of dissensus are broadly political, while Szabo specifies generational change as the source of the breakdown. By studying the traces of cleavage in public opinion, perhaps we can begin to identify the nature of change in élite as well as public opinion.

To study élites directly would require an additional book. None the less, I address the issue in two ways. First, in Chapter 7, I compare élite opinion to public opinion to ascertain the extent to which the élite and the public diverge in their opinions. This examination includes a review of available surveys of governmental élites and the "influential" élite in the press, educational system, and interest groups. Secondly, I review contextual, historical evidence of political debates within NATO countries for evidence of governmental and partisan debates that may have anticipated – perhaps precipitated – change in public opinion.

The second way to examine the source of change and the impact of public opinion is broader. In Chapter 7, I return to the question of "who is leading whom" by comparing those countries in which opinion has changed most or shows the most severe polarization. I also examine the impact of opinion on policy and trace that impact to the nature of political institutions and their susceptibility to popular pressure.

A NOTE ON DEFINING GENERATIONS

One goal of this book is to assess the degree of generational polarization in security policy opinions. That task obviously requires a definition of generations, for there are a large number of age combinations that could conceivably guide the study. In addition, there are some practical limits to the number of age combinations that can be analyzed and presented in a comparative study, but there is also a more fundamental question: what defines a political generation?

One answer is to construct a definition empirically. One can compute and compare a number of age groups in opinion surveys in an inductive search for those age cohorts that most clearly differentiate members of the population. That approach has, in fact, been employed in other studies.[45] However, the empirical approach has obvious practical limitations in a study such as this. In the first place, there are an infinite number of age combinations that one could explore, a strategy that would be inordinately time-consuming (and perhaps impossible) in a study that must compare a large number of opinion surveys. The task would be truly herculean were I to attempt to ascertain "the" pattern of age differences inductively across four countries, multiple issues, and several points in time. For practical reasons, then, I ruled out the empirical approach to defining generations.[46]

Most students of generational change have followed a more theoretical approach to the definition of generations. This approach is based on the classic description of generational politics offered by Karl Mannheim:

> The fact of belonging to the same class, and that of belonging to the same generation or age group, have this in common, that both endow the individuals sharing in them with a common location in the social and historical process, and thereby limit them to a specific range of potential experience, predisposing them for a certain characteristic mode of thought and experience, and a characteristic type of historically relevant action.[47]

The question raised by Mannheim's observation is exactly what constitutes a common "social or historical process". In many studies, it is defined as a dramatic event, such as a war or revolution. For example, students of generational change in American foreign policy often divide the body politic into the "Munich generation" and the "Vietnam generation", for these events were presumably critical to the formation of attitudes towards national security.[48]

This approach is rarely applied in post-war European studies. One reason is practical: it could hinder comparison were a cross-national study based on a variety of different generations defined in terms of unique "critical events". Moreover, it is not at all clear that there *is* a critical event in post-war European history that would qualify as a defining characteristic of generations. True, the Second World War itself is a clear dividing line, but should one also partition the post-war generations according to their exposure to crises (Suez, Berlin, Czechoslovakia) or domestic turmoil (Paris, 1968)? Is a common event of equal significance for all countries in a comparative study?

There is a second reason why the "critical event" approach has not been employed in comparative studies of generations: recent theories of generational change are based on gradual, incremental change rather than on the impact of critical events.[49] Inglehart's theory, for example, is based on the gradual effect of prosperity and security rather than on any single occurrence. For Inglehart, the prosperity and security of the post-war period have produced a generation with "a common location in the social and historical process . . . predisposing them for a certain thought and mode of action".

This "gradualist" approach has also characterized research on the security attitudes of the post-war "successor generation". What distinguishes the post-war generation is not exposure to a single, dramatic event. Rather, they matured politically during a period of gradual but unprecedented change in the international environment. Inglehart, for example, points to the fact that the post-war generation has enjoyed a sustained period of peace: "although the older generations have experienced total war in one form or another, the younger generation in these countries has never experienced invasion of the homeland by hostile forces. For them, war has been something that happens in other countries."[50] Furthermore, people born after the Second World War reached the crucial stage of young adult socialization during the mid 1960s, the beginning of the period of détente, arms control, and reaction against Vietnam.[51] As I argued above, the "social and historical process" of this period was one of rapid change in the nature of national security. The Cuban missile crisis and the beginnings of arms control negotiations highlighted the "stalemate" effect of nuclear weapons. The Vietnam War raised loud debates about the utility of military force. Finally, there was widespread speculation that economic interdependence had changed the nature of international politics, especially concerning the relevance and cost-effectiveness of military force as an instrument of national policy. This was a much different world than had been experienced by the pre-war generation.

Given the practical limitations to an inductive, "empirical" approach to generations, I adopted the strategy of treating generational change in the post-war period as a gradual process rather than as a reaction to specific events. My strategy was to divide the population by age so as to emphasize the differing security environments of the generations. I defined the generations to maximize attention to the

Table 2.1 The Generations Studied in this Book

Generation	Year of birth	Period of higher education	Age in 1980	Age in 1985
Pre-war generation	pre-1945	pre-1964	35+	40+
Détente generation	post-1945	post-1964	−35	−40

NOTE: The analyses in this book describe those older and younger than 35. This refers to age in 1980.

crucial years of the mid 1960s. A cutting point based on year of birth before and after 1945 places the post-war generation in the phase of adult socialization during the mid 1960s. Because special attention will be given to the views of the educated segment of the "successor generation", 1945 is a particularly useful cutoff point, for those born in 1945 began entering university about 1964 – at precisely the time that détente, Vietnam, and arms control had reached the agenda of Western governments.

Table 2.1 summarizes the generations that will be used throughout this book. In all of the analyses to follow, I present results for those born before and after 1945. As noted below, I use 1980 as the reference year, so the generations listed in tables refer to those "under and over 35 years of age" in 1980. Although the term is arbitrary, for ease of reference I occasionally refer to the younger group as the "détente generation" (one could just as easily label them the Vietnam generation or the arms control generation). The older generation is referred to simply as the "pre-war" generation.

A few final notes are necessary. The generational analyses presented below are based on the age of these two cohorts in 1980. That is, I wanted to maintain the focus on the détente generation even after they "aged" beyond their thirty-five years in 1980 (surveys inquire of chronological age, not date of birth). Thus, although the tables list generations based on the "over/under 35" cutoff, it should be understood that this refers to the respondents' *age in 1980*. Finally, it is worth noting that I did experiment with additional age cutoffs. These analyses suggest that age differences proceed rather smoothly from young to old. Thus, my use of a dichotomous definition of generations does not seem to do violence to the broader age distribution of security opinions.

RECAPITULATION: THE PURPOSE AND PLAN OF THE BOOK

This book describes change and cleavage in public opinion on national security issues in France, West Germany, Great Britain, and the Netherlands. In the chapters to follow, I trace historical trends and patterns of domestic polarization in four important domains of security policy: perceptions of change in the power balance and confidence in deterrence; nuclear weapons and arms control; the popularity of the NATO Alliance and partnership with the United States; and support for defense spending.

Each chapter contains an examination of historical trends in opinions and of important societal cleavages. Further, each chapter is guided by a theoretical theme most relevant to the issue at hand. Overall, I hope to assess the relevance of three theoretical perspectives – changes in international politics; generational change; and the effects of ideology and parties. The final chapter of the book contains an assessment of the impact of opinion, and it also includes a comparison of American and European public opinion, an important topic given recent discussions of a "crisis" in transatlantic relations.

3 The Ambiguous Politics of Parity: Power and Deterrence in European Public Opinion

It is ironic that a "crisis" in Western security began in 1979. This was the year of NATO's 30th anniversary, and among scholars the stability of the Alliance remained a prominent – even dominant – point of view. In fact, it was in 1979 that Anton DePorte convincingly analyzed the historical roots of the Western security "sub-system" that had endured for thirty years. In DePorte's view, the most important features of that sub-system remained intact. Since the end of the Second World War, the crucial consideration had been the rise to pre-eminence of the United States and the Soviet Union, with all its implications for the security dependence of Western Europe and the subjugation of Eastern Europe. For West Europeans, Soviet power combined with geography to produce a threat that was palpable, however much it might vary with circumstances. And failing a unified European effort in defense as in the economic sphere, alliance with the United States remained a *sine qua non* of security and perhaps even of survival. Although NATO had seen many bitter controversies, the Alliance endured because the forces of change had been insufficient to overturn the "profound, precise and lasting consequences" that had been wrought by the Second World War.[1]

Other scholars argued that forces of change had accelerated during the 1970s. By far the most frequent topic of discussion was the relative decline in American military power, symbolized by the codification of strategic parity in the SALT Agreements in 1972. The United States had also lost its dominance and leadership in the world economy, as revealed by the lack of consensus on the economic and energy issues of the 1970s.[2] To these changes in the international system were added more general theories about the transformation of military power in international politics. As power became attenuated by nuclear parity and as economic interdependence increased, the relative utility of military force had declined. The attention and resources of governments were shifting to the problems of global interdependence and national welfare. The marginal utility of investment in military power could become a subject of political debate – domestic as well as transatlantic.

Thus, just as NATO celebrated its 30th anniversary, the Alliance faced a tension between forces of stability and forces of change. Discussion of the impact of these changes involved domestic audiences in important ways, for the perceptions of the public were increasingly seen as critical to Alliance cohesion and domestic consensus. Indeed, for many theorists as for government officials, European public opinion was now the single most important concern. Ultimately the durability of the Alliance depended not just on the nature of military power or the objective state of the military balance. It also rested on the perceptions and confidence of citizens.

The purpose of this chapter is to analyze how European public opinion perceived these forces of change and continuity. In the following sections, I describe in more detail the arguments of theorists and strategists about the extent of change in the military balance and the consequences of these changes for the perceptions and confidence of citizens. Following this review, I examine opinion surveys that trace the public's perceptions of the military balance as well as their confidence in Western deterrence and defense capabilities.

The data suggest a paradoxical conclusion: although the public, like the experts, has perceived an adverse change in the East–West military balance, they do not feel less secure as a result. Indeed, the data suggest that the public's confidence in security is not closely related to its perceptions of the military balance. In a subsequent section of the chapter, I draw on this conclusion to explain the emergence of domestic controversy after NATO's decision in 1979 to modernize its intermediate nuclear forces (INF).

THE AMBIGUOUS POLITICS OF PARITY

In a celebrated essay, Arnold Wolfers once wrote that "national security" is at best an ambiguous political symbol. Far from providing a clearcut guide to the necessary level and structure of defense efforts, "security" represents a general goal about which individuals and nations will disagree as a result of different perceptions and values. It is rare to find consensus on the level of security that is necessary or agreement on the acceptable level of sacrifice required to achieve a given level of "security".[3]

Nothing could confirm Wolfers' observation more than the debates that arose during the 1970s, not so much over the fact of change in the East–West military balance and in international politics more generally, but over the consequences of those changes for deterrence and for the domestic security consensus. One school of thought argued that the emergence of US–Soviet parity, coupled with dramatic transformations in both international and domestic politics, had brought with it a decline in the relative utility of military force as an instrument of national policy. The most influential statement of these changes came in the works of Robert Keohane and Joseph Nye.[4] Keohane and Nye argued that the emergence of strategic parity had further accentuated what had long been apparent in the nuclear age: that the use of nuclear weapons as an instrument of policy would rarely bring benefits in proportion to the enormous costs. The threat of mutual assured destruction had lowered expectations of conflict through the "stalemate" effect, a perception that was reinforced by the détente and arms control agreements of the 1970s. Moreover, the most pressing problems of the 1970s – economic stagnation, inflation, exchange rate instability, global resource problems – could not be solved with military force. Thus, although Keohane and Nye did note that military force retained its potential as the ultimate – in their words, "dominant" – instrument of policy, the decline in the applicability of force and the costs associated with its use indicated that its utility relative to other policy instruments had been attenuated.[5]

Other scholars took this analysis one step further, arguing that strategic parity and the decline in the utility of force could contribute to a lack of cohesion in NATO and to the emergence of domestic debate and polarization. In fact, nervousness among allies had become apparent as early as 1972, when the ratification of the SALT I Agreements raised uncertainty about the ability and willingness of the United States to commit its nuclear weapons to European defense in an age of codified strategic parity. Moreover, some analysts argued that shifts in the military balance had led to domestic polarization. One German analyst observed that "the misleading term 'strategic overkill' raised questions about the meaning of further military efforts".[6] In 1987, Josef Joffe ascribed the emergence and emotion of the peace movements to the shock brought on by the growth of Soviet power: "Matched by the breathtaking expansion of the Soviet strategic arsenal, the three-generation jump [of Soviet missiles] in the European 'theater' spelled out the dreadful message that all of Western Europe, though a serene island of seemingly permanent détente, was an immovable target and a hostage to Soviet nuclear might."[7]

An additional prospect during the 1970s was that the cumulative effects of strategic stalemate, détente and economic stagnation could bring a conflict between domestic and external priorities – the age-old choice between guns and butter. Tracing the evolution of French defense politics in the 1970s, Edward Morse offered a prediction that seemed applicable to all Western societies in an age of strategic stalemate and budgetary scarcity:

> In a period when the costs of defense have increased dispro-
> portionately to other costs and when the outbreak of war becomes
> less probable, the curtailment of defense expenditures appears as a
> logical source of revenues that can be diverted to other govern-
> mental imperatives. In such circumstances, the classical guns or
> butter issue is inevitably posed in politics.[8]

In summary, much of the theoretical literature of the 1970s suggested that changes in the international system, especially the emergence of US–Soviet parity, had important consequences for the cohesion of the Western Alliance and for the domestic consensus on which security policy rested. Strategic parity lessened the fear of war, reduced the confidence of Europeans in the American guarantee, and sharpened domestic debate over the utility of marginal in-crements to military forces. The growing importance of economic issues and welfare priorities further strained consensus. In an age of nuclear stalemate, domestic reform, and economic interdependence, why pay more for military force, when its utility was doubted in any case?

As discussed below, both the theoretical and policy implications of "complex interdependence" were much debated. Tellingly, Keohane and Nye were criticized both for exaggerating and understating the utility of military force.[9] Yet a close reading of their work indicates that they did *not* argue that military force had lost all utility or that its potential dominance over other instruments of policy had been lost for all possible cases. Rather, they argued that military and economic developments had rendered it *relatively* less useful given the costs, benefits, and effectiveness of force in the face of the growing import-ance of non-military problems. Force retained its potential utility, but whether the costs of the maintenance and use of force would be accepted domestically was a question that remained open in light of the economic and political changes that had occurred during the

1970s. To return to the terms used by Arnold Wolfers, the increasingly complex calculations of costs and benefits meant that "security" in an age of parity and interdependence had become more ambiguous than ever before.

Although much of this analysis addressed the options of the superpowers, for Europeans the ambiguities were equally severe. Although some strategists argued that parity had not removed the need to compete in the "dynamic balance" of the arms race, this need had questionable applicability to Europe. Strategically, the competitive parity of the superpowers had progressively raised the costs of competing in the nuclear club. Further, although strategic parity had accentuated the importance of the conventional balance in Europe, the lesser risk of war, together with the fear of decoupling or the prospect of budgetary tradeoffs, meant that appeals for increases in conventional forces would fall on ambivalent ears in Europe. Equally important, the European experience with decolonization and the American experience in Vietnam combined to lower the possibility that "force short of war" would be enthusiastically greeted in Europe. If parity, interdependence, and domestic priorities had complicated the politics of defense in the United States, for Europeans the effects seemed even greater.

POWER AND PERCEPTIONS

Among American officials and strategists, concern for the perceptions of Europeans led to critiques of both American strategy and of the view that the utility of force had declined. Interestingly, these critics agreed with the prevailing view of the effects of strategic parity, especially the effect on alliances, but their analyses were directed less at describing the long-range impact of parity on the international system as they were animated by a desire to reform American strategic policy so as to assure Europeans of the reliability of extended deterrence. For example, Edward Lutwak criticized the calm attitude of many strategists in the face of "asymmetric parity" and argued that quantitative or qualitative imbalances could affect the more ephemeral, but no less important, perceptions of allies: "The political utility and military effectiveness of armed forces exist in different worlds: one, the world of appearances, impressions and culturally determined value judgments of international politics; the other, the world of physical reality in actual warfare."[10] Such analyses, concerned with what Richard Betts called the "Madison Avenue" view of deterrence, are significant because they suggest, not just that changes in the strategic balance itself could erode the confidence of the allies, but that alliance cohesion could also be weakened by the appearance – the *perception* – of declining American power or will.[11]

This concern had influenced American strategic policy even before the signing of the SALT I Agreement in 1972.[12] In February 1972, President Nixon posed the now-familiar "self-deterrence" dilemma of assured destruction and declared that greater flexibility in strategic options would be pursued: "A simple 'assured destruction' doctrine does not meet our present requirements for a flexible range of strategic options. No President should be left with only one strategic course of action, particularly that of ordering the mass destruction of enemy civilians and facilities."[13] In 1975, Secretary of Defense Schlesinger announced a renewed emphasis on "flexible options" in his *Annual Report*. What was significant about this statement was the concern that, despite strategic parity, "force asymmetries" could undermine the confidence of the European allies by calling into question not just the actual American guarantee of Europe, but also European assessments of American will and resolve more generally. As Schlesinger put it: "Friends may believe that a lack of willingness on our part to accept less than equality indicates a lack of resolve to uphold our end of the competition and a certain deficiency in staying power."[14]

Thus, the predictions of political theorists were confirmed by the worries of strategists and governments. The shift to strategic parity could undermine the cohesion of the Alliance by reducing confidence in the United States guarantee. To this observation the strategists added an additional concern: in an age of "asymmetric parity", the *perception* of inequality could further undermine confidence. Although strategic parity may have produced a superpower "stalemate" and an environment conducive to arms control, the utility of competition in nuclear (and, by implication, other) arms remained compelling for reasons of alliance confidence, especially the confidence of the Europeans.

DISSENTING VOICES

The upshot – indeed the purpose – of these arguments was to counsel the continuing political utility of American military power, especially to maintain confidence within the NATO Alliance. Not all analysts were convinced, however. Indeed, both the diagnosis and the prescription were challenged on several grounds. The strongest challenge came from those who doubted that strategic parity, assured destruction, or "force asymmetries" had wrought an unambivalent effect on perceptions or confidence in the Alliance. Lawrence Freedman argued that the cohesion of the Alliance depended not just on the military balance or the credibility of security guarantees, but also on faith in the policies, institutions, and self-confidence of the Alliance leader. If these were shaken during the 1970s, it was probably due more to these latter factors than to putative shifts in the military balance: "It was arguable that the problem, if there was one, had much to do with the collapse of self-confidence in the United States following the debacle in Vietnam and the Watergate scandals. . . . America appeared hesitant and fumbling, overwhelmed by the limits of power . . .".[15] Further, Freedman criticized both the assumption and the result of the shift toward the "perceptual school" of strategic policy. The assumptions were questionable, he argued, because it was not clear that putative inferiorities resulting from force structure asymmetries were perceived even by governments: "it would have been surprising if their views of the military balance were influenced by arcane and complex calculations which could only be performed with the aid of a computer".[16]

Warner Schilling went even further, arguing first, that it was unclear exactly *which* military balance most affected the perceptions of allies. More often than not, he hypothesized, assesments of the balance are confused, incorrect, or colored by the conventional military balance rather than the strategic one. Broader components of power – such as the strength of the economy – are equally influential. Moreover, once parity and assured destruction had been established, it was unlikely that force asymmetries would much affect assessments of extended deterrence in Europe. Given the ultimate inability of either superpower to avoid large amounts of death and destruction in a nuclear exchange, extended deterrence was largely unaffected. The American nuclear guarantee, Schilling asserted, "is about as good as it ever was".[17]

Finally, a challenge to the theoretical thinking of the 1970s came from specialists in European security affairs. Like the strategists, these scholars argued that global and domestic constraints on the acquisition and use of military force did not necessarily preclude their usefulness as political instruments even for the "second-tier" powers of Europe. So long as the American nuclear force was the ultimate guarantee of European security, maintenance and even improvement of substantial conventional forces was the price to be paid.[18] And although the policy was a delicate one, pursuit of détente or *Ostpolitik* had always been predicated on the maintenance of a secure balance of forces and firm ties to the West. Moreover, although it was certainly true that substantial expeditions outside the NATO area were skeptically greeted by Europeans, there remained considerable opportunities for influence in the supply, advising and even reinforcement of Third World military forces.[19] More generally, one could raise the objection that, whatever the shift in the balance of power, the nature of international issues or competing domestic priorities, the maintenance of standing military forces remained the *sine qua non* of the modern nation state, and there was still a substantial reservoir of domestic support for this symbolic function and for other, nonmilitary purposes of the defense establishment, especially the maintenance of jobs in crucial economic sectors. Although superpower parity, interdependence and the pull of domestic priorities may have rendered European security policy more ambiguous and therefore more contentious, it was not altogether clear that the debate would produce a rejection or even a stagnation in the European investment in military force.

To summarize, the 1970s saw a lively debate about the nature of military power in an age of nuclear parity, but there was widespread agreement on the shift to nuclear parity and mutually assured destruction. What divided analysts was differing assessments of the consequences of that shift. Some theorists had predicted a weakening of the NATO Alliance. Others argued that confidence was a product of factors other than the state of the US–Soviet military balance. Some even argued that the emergence of strategic parity had not been such a dramatic event. Since at least 1957, debate about the nuclear guarantee had raged, yet the Alliance had not dissolved. The heart of deterrence had always been the depth of American interest and commitment and the risk of escalation.[20] Finally, since the American commitment to European deterrence was dependent on European contributions to conventional forces, the maintenance of military force remained a potent argument in domestic political debates even at a time of competing priorities and the apparent futility of competing with the superpowers.

PUBLIC OPINION AND THE MILITARY BALANCE

The first question is whether European publics have perceived the changes in the military balance discussed by theorists and strategists. Perceptions of the "overall military strength" of the Soviet Union and the United States are displayed in Table 3.1. Between 1957 and 1981, the data seemed to confirm the arguments of those who fear the adverse effects of Soviet power on European calculations. Especially between 1969 and 1977 (when, unfortunately, there was a lapse in the surveys), public perceptions of Soviet power grew appreciably. By the end of 1981, a majority of the British and a plurality of West Germans saw the Soviets as militarily superior. In France, the public was about evenly split between Soviet superiority and parity between the superpowers. In no country was there a significant percentage who saw the United States as stronger than the Soviet Union.

None the less, the historical figures also indicate that these perceptions do not represent a substantial change over previous years. Although only one survey from the 1970s is available for all countries, the polls from the 1950s and 1960s show that pluralities and even majorities of the British have almost always seen the Soviets as superior to the United States in overall strength. In Britain, the major change through 1981 was a reversal in the percentage who saw parity (increasing) and the percentage who saw American superiority (declining). Although the degree of change is much less dramatic, the same pattern is also visible in France.

Only in West Germany were past patterns dramatically reversed. In USIA surveys conducted in West Germany, the Soviets had been considered superior by a plurality in only one survey (significantly, just after the Berlin crises), but by 1981 Soviet superiority had become the plurality view. And while the percentage who perceived parity remained largely stable in West Germany between 1964 and 1981, perceptions of American strength none the less dropped more than in any other country. In the second set of West German surveys (done by EMNID for the Federal Ministry of Defense), opinions are more sanguine about American power. Since the late 1960s, equality with the Soviets has been the dominant and even the majority view. None the less, like other surveys, these polls also show a perception of declining American power together with a growth in Soviet power. Notice, however, that the availability of yearly polls for the 1970s shows that the largest single increase in the perception of Soviet strength occurred suddenly rather than gradually – beginning in 1975

Table 3.1   Perceptions of Overall US–Soviet Military Strength

"All things considered, which country do you think is ahead in total
military strength at the present time – the United States or the Soviet
Union?"

		US ahead (%)	Both equal (%)	Soviets ahead (%)	Don't know (%)
FRANCE					
	1957	17	20	25	38
	1958	19	34	29	18
	1960	16	16	37	31
	1961	12	20	43	25
	1963	24	19	28	29
	1964	28	25	25	22
	1965	25	32	20	23
	1968	23	30	30	17
	1969	41	18	23	18
	1977	16	27	34	23
Mar	1981	16	38	30	16
July	1981	16	42	25	18
Oct	1981	15	33	34	19
July	1982	18	37	24	22
Aug	1985	25	41	19	15
Dec	1985	21	39	19	21
BRITAIN					
	1957	19	6	50	25
	1958	26	8	41	25
	1960	14	5	57	25
	1961	15	8	56	21
	1963	26	7	41	26
	1964	27	7	42	24
	1965	26	15	37	22
	1968	27	12	45	16
	1969	36	13	32	19
	1977	10	19	50	22
Mar	1981	11	27	52	11
July	1981	9	18	50	13
Oct	1981	10	29	51	10
Dec	1981	10	20	56	14
July	1982	14	28	46	12
June	1985	23	38	34	6
Dec	1985	22	34	28	16

		US ahead (%)	Both equal (%)	Soviets ahead (%)	Don't know (%)
WEST GERMANY (USIA)					
	1957	38	20	23	19
	1958	24	22	23	31
	1960	24	12	35	29
	1961	26	17	38	19
	1963	50	18	16	16
	1964	41	30	14	15
	1965	41	32	10	17
	1968	28	35	26	11
	1969	39	32	18	11
	1977	15	35	34	17
Mar	1981	18	33	35	14
July	1981	15	33	38	15
Oct	1981	15	29	38	19
Dec	1981	13	24	44	19
July	1982	18	30	40	11
June	1985	17	46	25	11
Dec	1985	17	47	20	16
WEST GERMANY (EMNID)					
	1962	20	39	10	31
	1965	34	39	8	19
	1967	22	49	13	16
	1968	17	46	19	18
	1969	21	49	14	15
	1970	17	50	19	14
	1971	16	60	19	5
	1972	16	54	16	14
	1973	15	50	17	18
	1974	10	53	18	19
	1975	10	51	26	13
	1976	9	48	24	18
	1977	14	52	22	13
	1978	11	57	28	4
	1987	14	60	23	3

NOTE: From 1977 to 1985, response categories were more detailed (US or USSR considerably ahead, somewhat ahead). These categories have been combined in this table. The EMNID surveys in West Germany asked: "Taken altogether, are the armed forces of the USA as strong as, superior to, or weaker than those of the Soviet Union?"

and continuing through 1978. This suggests that assessments of military power were affected more by events than by the actual evolution of the military balance.

In fact, there is much in these data to suggest that perceptions of military power are affected more by events that give the appearance of strength than by changes in military power itself. This pattern is visible in a number of shifts in the survey responses. Between 1961 and 1963, perceptions of Soviet power declined rapidly, presumably due to American success in the Cuban missile crisis. Perceptions of Soviet power then increased after the invasion of Czechoslovakia in 1968. Finally, the yearly EMNID surveys for West Germany suggest that Freedman was correct when he argued that America's lack of self-confidence in the mid 1970s had an impact on perceptions. West German perceptions of American strength declined during the period of Watergate, withdrawal from Vietnam, and the recession that followed the Arab oil embargo.

The implication of this pattern is that appearance of greater self-confidence can improve the perception of allies. That is what happened during the early 1980s. As Table 3.1 shows, in July 1982, after only nineteen months of the Reagan presidency, Europeans' perceptions of Soviet strength declined, and the perception of parity grew. Although it is true that the Reagan military buildup was begun during this time period, one could hardly argue that the military balance had changed all that much. What seems more probable is that the rhetoric of strength, together with policies that challenged the Soviets, had impressed Europeans. In any case, by 1985 the perception of parity

Table 3.1 – cont.

SOURCES: USIA surveys are from the following sources. 1957–80: Kenneth Adler and Douglas Wertman, "West European Security Concerns for the 1980s: Is NATO in Trouble?", paper delivered to the 1981 Annual Meeting of the American Association for Public Opinion Research, Buck Hill Falls, Pennsylvania. 1981–5: Office of Research, United States Information Agency, *West European Public Opinion on Key Security Issues, 1981–1982* (Washington, D.C.: Report R–10–82, June 1982) Table 4; *July 1982 NATO Summit Follow-Up* (Washington, D.C.: Machine-Readable Branch, US National Archives and Record Service, Study nos. I8235, I8229, and I8230); *Foreign Opinion Note* (Washington, D.C.: 22 January 1986); and *Post-Geneva Survey: December 1985 [Contractor's Reports]* (Washington, D.C.: mimeographed).

The EMNID surveys for West Germany are from Federal Ministry of Defense, Information and Press Staff, *Meinungsbild zur wehrpolitschen Lage* (Bonn: annually) mimeographed.

was once again the dominant view in these three European countries.

For NATO governments, these polls are a good illustration of a public opinion glass that is both half-empty and half-full. On the one hand, even in the early 1980s, the combined percentage who perceived American superiority or superpower parity was substantial in all countries. By 1985 it was a clear majority. To the extent that the public understands that NATO's deterrence strategy rests on maintaining uncertainty in Soviet minds about the likely costs of military action against NATO, one could argue on the basis of these figures that their confidence has not been undermined. After all, Alliance planning and rhetoric usually emphasize balance and equality rather than superiority.

None the less, the long-term erosion in perceptions of American strength cannot be reassuring. Moreover, the fact that West German attitudes have deteriorated most noticeably is likely to cause unease about the calculations and strategies of this key member of the Alliance. Finally, to the extent that confidence in the Alliance rests not on judgments about uncertainty and deterrence but on the "Madison Avenue" effect of perceptions, the growing appreciation of Soviet power will surely be a source of worry.

Precisely for that reason, it is important to examine perceptions of more specific elements of the military balance. Most important are assessments of the Soviet–American strategic nuclear balance, because nuclear weapons are more visible to the public and because NATO's deterrence strategy rests heavily on the American strategic guarantee. On this question Europeans are less pessimistic (Table 3.2). In general, perceptions follow much the same pattern as assessments of "overall" US and Soviet military strength. The British are most pessimistic (a plurality saw Soviet strategic superiority in 1982). The French and West Germans, in contrast, are much more inclined to see Soviet–American parity. Like perceptions of overall American and Soviet military strength, the perception of growing Soviet strength and of parity in strategic power has increased in all three countries. In fact, the perception of strategic nuclear parity is higher than it is for the overall military balance: 30 to 40 per cent saw nuclear parity in 1982 whereas only 20 to 30 per cent saw "overall" parity in 1981. The perception of nuclear parity is higher than "overall' parity in earlier years as well.

Why should this be the case? Geography plays a role. For Europeans, perceptions of the "overall" relative strength of the Soviet Union and the United States is in part a function of the Soviet

Table 3.2   Perceptions of the US–Soviet Nuclear Balance

"Which country do you think is ahead at the present time on strength in nuclear weapons – the US, the USSR, or do you think they are about equal?"

	US ahead (%)	About equal (%)	Soviets ahead (%)	Don't know (%)
FRANCE				
June 1955	20	35	6	39
Nov 1957	14	28	20	38
June 1962	12	14	48	26
Jan 1963	24	20	29	27
Feb 1964	21	23	37	19
May 1965	23	22	28	27
July 1971	43	11	25	16
June 1972	27	53	27	7
July 1979	18	47	27	8
Apr 1982	11	46	35	9
BRITAIN				
June 1955	39	27	5	29
Nov 1957	26	31	21	22
June 1962	26	7	42	25
Jan 1963	26	10	34	30
Feb 1964	26	10	39	25
May 1965	27	19	37	17
July 1971	39	8	32	18
Mar 1972	21	47	23	9
June 1972	29	47	19	5
July 1979	18	19	54	9
Apr 1982	22	33	37	9
WEST GERMANY				
June 1955	39	36	6	19
Nov 1957	31	40	10	19
June 1962	32	20	25	23
Jan 1963	46	26	11	17
Feb 1964	40	28	14	18
May 1965	40	33	13	14
July 1971	46	16	19	18
Mar 1972	36	39	14	11
June 1972	46	30	14	10
July 1979	14	42	27	17
Apr 1982	16	38	35	11

NOTES: Wording varies slightly. In 1955 and 1957, the question refers to "Western forces" and to "atomic weapons". In 1962, the comparison is proximity to Europe. The Soviet Army is literally on the European doorstep. While nuclear weapons are also relevant here, both the tradition of arms control and the broader purposes of strategic forces suggests that they are in part a US–Soviet matter. Indeed, as Kissinger so wryly suggested, this may be a hope as well as an observation in Europe.[21] Secondly, the visibility of arms control negotiations during the 1970s, with their emphasis on the goal of negotiated equality, may have contributed to the opinion that parity in fact existed. Further, this feeling would be reinforced by the very nature of nuclear weapons, especially during a period in which the "stalemate" effect of parity was a well-publicized view (recall the comments of Henry Kissinger quoted above). To the extent that the deterrent effect of nuclear weapons in an age of parity and mutual destruction had penetrated the public consciousness, it seems understandable that the *nuclear* balance would be perceived as more "equal" than other types of military force.

In any case, the surveys on the nuclear balance are notable in one final respect: they confirm the sensitivity of power perceptions to major international events. Note that the most visible changes in assessments of the nuclear balance occur after 1957 (Sputnik), 1962 (Cuban crisis), and 1972 (SALT Agreements). The SALT period in particular seems (predictably) to reinforce the perception of parity. Although yearly polls would be helpful in fully documenting the pattern, it seems probable that assessments of the nuclear balance, like assessments of the overall balance, are more sensitive to major events than to close attention to the balance of military forces themselves. This in itself does not obviate the relevance of power perceptions to popular confidence in national security. Rather, it suggests that the perceptions reflect success and failure internationally rather than a fine-tuned reading of the military forces themselves.

Like opinions of the overall US–Soviet balance, these opinions of

---

Table 3.2 – cont.

between "Communist and anti-Communist countries". From 1963 to 1965 the question was prefaced by the phrase "All things considered".

SOURCES: United States Advisory Commission on Information, *The 28th Report* (Washington, D.C.: Government Printing Office, 1977) pp. 135–8; and two reports from Office of Research, United States Information Agency: *West European Perceptions of NATO and Mutual Defense Issues* (Washington, D.C.: Report R–27–79, 20 December 1979) p. 30; and *Key Security Issues, 1981–1982*, Table 6.

the strategic nuclear balance are not unambiguous in their meaning. Certainly, the substantial perception of parity will not trouble those who see deterrence as a function of the balance of risk and uncertainty. Especially for publics who are well aware of the implications of escalation, the growing perception of Soviet strategic power is less important than the still substantial view that strategic parity exists. None the less, it is precisely the emergence of parity that is most often mentioned as the source of European uncertainty about the credibility of the American guarantee, and it is in the area of visible strategic systems that strategists and policy-makers have been most troubled by the perceptions of allies.

Of course, it was the effect of strategic nuclear stalemate that focused the attention of Chancellor Helmut Schmidt on the problem of the theater nuclear balance. His 1977 speech on the subject eventually led to the INF missile deployment. Further, it was precisely this type of concern for the credibility of extended deterrence that has animated American shifts to variants of "flexible options" to dispel any notion that parity had weakened the US commitment to use nuclear weapons, if necessary, to deter and defend in Central Europe. It is testimony to the concern of the American government on this score that it commissioned a number of polls in the late 1970s and early 1980s to measure popular perceptions of the US–Soviet balance in Central Europe, both in intermediate nuclear forces and in conventional forces.

These polls are fraught with ambiguities. In the first place, Schilling's warning about confusion as to which forces influence perceptions of military power seems appropriate: do surveys inquiring of "US nuclear strength in Europe" refer to missiles, and in the event, does it include US forces (such as sea-based forces) assigned to the NATO command? Does it include weapons assigned to allied forces under the dual-key arrangement? And of course, as the Soviets have been quick to point out, one must ask if British and French national forces should be considered in any assessment of the "Eurostrategic" balance. These uncertainties must be multiplied when one considers the conventional balance in Europe: does it make sense to attempt to ascertain European perceptions of the US–Soviet conventional balance in Europe, when it is the very purpose of the Alliance to combine military forces?[22]

Given these ambiguities, the meaning of polls on "theater" balances is unclear. Perhaps it is a surprise to find that in 1981, after two years of official justification of the INF decision that repeatedly emphasized the imbalance created by deployment of the Soviet

SS-20, the plurality view in all European countries but two (Britain and Norway) was that the INF balance between the United States and the Soviet Union was about equal (the plurality averaging 34 per cent), although almost identical percentages did see Soviet "theater" superiority.[23]

Compared to most quantitative counts of the theater nuclear balance, these perceptions are inaccurate.[24] None the less, the critical question is whether quantitative imbalances have affected political calculations, and here the significance of strategic and theater balances remains unclear if the issue is *public confidence*. One view, put bluntly, is that stalemate is stalemate. As seemed to be the case for the US–Soviet strategic balance, it is possible that European publics have come to believe that mutual deterrence in Europe and elsewhere was long ago established at all levels given the destructive power available at the theater and strategic levels. Nor is this a view that is confined to the public. In Schilling's analysis cited above, the crucial balance is that of destructive capability – not the numerical balance of forces. Moreover, this was a view that was frequently stated during the debate over INF deployment. For example, in the arguments of one prominent European politician, the primary lesson of the entire INF controversy was that the quantitative balance of nuclear forces is not the overriding factor: "in view of the nature of nuclear weapons and the numbers and types available to either side, we must avoid an excessive preoccupation with imbalances in certain categories of systems. . . . to suggest that the SS-20 could be used for any conceivable political or military objective, except to secure mutual suicide, is to exist in an unreal world."[25]

Nevertheless, disagreement on the adequacy of NATO's nuclear deterrent has renewed a long-standing tradition in the Alliance: the ambiguities of nuclear deterrence, theater and strategic, lead directly to the problem of conventional deterrence. If there is at best a stalemate in nuclear forces, NATO's putative weakness in conventional forces takes on added significance. By all accounts, this should be the area of greatest pessimism among Europeans, whose attachment to the nuclear deterrent stems in part from the recognition of weakness in conventional forces and in part from aversion to the costs that would be required to improve them.

Surprisingly, the balance of conventional forces has not received great attention in public opinion polls. Those polls which have been done indicate that European opinion is fairly pessimistic. In 1978 and 1979 the British saw Warsaw Pact superiority rather than parity by a margin of 59 per cent to 22 per cent, while the West

Germans were more closely divided (52 per cent Warsaw Pact superiority and 40 per cent equality of the alliances). In France and the Netherlands, large percentages saw parity of the alliances (64 per cent and 49 per cent respectively). In a 1980 survey that simply asked which alliance was superior (excluding the "both equal" option), opinion was almost perfectly divided: similar percentages in Britain (57 per cent), West Germany (55 per cent) and France (50 per cent) believed in March 1980 that the Warsaw Pact was "superior" to the NATO Alliance. By 1986, there appeared to be some improvement in a survey on the "conventional strength of the United States and its allies versus the Soviet Union and its allies". The British remained the most pessimistic (45 per cent saw Warsaw Pact superiority versus 31 per cent who perceived parity), but the West Germans and the French were more inclined to see parity (in both countries, the margin of parity versus Warsaw Pact superiority was 43 per cent to 27 per cent).[26]

Only in West Germany are there trend surveys on the NATO/ WTO military balance (Figure 3.1). Consider the first poll displayed in Figure 3.1, an evaluation of the strength of "the US and the West and Russia and the East". Here West German responses are very similar to the earlier polls on "overall US and Soviet Strength". The perception of Western strength has declined while perceptions of parity and Soviet strength have grown. However, note that these "allied" assessments are more optimistic than the "US–Soviet" survey. Here the perception of parity was a *majority* view in 1982, compared to less than 30 per cent in the US–Soviet poll in late 1981, and while the Soviets were considered superior to the United States in "overall strength" by 40 per cent, in this poll the figure is 25 per cent. Substantially the same pattern is evident in the second poll shown in Figure 3.1, which shows a blunt survey question asking "Who is militarily superior: NATO or the Warsaw Pact?" Although there has been an increase in the perception of the Warsaw Pact's power, the plurality view in the late 1970s and early 1980s was that the alliances were equal. By 1985, alliance parity was the majority view.

This certainly goes against the grain of many assessments of NATO's conventional capability, although even here there is a substantial scholarly debate.[27] None the less, perhaps the surveys should be read less in terms of their "accuracy" than for their political significance and consistency with the type of confidence that NATO strategy and force posture are designed to evoke. If NATO forces are

US and West or Russia and East?

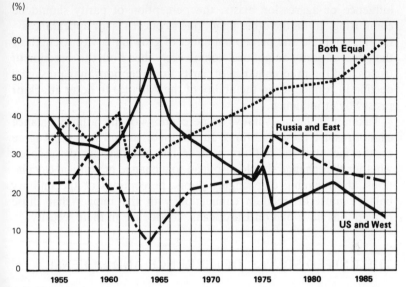

NATO or Warsaw Pact?

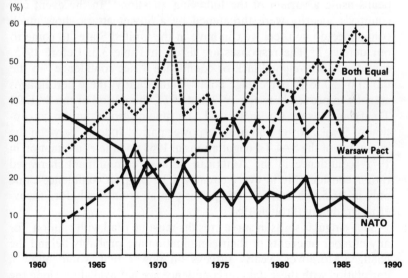

Figure 3.1   West German Responses: Who is Stronger in Military Strength?

SOURCE: West German Ministry of Defense, *Meinungsbild zur Wehrpolitis-chen Lage* (Bonn, annually).

meant to reassure public opinion that a sufficient deterrent to Soviet influence or aggression exists, the perception of parity should be comforting. If, on the other hand, one's concern is for appearances – for the symbolic and perceptual effect of growing Soviet strength or the effect of parity on political confidence – then both the direction of trends and the predominance of parity in perceptions may presage a decline in confidence in the ability of the Alliance to deter attack or resist Soviet influence.

Taken in isolation, surveys on perceptions of the military balance cannot resolve these questions. Just as theorists and strategists agree on the fact that the military balance has changed but disagree on whether that change should also lead to a change in political calculations, the meaning of changing public perceptions of the military balance must be read in connection with the impact that those perceptions have had on Europeans' confidence in their security.

THE UNITED STATES, DETERRENCE AND DEFENSE

Between 1968 and 1981, the American government queried Europeans using a variant of the following question: "In the event our country's security were threatened by a Soviet attack, how much confidence do you feel we can have in the United States to come to our defense?" The responses are listed in Table 3.3. Before 1975, confidence outweighed lack of confidence ("net confidence" in the table) by 50 to 70 percentage points. Significantly, these percentages actually improved between 1972 and 1974, the period of the SALT I Treaty and (as we saw in Table 3.1) a time of growth in the perception of Soviet power and of superpower parity. Indeed, between the beginning of the SALT I negotiations in 1968 and their culmination in 1972, confidence in the American defense commitment increased rather considerably in every country. The drop in confidence came only in 1975, when it fell precipitously in all countries before recovering gradually through 1981.

Such singular shifts in survey results must be read with caution, for any number of events or their combination are probably behind the change. Moreover, yearly surveys on power that would allow a correlation with these data on confidence are not available. None the less, the evidence is sufficient to indicate that European confidence in the United States does not result solely from their perceptions of military power. Between the 1960s and 1972 the British saw Soviet

Table 3.3   Confidence in the US Commitment to Defend Western Europe

"*In the event our country's security were threatened by a Soviet attack, how much confidence do you feel we can have in the United States to come to our defense – a great deal, a fair amount, not very much, or none at all?*"

	Great or fair (%)	Not much or none (%)	Don't know (%)	Net confidence (%)
FRANCE				
1968	50	30	20	+20
1972	73	18	9	+55
1974	72	14	14	+58
1975	49	34	17	+15
1978	53	25	22	+28
1979	58	32	10	+26
1980	65	23	12	+42
1981	66	21	13	+45
BRITAIN				
1968	67	14	19	+53
1972	82	16	2	+66
1974	84	11	5	+73
1975	63	29	8	+34
1978	73	20	7	+53
1979	68	28	4	+40
1980	71	24	5	+47
1981	74	19	7	+55
WEST GERMANY				
1968	53	41	6	+12
1972	67	23	10	+44
1974	72	20	8	+52
1975	49	41	10	+ 8
1978	61	28	11	+33
1979	53	35	12	+18
1980	66	25	9	+41
1981	59	28	13	+31

NOTES: Wording varies slightly. The 1978 question refers to a "threat to Western Europe's security". The 1975 question refers to "trust" rather than confidence in the United States. The 1974 question refers to a Soviet attack on Western Europe, "without involving the United States directly".

"Net confidence" is calculated by substracting the percentage of "not much/ none" confidence from those with "great/fair" confidence.

SOURCE: See p. 56.

superiority, yet their confidence in the American commitment *increased* during this period, as did that of the French and West Germans who also saw growth in Soviet power. In West Germany, where a yearly poll on American power is available (recall Table 3.1), the perception of declining American power was not gradual, but – like this poll on confidence – appeared suddenly in 1975. Taken together, these trends confirm once again that dramatic events color perceptions of power. Secondly, they focus attention on the year 1975. Of course, that year culminated a period of considerable turmoil: the climax of the Watergate episode; the withdrawal of American troops from Vietnam and the fall of Saigon; and the worst recession of the post-war period. Although the effect of none of these events can be isolated with certainty, it seems clear that they were more influential than the actual state of the military balance. Indeed, although the American defense debate after 1975 had highlighted the putative *weakness* of American military forces after a "decade of neglect", these polls show that confidence in the American commitment actually began *improving* in 1975.

Moreover, confidence in the American *nuclear* guarantee in the 1980s is at a level that must be considered surprising in light of the interminable debates that have raged over the subject. When asked about confidence in the American commitment "to do whatever is necessary to defend [your country] *even if this would risk the destruction of US cities*", pluralities and even majorities in all countries express a great or fair amount of confidence in the United States (Table 3.4). Perhaps paradoxically, the French, with their ambivalent attitude toward the American deterrent, are among the *most* confident in the American guarantee!

These data also provide additional evidence that confidence is not closely related to perceptions of military power. We saw in Table 3.1 and 3.2 that perceptions of American power and perceptions of parity increased during the early to mid 1980s. Yet these data on the nuclear commitment show that the 1980s were generally a time of declining confidence in the United States. Clearly, something other than changing perceptions of power had affected European con-

Table 3.3 – cont.

SOURCE: Kenneth Adler and Douglas Wertman, "West European Concerns for the 1980s: Is NATO in Trouble?", paper presented to the 1981 Annual Meeting of the American Association of Public Opinion Research, Buck Hill Falls, Pa, Table 7.

Table 3.4　Would the United States Risk its Cities for Western Europe?

"If our security were threatened by a Soviet attack, how much confidence do you have in the US to do whatever is necessary to defend our country, even if this would risk the destruction of US cities – a great deal, a fair amount, not very much, or none at all?"

	Great or fair (%)	Not much or none (%)	Don't know (%)	Net confidence (%)
FRANCE				
July 1981	52	31	17	+21
May 1982	56	37	8	+19
Dec 1985	45	34	22	+11
BRITAIN				
July 1981	56	37	7	+19
Mar 1982	56	40	3	+16
May 1982	49	47	4	+ 2
Dec 1983	44	52	4	- 8
July 1984	52	43	5	+ 9
Dec 1985	38	50	12	-12
WEST GERMANY				
July 1981	48	38	14	+10
Jan 1982	49	39	12	+10
Apr 1982	52	37	11	+15
July 1982	49	39	12	+10
Aug 1983	43	50	7	- 7
Nov 1983	41	43	15	- 2
July 1984	27	63	10	-36
Dec 1985	40	46	14	- 6
NETHERLANDS				
July 1981	53	42	5	+ 9
July 1984	41	42	17	- 1

NOTE: In 1983, the question refers to a "direct attack against the United States itself" rather than to "the destruction of American cities".

SOURCES: Through 1982, Office of Research, USIA, *West European Public Opinion on Key Security Issues, 1981–82*, Report R–10–82 (Washington, D.C.: 1982) Table 3. For 1983: Social Surveys Ltd, *Gallup Political Index*, no. 280 (December 1983) p. 12. For 1984 and 1985: Office of Research, United States Information Agency, *NATO and Burdensharing* (Washington, D.C.: Report M–9/11/84, 11 September 1984) Tables 3 and 4; and *Post-Geneva Survey: December 1985 [Contractor's Reports]*.

fidence. Perhaps it was the transatlantic economic disputes of the 1980s or the negative implications for Europe of the Strategic Defense Initiative (SDI) that shook European confidence. In any case, the irony is that the strengthening of America that was designed to improve the confidence of allies did not have the intended effect, despite the fact that evaluations of American power did improve.

Somewhat surprisingly, the faith in the American commitment (still rather high) does not translate into an overwhelming confidence in the ability of NATO to deter attacks. In surveys in 1981 and 1984 that inquired of confidence in "NATO's ability to prevent an attack on Western Europe", the percentages split about evenly. An average of 40 per cent in 1981 and 50 per cent in 1984 thought that NATO could "prevent a Soviet attack". Confidence in NATO's ability to *defend* Europe against attack is at about the same level.[28] But if opinions are less than totally confident on the question of defending Europe, historical polls indicate that this state of affairs is nothing new. The USIA has surveyed Europeans on this issue since the 1950s. In the 1950s and early 1960s, confidence in NATO's ability to defend Western Europe averaged 41 per cent in Britain and 53 per cent in West Germany. In 1984, the figures were 54 per cent and 51 per cent respectively. In France, confidence in NATO's capabilities actually increased, from 23 per cent in the earlier period to 40 per cent in 1984. Although confidence in NATO defense is barely a majority, current figures are none the less higher than in the age of American nuclear superiority.

Table 3.5 provides some final evidence on the evolution of confidence in NATO's defensive capabilities. From 1961 to 1986, the percentage of West Germans who thought that NATO is "strong enough to protect us" versus those who thought that "the Russians would overrun us" has fluctuated between 35 and 55 per cent in both directions, with no negative trend evident. Indeed, beginning in the mid 1970s, West Germans were growing slightly more confident in NATO's abilities (Table 3.5). An additional survey with slightly different response categories produced essentially the same picture. From 1960 to 1979, a stable average of 30 per cent thought that West Germany and NATO could not defend against a Soviet attack.[29]

Overall, surveys on confidence in deterrence reveal a clear picture. Although there have been substantial changes in perceptions of both the US–Soviet and NATO–Warsaw pact military balances, confidence in the US and in the Alliance as a whole appear to have changed little *in response to perceptions of the military balance*. To

Table 3.5 *West German Views of NATO's Defensive Capabilities*

"Assuming the Russians and the People's Army of the GDR attack us: do you believe that NATO including the Bundeswehr is strong enough to protect us effectively, or would the Russians in your opinion overrun us?"

	Strong enough (%)	Russians would overrun (%)	Don't know (%)	Net confidence (%)
1962	31	29	40	+ 2
1967	36	42	22	– 6
1968	34	44	22	–10
1969	36	46	19	–10
1971	49	45	6	+ 4
1974	38	37	25	+ 1
1976	33	41	26	– 8
1977	40	39	21	+ 1
1978	48	47	5	+ 1
1979	51	44	4	+ 7
1980	51	44	5	+ 7
1981	49	48	3	+ 1
1982	55	43	1	+12
1983	49	47	3	+ 2
1984	52	46	2	+ 6
1985	50	47	2	+ 3
1986	58	40	2	+18
1987	56	41	3	+15

NOTE: "Net confidence" is calculated by subtracting the percentage who answer that the "Russians would overrun" from the percentage answering "strong enough to protect us".

SOURCE: Press and Information Office, [West German] Federal Ministry of Defense: *Hinweise für Öffentlichkeitsarbeit*, no. 7/79 (Bonn: 14 September 1979) p. 77; *Meinungsbild zur Wehrpolitischen Lage: Herbst 1983* (Bonn: July/August 1983) p. 14; and *Material für die Presse*, no. 23/19 (Bonn: 17 November 1986) p. 2.

paraphrase Schilling, it appears that European confidence in their security is, at a minimum, about as good as it ever was. It may even be slightly higher than it was in earlier years.

THE BALANCE OF POWER IN DOMESTIC POLITICS

If European confidence in deterrence has been largely immune to shifts in the balance of power, there remains the additional question of whether all sectors of the population share this sentiment. That is, what patterns of domestic division have resulted from the evolution of perceptions of the military balance? Based on existing theory, what domestic alignments would one predict in perceptions of the contemporary balance of power? Are there inherent tendencies for certain societal groups to see one side or the other as stronger or weaker in military strength, or are the views of all social groupings a uniform reflection of the information available as public discussion proceeds?

The most appealing hypothesis is based on the ideological arguments discussed in the previous chapter. After all, the crucial distinction in the security attitudes of the Left and the Right involves the relevance of military force to problems of national security. For the Left, military force – a balance of power – has always been the problem rather than the solution. The accumulation and balancing of military force is seen as a symptom of political conflicts of interest. Threats to security, therefore, can only be addressed by reconciling underlying differences politically (or by encouraging the economic and social ties that would ameliorate those differences). Indeed, the tradition of the European Left has been to criticize policies of power balance as irrelevant at best or at worst as destructive, for the balance of power encourages an arms race without addressing underlying conflicts of interest. In its modern variant, the Socialist and Labour parties of Europe have argued that national security requires a dual policy of strength *and* negotiation, although the rhetorical emphasis of the Left has generally been more on negotiation than on strength.

Does this suggest that ideological affinities will produce inherently different perceptions of military power? In several indirect ways, it should. First, parties of the Left view military force as a less relevant component of overall security policy. To that extent, they may be inherently less amenable to arguments that the military balance has shifted one way or the other. If force is not the primary determinant of "security", the *perception* of a force imbalance may be less prominent on the Left. A second reason is fairly obvious: political arguments about the need for stronger military forces often turn on competing arguments about the state of the military balance. To accept the view that the balance has deteriorated would therefore admit of the solution that the Left rejects, for in their view a balancing of forces is either irrelevant or an invitation to an arms race. Further, partisans of the Left are likely to be skeptical of investing additional resources in defense when these would compete with social priorities. For the Left, therefore, arguments about the military balance are part irrelevant and part red herring. In both cases, the result could be an inherent tendency to see the balance as less threatening or less crucial to national security.

A second theoretical perspective would focus less on ideological tradition and more on the social and political changes of the post-war period. Inglehart's generational theory is most applicable. In his formulation, younger Europeans feel inherently more "secure" than their elders because they grew to maturity during a period of détente and escaped the hot and cold wars experienced by older Europeans. For these younger cohorts, matters of security and military force are simply less salient parts of existence. Indeed, younger Europeans grew to political maturity at precisely the time that strategic parity and arms control agreements were prominent topics of public discussion. In Inglehart's words, the more secure environment of the younger generation has produced a cohort of Europeans for whom national security is not a dominant concern: "Although the older generations have experienced total war in one form or another, the younger generation has never experienced invasion of their homeland by hostile forces. For them, war has been something that happens in other countries."[30]

This tendency to feel "unthreatened" is presumably reinforced by an additional factor: the much higher educational achievements of the post-war generation. Attendance at European universities grew two- to threefold during the 1960s and 1970s. In Inglehart's view, the emergence of a more highly educated younger generation will have important consequences for national security views because the educated are more cosmopolitan and are better able to deal with remote ideas and threats.[31] In addition to these cognitive effects of higher education, it seems obvious that the more highly educated should also be better informed about the ambiguities of defense policy that divided strategists and preoccupied governments during the 1970s. To the extent that security problems have become more contentious, one would expect evidence of these debates to be reflected first and foremost among the better educated members of society. The British Defence Minister, whose concern for the domestic security consensus was cited in Chapter 2, was particularly concerned with the views of the educated youth: "The educated and sophisticated young people of today are less likely to accept without question a description of world affairs that attributes to the East–West balance a primary and fundamental importance."[32]

POWER POLITICS IN DOMESTIC POLITICS

A breakdown of surveys on the military balance indicates a moderately strong – but comparatively uneven – relationship between the political leanings of respondents and their evaluation of the military balance. Table 3.6 sets out these breakdowns for two survey questions. The 1979 poll inquires "Which side do you think is ahead in total military strength – the Soviet Union and its Warsaw Allies . . . the United States and its NATO allies . . . or are both sides about equal . . .?" The 1986 question was the same, but it referred to the "conventional military strength" of the two sides.[33]

Table 3.6 shows that the parties of the Left generally give more optimistic evaluations of the power situation than do parties of the Right. They are more likely to respond that there is equality of power and less likely to see the Warsaw Pact as stronger than NATO. However, while the partisan alignment is strong in the 1979 survey, in 1986 they are clear only in France. In Britain and Germany in 1986 they are far more modest. Given the difference in wordings in the two years, it is difficult to say why this is the case. Perhaps the growing attention given to conventional forces had impressed *all* political parties by 1986, thus reducing the differences among them. It is also possible that, because of the inherent difficulty of assessing the balance of military forces, the distribution of public opinions on these issues is changeable in ways that are not related to partisan sentiments. Of course, the French data suggest that these explanations do not always apply, for the gap among French parties remained in both surveys. A cautious conclusion from these data would therefore be that they suggest different predispositions on the part of Left and Right in evaluations of military power, but the evidence is not overwhelming that they are deep or firmly engrained.

None the less, more continuous surveys conducted in West Germany indicate that partisan cleavage is consistent, if not stable. Figure 3.2 displays the evolution of division between the West German Social Democrats and the CDU/CSU. The question asked bluntly: "Which bloc is militarily superior at the moment: NATO or the Warsaw Pact?" Beginning with the first survey in 1973, Social Democrats have always been less inclined to see "the East" as superior in military power. By 1979, when tensions had risen considerably and a domestic debate on security issues had broken out, the gap between the parties became much larger. These West German figures suggest that ideological differences were focused and

Table 3.6   Opinions of the NATO–Warsaw Pact Military Balance by
Political Party Affiliation

*"Which side do you think is ahead in total military strength at this time –
the Soviet Union and its Warsaw Allies on the one side, or the United States
and its NATO Allies on the other, or do you think both sides are about
equal in military strength?"*

	May 1979		March 1986	
	WTO stronger (%)	About equal (%)	WTO stronger (%)	About equal (%)
FRANCE				
Total population	**27**	**64**	**24**	**42**
PCF	22	64	28	47
Socialist	28	61	20	48
UDF	30	62	31	40
Gaullist (RPR)	32	66	34	37
BRITAIN				
Total population	not available		**45**	**31**
Labour			42	29
SDP/Alliance			52	28
Conservative			48	31
WEST GERMANY				
Total population	**52**	**40**	**27**	**43**
Greens	–	–	22	45
Social Democrats	46	46	26	43
Free Democrats	49	40	32	48
CDU/CSU	59	33	30	44
NETHERLANDS				
Total population	**44**	**33**	not available	
PvdA (Labour)	40	37		
D'66	43	36		
CDA	49	30		
VVD	56	26		

NOTES: The percentage responding that NATO is superior is not shown
here.

The 1979 survey in the Netherlands uses slightly different wording; it
explains the membership in the alliances ("the United States and most
countries of Western Europe . . . . and Russia together with other countries
of what is called the East bloc"). The 1986 survey refers to "conventional
military strength" rather than to "total military strength."

In this and all following tables, a dash (" – ") is used when data is not
available; an asterisk (" * ") is used when the number of responses is too

exacerbated by the contentious climate of the late 1970s and early 1980s. This conclusion is reinforced if one considers the military situation *preferred* by adherents of the two parties. In polls conducted during the INF missile debate, 63 per cent of SPD adherents preferred US–Soviet equality as the best protection for German security, versus 52 per cent of the Conservative coalition.[34]

The importance of party views to these issues is further accentuated by the fact that the breakdown of responses to these same questions by the age and by the educational level of the respondents reveal only minor differences in views of the military balance. Summarizing a number of analyses, it is fair to say that the young do not see the military balance much differently than their elders. Nor do the higher educated differ much from those with lesser education.[35] There is only one circumstance in which generational and educational experience prove noteworthy, and that is when they are combined. Consider Table 3.7, which shows views of the military balance broken down by the age *and* educational level of the respondents. In France, younger respondents with higher education are moderately more likely to see alliance equality.[36]

The same pattern of a more optimistic "successor" generation is evident in the Netherlands and West Germany. Indeed, the distinctly more optimistic assessment of the young educated in the Netherlands stands out with particular clarity. Only in Britain do the "successor generation" not show a distinct profile.

To this point, polarization in perceptions of the military balance could hardly be termed dramatic. When party affiliation is examined, divisions are visible but not dramatic or stable. The views of the young, educated "successor generation", although certainly more optimistic, are not overwhelmingly so. Further analysis of these surveys indicate that clearer patterns emerge when age, education and political affiliation are analyzed together, although there are some additional complications.

Table 3.6 – cont.

small to calculate percentages. Unless otherwise noted, those without an opinion are excluded from calculation of percentages.

SOURCES: Machine-Readable Division, US National Archives and Record Service, *Perceptions of the Soviet Military Threat [France, West Germany]* (Washington, D.C.: Study no. I7904); Netherlands Institute for Public Opinion (NIPO), Report A–407/41 (Amsterdam: October 1979) p. 1; Office of Research, USIA, *March 1986 Multi-Issue Survey [Contractor's Reports]* (Washington, D.C.: mimeographed).

Percentage Responding East is Superior

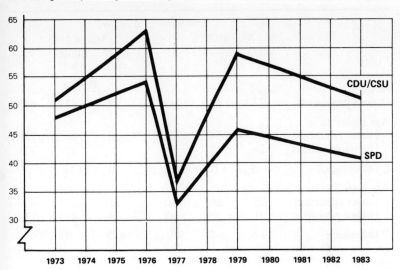

Difference Between SPD and CDU/CSU

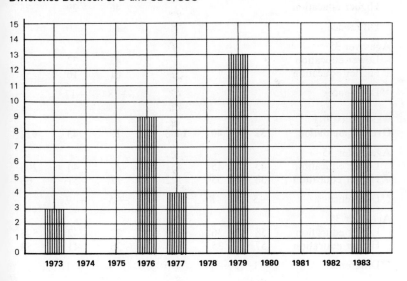

Figure 3.2   West German Party Views of the Military Balance

SOURCE: See Figure 3.1.

Table 3.7   Opinions of the Military Balance by Age and Educational Level

| | Which side is stronger? | | | | | |
| | May 1979 | | | March 1986 | | |
	WTO (%)	Equal (%)	n	WTO (%)	Equal (%)	n
FRANCE						
Overall population	27	64	749	24	42	947
Age under 35						
Lower education	31	58	215	26	40	228
Higher education	26	68	84	26	52	134
**Difference	−5	+10		0	+12	
Age over 35						
Lower education	25	66	402	21	40	459
Higher education	31	63	48	34	40	126
**Difference	+6	−3		+13	0	
BRITAIN						
Overall population	not available			45	31	1011
Age under 35						
Lower education				45	29	287
Higher education				46	29	75
**Difference				+1	0	
Age over 35						
Lower education				43	33	590
Higher education				61	16	58
**Difference				+18	−17	
WEST GERMANY						
Overall population	52	40	1468	27	43	922
Age under 35						
Lower education	43	45	431	27	44	206
Higher education	38	53	122	22	51	66
**Difference	−5	+ 8		− 5	+ 7	
Age over 35						
Lower education	58	36	840	27	42	596
Higher education	57	35	75	36	41	53
**Difference	−1	− 1		+ 9	− 1	

NETHERLANDS (1978)				
Overall population	**34**	**49**	**879**	**not available**
Age under 35				
Lower education	36	45	299	
Higher education	25	61	74	
**Difference	−11	+16		
Age over 35				
Lower education	33	50	459	
Higher education	42	45	47	
**Difference	+ 9	− 5		

NOTES: In this and all following tables, higher education is defined as nineteen years or older on completion of full-time education. The "Difference" figure subtracts the views of the lesser educated from those with higher education.

SOURCES: See Table 3.6. In addition, the Dutch survey is from Machine-Readable Branch, US National Archives and Record Service, *1978 NATO Summit Rider: Netherlands* (Washington, D.C.: Study no. 7801).

Table 3.8 shows responses to the 1979 survey arranged by the political affiliation of each age and educational group. Note that younger *and* older French Socialists with higher education stand out: both are more likely to see alliance equality than are their cohorts with lesser education, a pattern that is not evident for other parties. The same is true of the educated among both younger and older German Social Democrats and Dutch Labour Party members. In addition to this polarization by education, the German figures also show that, with one exception, the Left-Right division in West Germany is fairly general: all but the young with lower educational achievements are polarized according to political views. Thus, in this 1979 survey, evaluations of the military balance are divided in several ways. The young are more optimistic about the military balance; the young and educated of the Left are most optimistic (and most divided from their cohorts in the conservative parties); and respondents of most age and educational groups are divided along party lines.

Finally, the Dutch provide an additional complication. The young educated are indeed the most optimistic about the power balance (and by a wide margin), but this pattern characterizes the views of *all* political parties. Indeed, it is the young, educated adherents of the conservative CDA who are most optimistic. For other age and educational groups in Holland, the division is along the more familiar

Table 3.8   Percentage Responding that NATO and the Warsaw Pact are "Equal" by Age, Education and Party Affiliation (May 1979)

	Under 35 Education		Over 35 Education	
	Lower (%)	Higher (%)	Lower (%)	Higher (%)
FRANCE				
Total population	**58**	**68**	**66**	**63**
PCF	50	*	69	*
Socialist	56	66	62	70
UDF	55	52	67	46
Gaullist (RPR)	71	68	65	60
n =	191	77	366	46
WEST GERMANY				
Total population	**45**	**53**	**35**	**35**
Social Democrats	49	64	42	48
Free Democrats	43	80	32	*
CDU/CSU	44	31	31	26
n =	398	111	774	69
NETHERLANDS (1978)				
Total population	**45**	**61**	**50**	**45**
PvdA (Labour)	53	56	58	100
D'66	38	56	63	*
CDA	43	80	46	40
VVD	47	68	43	25
n =	299	74	459	47

NOTES AND SOURCES: See Table 3.6.

Left–Right axis and is especially prominent among older adherents of the Dutch Labour Party (PvdA).

This detailed breakdown of views of the military balance suggest a more complicated picture than any one theory would have it. Certainly the ideological divisions represented by party loyalties are a visible pattern. Evaluations of the military balance are aligned by party within most age and educational groups. Yet age and educational achievements are also significant in important, if different, ways. One uniformity is the more optimistic assessments of the young educated, as would be suggested by theories of generational change. Yet there are apparently other factors at work as well. Much of the difference in the views of the younger educated can be traced to members of parties of the Left, suggesting that ideology combines with education to produce a distinct set of views. In addition, there is some evidence that *older* educated adherents of the Left are also more optimistic about the military balance. Finally, we have seen that ideological division is not confined to the young or the young educated. Among older groups as well, adherents of different parties also see the military balance differently.[37]

Thus, issues of military power evoke both the "old" traditional ideological cleavages and the "new" cleavages resulting from the experience and educational achievements of the "successor" generation. The data therefore suggest a "glacier" process in the politics of national security. The distinct views of the successor generation indicate that they are indeed less inclined to see an imbalance of power. This is likely due to the prevalence of arms control and détente during their early adulthood, although the concentration of this viewpoint in the young, educated Left would suggest that traditional ideological arguments about the irrelevance of force may also be at work. And the fact that older citizens of all levels of education are similarly divided would suggest that ideological arguments retain their salience. Although scholars – and statesmen – have become preoccupied with the views of the "successor" generation, these surveys suggest that domestic conflict over the state of the military balance also joins divisions that predate the experience of the "détente generation".

THE POLITICS OF PARITY . . . AGAIN

Earlier sections of this chapter established that trends in public assessments of the military balance have not had a decisive impact on perceptions of security. Although perceptions of the power balance have changed, confidence in deterrence and in the United States defense commitment have not changed as a consequence. The existing evidence suggests that views of the balance and confidence in deterrence (and the United States) are influenced more by the flow of international events than by a "tracking" of the military balance.

This by itself indicates that theorists and policy-makers have exaggerated the importance of the size and structure of military forces to citizens' evaluations of their nation's security. Yet their concern is understandable, for common sense alone would suggest that assessments of the military situation should condition other attitudes that are important to the domestic politics of defense. For example, one would expect that evaluations of the military balance would condition support for defense spending and other Alliance policies.

But do individuals actually see a relationship between the international situation – including the military balance – and their views of other issues? There is some evidence to suggest that they do not. Perhaps most important, it is now well-documented that public knowledge of security issues is low, and this is especially the case with a complicated question such as the balance of military forces. Indeed, it is probably the low level of citizen information on defense issues that explains the sensitivity of public perceptions to dramatic events. The latter are far more publicized and understandable than descriptions of warheads or counts of infantry divisions. On these complicated issues of security policy, opinions may not be deeply rooted in information or beliefs. The correspondence of power perceptions with other defense issues is therefore open to question.[38]

A second reason is that citizen views of specific defense issues are in all likelihood affected by factors other than their assessment of the balance of power. We shall see in Chapter 6, for example, that support for defense spending is heavily conditioned by the economic climate and by government spending priorities. There is also evidence that support for nuclear deterrence and for the INF missile deployment was related to general citizen fears as much as to perception of the missile balance. Although a lack of correspondence between views of the military balance and views of specific defense questions may be due to a lack of information, it is also the case that other factors mediate such opinions. Put simply, citizens may come to their opinions of specific defense questions in spite of, rather than because of, their assessment of the military balance.[39]

In later chapters, I shall examine public opinion on specific defense issues in great detail. Here the question is whether opinions on these issues are related to perceptions of the military balance. Tables 3.9 and 3.10 provide a summary of opinions on a number of separate security questions, arranged according to the respondents' assessment of the NATO–Warsaw Pact balance. The May 1979 survey in Table 3.9 shows that these opinions are in fact very strongly correlated with assessments of the military balance. Statistically, assessment of the Soviet threat and support for defense spending are highly dependent on whether respondents see the military balance in favor of NATO, the Warsaw Pact, or in essential equality.[40]

None the less, a close examination of the percentages reveals that

Table 3.9   The Effect of Perceptions of the Military Balance on Opinions
of Other National Security Issues (May 1979)

	Which side is stronger?		
	NATO (%)	WTO (%)	Equal (%)
FRANCE			
Concerned about Soviet intimidation	42	44	31
Concerned about Soviet attack	24	32	23
Defense spending should be increased	16	26	14
WEST GERMANY			
Concerned about Soviet intimidation	44	58	32
Concerned about Soviet attack	34	36	22
Defense spending should be increased	21	33	17
NETHERLANDS (1978)			
Fear Soviet threat	18	26	17
Fear Soviet attack	26	26	8
NATO is essential	89	90	82
Confidence in NATO	78	63	62
Confidence in USA	86	75	81

NOTES: The table shows the percentage expressing particular views on
defense issues, arranged by their assessment of the military balance. For
example, 42% of the French who think that NATO is superior are concerned
about Soviet intimidation, versus 44% of those who believe that the WTO is
superior and 31% of those who think the Alliances are equal.

The responses shown on the left-hand side of the table are partial responses to *separate* questions. Complete responses are described in detail in
subsequent chapters.

SOURCE: See Table 3.6.

the distribution of differences is not exactly as might be expected. To
be sure, those who see Warsaw Pact superiority are generally more
likely to feel intimidated by the Soviets, to fear a Soviet attack, or to
favor an increase in defense spending. More interesting, however, is
the fact that those who see the power balance as essentially equal

show the most distinctly optimistic views. In all three countries, those who see equality are the *least* likely to fear Soviet attack or intimidation. Indeed, their fear of the Soviets is lower than among those who see NATO superiority! In France and West Germany, those who see alliance equality are also less likely to support increased defense spending than are those who see NATO as superior. Put simply, those who saw equality between the two alliances in 1979 were even more confident of their security than those who saw NATO superiority.[41]

The 1980 survey shown in Table 3.10 did not include the "equal" response, and generally the responses of those who saw NATO inferiority differ less from other responses than in the 1979 survey. In France the differences are marginal, except for the question on the US commitment that was no doubt colored by events in Afghanistan. The same is true of Britain and West Germany (although the question on defense spending shows some sensitivity to power perceptions in the latter country).

Most interesting are the responses in Britain, the only country in which the survey allowed the "equal" response in this question. The result is the same as in the 1979 survey: the British who saw the alliances as militarily equal were less supportive of defense spending and more supportive of "out of area" operations than those who saw NATO as superior. Their confidence in the United States was no different than those who saw NATO as superior. In short, these British responses, as well as all the responses in 1979, indicate first, that the views of those who perceive parity differ most from others, and secondly, that this group tends to be the most optimistic about a range of other security issues.

The argument made earlier about the "ambiguous" politics of parity takes on additional significance in the light of these data. Recall that in most countries it was the perception of parity that increased during the 1970s and 1980s. Since these people differ decidedly in threat perception and support for defense spending from those who see the Warsaw Pact as superior, the opposition of views in the security debates of the early 1980s are understandable. Overall, views of the military balance had changed noticeably; but more importantly, the consequences of these changes were also perceived differently by different sectors of the population. The growth of Soviet military power and the emergence of parity had produced competing views, both of the military balance and of the consequences for European security.

Table 3.10   The Effect of Perceptions of the Military Balance on Opinions of Other National Security Issues (March 1980)

	Which side is stronger?		
	NATO (%)	WTO (%)	Equal (%)
FRANCE			
Prefer NATO to Alternatives	15	13	–
Approve Use of Force "Out of Area"	71	69	–
Defense Spending Should be Increased	18	17	–
Confident in US Defense Commitment	78	69	–
BRITAIN			
Prefer NATO to Alternatives	52	48	55
Approve Use of Force "Out of Area"	75	75	87
Defense Spending Should be Increased	55	58	47
Confident in US Defense Commitment	82	70	81
WEST GERMANY			
Prefer NATO to Alternatives	55	61	–
Approve Use of Force "Out of Area"	57	58	–
Defense Spending Should be Increased	19	31	–
Confident in US Defense Commitment	82	67	–

NOTES: The table shows the percentage expressing particular views on defense issues, arranged by their assessment of the military balance. For example, 71% of the French who think that NATO is superior approve of NATO's use of force "out of area", versus 69% who believe that the WTO is superior.

The responses shown on the left-hand side of the table are partial responses to *separate* questions. Complete responses are described in detail in subsequent chapters. The "both equal" response was allowed in Britain only.

SOURCE: Machine-Readable Division, US National Archives and Record Service, *USIA Multi-Regional Security Survey* (Washington, D.C.: Study Numbers I8007, I8010, and I8005).

INF: THE DEBATE FINALLY HELD

European opinions of the military balance and the quality of deterrence are fairly clear. Although the growth of Soviet power and the emergence of strategic parity were acknowledged in European opinion, confidence in the United States and in NATO deterrence were not affected. The evidence suggests that it is dramatic international events – not all of them related to successful or unsuccessful military confrontations – that most influence perceptions of power and confidence in deterrence.

To Americans, this set of attitudes may be perplexing or even reflective of wishful thinking. After all, Soviet power has grown both in relation to the United States and in the Central European theater. European attitudes, it might be argued, reflect an unwillingness to recognize the consequences of these facts. Although both public opinion and defense policy in the United States reacted to the growth in Soviet power, Europeans have recognized the shift in the balance of power but have lagged in actions that would counter it.

Explanations of this difference in American and European threat perceptions are familiar, if not uncontested. Perhaps the primary one is the most obvious: in Europe, deterrence has worked for almost forty years, despite a succession of crises and periodic predictions of Soviet adventurism or American distraction. As Viscount Davignon put it in 1983:

> *The* great fear has gone. The Soviet Union is no longer the bogeyman it was in the immediate postwar period, and in any case we have grown used to it. We in Europe have grown used to seeing the "Beware of the Dog" sign on the gate next door, and the dog itself no longer really bothers us or our children as we make our way home on an evening. There is just the sign itself, a representation of a threat.[42]

But if the success of deterrence is one reason for the lesser fears of Europeans, the divergence in threat perceptions is even more frequently attributed to the differential rewards of the détente of the 1970s. By the late 1970s at least, most Americans – and certainly the American government – had come to doubt the wisdom of détente, while for Europeans the benefits in human contacts, trade, *and* security remained visible and desirable. In its most strenuous versions, American critiques of Europe included the charge of "détente euphoria", if not Finlandization. Given the benefits of détente, Europeans either refused to see the growing threat of the Soviets or were fooled by détente into the belief that security could be increased by negotiation rather than through military strength. Neither the national interests of the Europeans nor their attachment to negotiation would admit of the growing threat and the need to redress the military balance.

Such arguments are not inconsistent with the surveys described above, but a look at additional evidence indicates that in many respects they are flawed or simplistic. For example, it is simply not the case that Europeans do not perceive a Soviet threat. Nor are they convinced that détente alone represents a solution to the threat. In fact, as early as the mid 1970s, opinion polls showed a sharp deterioration in European views of the Soviets. In Britain, polls on the Soviet military threat and on general "suspicions" of the Soviets tracked this shift clearly. In 1967, 36 per cent of the British thought that "we should treat Soviet advances with suspicion", but in 1974 the figure was 52 per cent, and it grew to 67 per cent in 1976 and 1979. In 1968, 49 per cent of the British characterized "Russia" as a "military threat", but the figure grew to 62 per cent in 1974 and 78 per cent in 1978 (by 1980 the figure was 85 per cent). In West Germany, a "threat index" based on surveys inquiring of the "Communist threat" began increasing in 1974 after declining for most of the late 1960s and early 1970s. In 1976, the German threat index reached a level it had not seen since the Soviet invasion of Czechoslovakia in 1968 – in fact, it was higher in 1976 than after the Soviet invasion of Afghanistan. The evidence therefore indicates that European threat perceptions began increasing soon after détente reached its peak in the early 1970s.[43] Moreover, we shall see in the following chapter that expectations for the *results* of détente were largely skeptical, although the desire to maintain negotiations remained strong.[44] In any case, the opinion surveys hardly document a trivialization of the Soviet Union. Surveys on the Soviet threat track a deterioration of the East–West climate beginning in the mid 1970s.

The stability of Europeans' confidence in their security in the face of these developments must therefore be explained by something other than an ostrich-like refusal to recognize a threat. Given the generally low level of expertise of the average citizen in defense matters, one plausible explanation is that public opinion was simply reacting to what governments were doing in the security field. And in fact, although we normally associate the period of détente and arms control with the relaxation of defense efforts, the fact is that all European governments were building up their defense forces during the 1970s. In all countries except Britain, defense budgets in the 1970s continued the real increases that had been maintained (with occasional reversals) throughout the 1960s. In the Netherlands, France, and West Germany, substantial modernization programs had been started in the early 1970s, either as part of the normal weapons cycle (West Germany, Netherlands) or as part of a reorientation in emphasis (France). Considerable attention was devoted to these efforts. In West Germany, orders for aircraft, tanks, and naval vessels under Defense Minister Leber were well publicized and justified as replacements needed under NATO commitments. In France, improvement of conventional forces under Giscard d'Estaing required monetary commitments after the past priority accorded the *force de frappe*. The Dutch defense program of 1974 received similar publicity – indeed, in typical Dutch fashion, a poll on the subject was conducted. Thus, the substantial defense efforts of these three countries was well known. Significantly, public opposition to the defense budget actually declined throughout the 1970s.[45]

Thus, although there was public recognition of growing Soviet power, there was also recognition that substantial investments in the defense budget were being made. The perception was also widespread that military equality already existed. But perhaps most important, public opinion during the 1970s had shifted dramatically to the view that *parity was desirable*. In a 1974 survey comparing general public attitudes to the attitudes of the most educated and wealthy "élites" of European countries, the "élites" favored US-Soviet equality of power even more than the general public: 61 per cent of élites and 47 per cent of the public in Britain favored equality. The figures were 61 per cent and 51 per cent in West Germany. In France, 62 per cent of both samples favored equality.[46]

These figures reflected a trend that had been developing since the 1960s. Unsurprisingly, French public opinion has always preferred superpower equality, but in other countries the shift is remarkable. In Britain and West Germany, the percentage favoring equality grew from about 20 per cent in 1958 to a majority in the 1970s. By 1981, it joined the French at or near 60 per cent favoring equality.[47] Although similar polls are not available for the preferred state of the NATO-Warsaw Pact balance, the strength of these figures suggest that they would not be much different. By the end of the 1970s, not only did large portions of European opinion perceive military parity – they very much liked it that way.

The perceived virtues of parity probably reflect a diffuse sentiment. For example, it is not clear from the polls whether it concerns the nuclear balance, the conventional balance, or – as in the Alliance's own strategy – a mixture of the two. None the less, the strength of the attachment deserves explanation. From what has been said above, several factors appear relevant. The first is the paradoxical comfort of nuclear weapons. Although the enormous destructive power of these weapons are certainly known to the public, it is precisely the deterrent effect of that destruction that can be seen as a contribution to stability. We saw above that public opinion is more likely to see parity in the nuclear balance than in more general assessments of military power. Thus, stable deterrence is apparently seen less in a strict comparison of forces and more in the balance of destructive capabilities. Just as some strategists endorse assured destruction for its stabilizing qualities, so the public may see a lining of virtue in the threat of nuclear destruction.

Moreover, parity offers other virtues, for the logic of mutual destructive capabilities is also the logic of arms control. I cited Henry Kissinger above to the effect that parity had reduced the marginal utility of additional increments of military force. Given the pull of domestic priorities, this equation offers the hope of an escape from the budgetary costs of the arms race. Further, given the size of existing nuclear arsenals, could equal security not also be achieved at *lower* levels of arms and spending? Finally, to this observation must be added the familiar dictum that, for Europeans, reliance on nuclear deterrence has resulted in part from recognition of the costs of conventional armaments.

Recent years have shown that these views are not uncontested. Indeed, the significant point is that European publics and élites are divided, both on the question of what the balance is and what it should be. The polls in previous sections of this chapter showed that by the late 1970s and early 1980s, public opinion in Europe was increasingly clustered around the views that the Soviets had become superior and that the military balance was essentially equal. When nuclear weapons are mentioned, the perception of equality is generally higher. Moreover, not only is the overall population divided between these two views, there are additional divisions among parties and educational groups who differ in their interpretation of the military balance and it consequences.

It is in this context that the détente of the early 1970s has a special significance, for during the détente period these divergent opinions were not contested in public debate. Europeans were increasingly unsettled by Soviet intentions, but the contacts and negotiations of the détente period were not directly challenged until the end of the decade. With the exception of the Middle East War in 1973, an open East–West confrontation did not occur. Moreover, until the INF deployment decision and the Soviet invasion of Afghanistan, the prospect of increasing military forces beyond what was already planned had not been raised. In short, before 1979 the implications of change in the military balance had not been widely debated. After the INF decision and the Soviet invasion of Afghanistan in 1979, all these questions became the subject of heated controversy.

Given the fragmentation that had evolved in public opinion, the vociferousness of that debate does not seem surprising. The INF decision – and the more general call for increased military force – set in opposition views that had become increasingly polarized during the previous decade. Although the Alliance justified its INF decision in part on the need to balance Soviet deployment of the SS-20, this argument would hardly impress the substantial percentage of public opinion who believed equality already existed and who were largely unconcerned about their security. Moreover, the 1970s had seemed to offer the prospect of arms limitations or perhaps even reductions that could bring budgetary savings, but now the prospect was of additional defense spending at a time of austerity and fears for social programs. And paradoxically, while many had become attached to the stability brought about by mutually assured destruction, increasingly the strategic discussion highlighted "flexible nuclear options" designed to reinforce strategic deterrence. The neutron bomb controversy and the INF decision further fanned this debate.

Finally, all these sentiments came together in the decidedly negative reaction of Europeans to the harsh tone of American foreign policy in the late 1970s and early 1980s. We shall see in Chapter 4 that at this time Europeans' confidence in American foreign policy dropped to the lowest level of the post-war period. In addition, the Reagan military build-up, together with the hardline language of the President's early years in office, apparently frightened Europeans. We saw above that overwhelming percentages of Europeans prefer parity in the military balance. In the early 1980s, however, about 60 per cent of all Europeans believed that the United States was seeking superiority.[48]

None of this is to suggest that the critique of INF was in some sense "correct". Rather, the point is that the public debate over the missiles was not as novel or puzzling as has often been supposed. Aside from the more radical critics who challenged the Alliance as well as the missiles, the debate covered much the same ground as the scholarly and strategic debates of the 1970s, especially on the crucial question of whether deterrence (and extended deterrence) required an elaborate quantitative balance or merely a balance of destructive potential. These questions remain unresolved to this day, although they have taken on added intensity, fueled by new issues (especially SDI and the "double zero" solution to INF) that have once again raised the puzzle of the nature of deterrence, power, and influence in an age as yet dominated by assured destruction. The controversy over INF – carried out both by and for public opinion – was a reflection of competing views of the military balance. As Freedman has said, the debate among strategists on this question had been "noisy, even cacaphonous". Given the divisions that had evolved in European public opinion, is it any surprise that the public discussion was equally boisterous?

SUMMARY AND IMPLICATIONS

The survey data examined in this chapter point to two major conclusions, both with important implications for domestic consensus and transatlantic consensus in the NATO Alliance.

The first is the disjunction between perceptions of power and confidence in security. Although both types of perception have changed over the last twenty years, they have not changed in unison. At times, perceptions of American strength have declined, but confidence in security did not. In the early 1980s, perceptions of American strength improved, but confidence in the American commitment declined. To the extent that perceptions of security fluctuate, they seem to do so not simply in response to the actual military balance, but to major events that appear to demonstrate the strength or weakness of the West (although not all of these events could be called military confrontations).

This pattern has obvious implications for American defense policy. As noted earlier, American strategic policy has frequently changed in response to fears about the assumed erosion of European confidence that could arise from perceived shifts in the military balance. Questioning this evolution, Warner Schilling observed that "there is no evidence that the United States government has engaged in any systematic research as to how relevant foreign élites reach their judgments about the state of the strategic balance".[49] I have touched on the perceptions of élites only peripherally in this chapter, but if we assume that the public takes "cues" from governmental and other élites (not unreasonable, given the low level of the public's information on defense issues), then our data would suggest that élites are entirely comfortable with parity. In fact, direct surveys of élites (discussed in Chapter 7) tend to confirm this observation. All of this occurred at a time of erosion in the perceived power position of the United States.

Of course, none of this suggests that the confidence of Europeans should not be a concern to the American government. Rather, it suggests that adjustments in military programs, taken alone, will not necessarily affect confidence one way or the other. Instead, the confidence of Europeans will be far more affected by success and failure abroad or by major pronouncements that affect perceptions of confidence. As we shall see in Chapter 4, the criticism that accompanied the SDI program and the Reykjavik summit (criticism that originated in part from European chancelleries) is a negative example in this regard.

In any event, these observations should not be read to suggest that Europeans are insensitive to Soviet power. Quite the opposite. The next chapter shows that, with regard to the INF deployment, concern for Soviet deployments was a factor in the evolution of European opinion on INF, and the Soviet walkout from the INF negotiations in 1983 was no doubt one reason for the calm reception that NATO's deployment eventually received. None the less, the apparent immunity of broader perceptions of "security" to the military balance makes the justification of military programs more difficult. The "stalemate" effect of nuclear parity has complicated the task even further.

The difficulty of reaching consensus on these issues is apparent from the second major finding described in this chapter: European societies are indeed divided in their evaluations of the military balance. Traditional ideological cleavages are apparent in all age and educational groups, and the more optimistic assessments of Left-wing parties are probably related to their skepticism of force as a solution to security problems, their preference for social rather than military investments, and their belief that negotiation – rather than a military balance – is the key to national security. These cleavages are further complicated by the fact that it is the most educated and presumably most active members of the Left who are also most skeptical.

Taken together, the data therefore suggest that a consensus on national security will take more than mere appeals to maintain the military balance. To return to Wolfers' terms, in an age of strategic parity and domestic polarization, national security appears to be even more ambiguous than before. That is nowhere more apparent than in the field of nuclear strategy and arms control, where public opinion has emerged as a major concern for NATO governments. That is the subject of the following chapter.

4 Collision and Collusion: The Public, Nuclear Weapons, and Arms Control

On 8 January 1985 US Secretary of State George Schultz and Soviet Foreign Minister Andrei Gromyko announced in Geneva that the United States and the Soviet Union would resume the arms control talks that had been interrupted in December 1983, when the Soviets walked out of negotiations to protest NATO's deployment of intermediate-range nuclear forces (INF). The new round of talks revived negotiations on both strategic and INF systems and initiated negotiations on the limitation of defensive weapons systems.

Three days after the US–Soviet announcement, Helmut Schmidt, the former West German Chancellor, published a commentary on the arms control talks under the title "Now Europe Must Act". Although Schmidt welcomed the thaw in East–West relations symbolized by the Schultz–Gromyko statement, he also expressed clear reservations:

> So far, so good. But it is not yet at all certain – assuming that arms control negotiations do materialize in 1985 – that the security interests of West European peoples and governments will be adequately taken into consideration (to say nothing of the interests of East Europeans). To be sure, all Europeans will welcome any limitation of strategic nuclear weapons. But we want not simply more security for the superpowers as between each other, we also want more security for ourselves!
>
> Only if the governments of Western Europe act together can they exert an effective influence on the emergence of a new phase of détente; [and thereby ensure] that European interests are not swept under the superpower table (as twice already, in SALT II and in the rejection of the 'walk in the woods' compromise for medium-range missiles); and [also ensure] that the new phase of détente once more opens room for maneuver for the nations of the European continent.[1]

These words will evoke an uncomfortable sense of *déjà vu* among students of Western security, for it was also Helmut Schmidt who called attention in 1977 to the failure of US–Soviet negotiations to address "disparities" in the balance of nuclear and conventional forces in Europe. As in his more recent commentary, in 1977 Schmidt had heartily endorsed the concept of strategic arms limitation, but he also underscored his concern for European interests: "We in Europe must be particularly careful to ensure that these negotiations do not neglect the components of NATO's deterrence strategy."[2]

Schmidt's 1977 speech led to NATO's decision in 1979 to deploy 572 intermediate-range missiles in Western Europe, a decision that sparked one of the most turbulent and bitter periods of debate in the history of the NATO Alliance.[3] In Europe the decision was denounced by hundreds of thousands of demonstrators, and each passing day brought reports of new public opinion surveys revealing the apparent pacifism of European populations. Strategists joined the debate as well, as in proposals for "no-first-use" of nuclear weapons. By the "hot autumn" of the scheduled deployments in 1983, it was not at all clear that every recipient country would accept its contingent of the Pershing and Cruise missiles.

It was therefore all the more surprising that the controversy passed so quickly. In the event, all countries accepted the deployments, and the missiles arrived with very little fanfare. Moreover, subsequent nuclear controversies, such as President Reagan's strategic defense initiative (SDI), did not produce the resurgence of public consternation that many had expected. Compared to the shrill and bitter arguments heard during 1981 and 1982, by 1984 the Alliance had entered a period of relative calm.

If only for this reason, Helmut Schmidt's later warning no doubt fell on unwelcome ears. Yet renewed attention to the problems of European arms control was bound to re-emerge, with or without the help of the former Chancellor. In the first place, the debate over the 1979 decision may have subsided, but it did not – perhaps it could not – resolve the thorny issues of defense and deterrence that have plagued NATO virtually since its inception.[4] Moreover, once the arms control process resumed, it was inevitable that these issues, ranging from the credibility of extended nuclear deterrence to the adequacy of NATO's conventional forces, would be emphasized once again. In this sense, Schmidt was prophetic, for the resumption of US–Soviet negotiations did indeed raise questions about European security. At their Reykjavik summit in October 1986, President

155223

Reagan and Secretary Gorbachev came close to agreeing to a "zero solution" for INF in which all American and Soviet intermediate forces would be withdrawn from Europe. They also briefly flirted with a zero option for the strategic forces that have long served as the ultimate guarantee of European security. Although the idea of eliminating strategic ballistic missiles soon gave way to less ambitious proposals, in December 1987 the two leaders signed the "double-zero" INF Treaty that will eliminate all intermediate and short-range nuclear forces from Europe.

The Treaty immediately stimulated renewed debate. One familiar concern was the European fear that removal of INF would "decouple" Western Europe from the American nuclear guarantee. In addition, the double-zero solution focused attention on the adequacy of NATO's conventional forces and on the battlefield (tactical) nuclear weapons that will not be limited by the agreement. As revealed in press reports from Europe and America, the Treaty negotiations produced yet another full-scale debate about the role of nuclear weapons in NATO's policy of flexible response.[5] While it appeared in 1982 that the major concern of Europeans was the prospect of new weapons deployments, by 1987 the fear was that these weapons might be reduced or eliminated completely.

These concerns point to a persistent paradox in European reactions to superpower arms control: they are worried both by the failure to negotiate (for this would symbolize a breakdown in the broader East–West relationship so crucial to European interests), but also by the willingness to negotiate (for negotiations raise the spectre of agreements that neglect or ignore European concerns). As Glenn Snyder has shown, Europeans are caught in the alliance dilemma of "abandonment and entrapment". As a result, Europeans fear both collision and collusion in US–Soviet relations.[6]

This paradox is a familiar part of the transatlantic relationship, but the recent history of European arms control has produced one development that is considered quite new by many observers: the growing awareness and polarization of public opinion. The most vigorous mobilization of the public came within the peace movements and peace parties that coalesced to oppose the deployment of INF. But as Michael Howard reminds us, these movements only underlined in more vocal form concerns that were felt both by a broader public and by many experts and government officials.[7] Now at first glance, the political significance of the public reaction might appear evanescent. Both before and after the INF deployment, elections throughout Western Europe saw the confirmation or election of governing parties that were firmly committed to INF. None the less, with the resumption of negotiations in 1985 and the signing of the INF Treaty in 1987, the evolution of public attitudes has taken on renewed significance. Indeed, press reports indicate that some European governments initially repressed their doubts about the prospective INF agreement to avoid a rekindling of public pressure.[8] More generally, despite the muted public reaction to the actual INF deployments, the assumption is widespread that successful arms control negotiations are essential to the restoration and maintenance of domestic consensus on security policy.

UNANSWERED QUESTIONS

The unsettled state of European public opinion has been closely monitored in Washington. According to Strobe Talbott's account of the first round of INF negotiations, in the Fall of 1982 Ambassador Paul Nitze made a series of appeals to his colleagues in Washington to fall back from the original American "zero–zero" proposal that would have required the Soviets to dismantle all their SS-20 missiles in return for American agreement to cancel the deployment of Pershing and Cruise missiles. As reported by Talbott, the basis of Nitze's argument was as follows:

"We have a political problem in Europe," he [Nitze] said at a meeting in the State Department. "A considerable percentage of European public opinion is not satisfied with our zero-zero position and *would* be satisfied with an outcome that left us with zero on our side. . . . There's another percentage of the European population that doesn't hold out any hope for zero-zero but might be satisfied if we seem to be exploring an equitable solution above zero. The first thing we've got to do is start exploring those solutions so that it becomes more likely that the requisite percentage will support deployment."[9]

These passages are significant for several reasons. The first is the dramatic illustration of the institutionalized role of public opinion surveys in the policy process.[10] Equally important, the episode recounted by Talbott illustrates the difficulty of predicting the evolution of public opinion. In this account, Ambassador Nitze had apparently concluded that the percentage of Europeans adamantly opposed to

INF deployment would persist in their opposition and pose severe political problems for European governments. This conclusion was no doubt encouraged by the presence of hundreds of thousands of demonstrators on the streets of European cities. Yet the polls themselves also revealed a not inconsiderable percentage of Europeans who would support deployment under some conditions – usually related to arms control negotiations. In retrospect, one might speculate that this more tolerant attitude toward INF eventually prevailed, obviously not because agreement was reached, but as a result of other considerations: the fact that negotiations had indeed been pursued; the fact that it was the Soviet Union, after all, that had abandoned the negotiations; or because the deployment itself was eventually begun in a much less crisis-ridden atmosphere than had prevailed earlier in the decade. In other words, it may be that opinions of the INF deployment were influenced far more by the general political climate of the times than by any judgment of the weapons themselves or of the details of particular negotiating positions as they unfolded. Although governments are increasingly attentive to public concerns as a result of the unrest that accompanied the INF debate, it is unclear that the monitoring of opinion surveys on specific weapons or negotiations will provide the guidance they seek.

The purpose of this chapter is to clarify this uncertainty. The resumption of Soviet–American arms control talks has already brought renewed speculation about the reaction and potential influence of European public opinion. This speculation is based in part on the putative "lessons" of the INF episode. Before that process gets too far underway, it would seem useful to take a comprehensive look at the views of Europeans on a broad range of issues relating to NATO's nuclear strategy, including the issue of arms control.

This chapter provides such an overview. First, I briefly review West European attitudes on such fundamental questions as nuclear deterrence and the acceptance of military force. A second section relates the upsurge of European nervousness about nuclear weapons to the dramatic rise in the fear of war and the increasing doubts of Europeans about American foreign policy. I then turn to the specific issue of nuclear weapons in Europe and to public evaluations of the 1983 INF deployment. A third section of the chapter returns to current issues of arms control and explores the likely reaction of European public opinion to the "denuclearization" of Europe that has been foreshadowed in the double-zero Treaty. The theme of this section is that the "lessons" of the INF deployment have been misread. This misreading could lead to serious political problems in reaction to the Treaty. The chapter concludes with observations about potential problems in the future of European arms control.

THE FUNDAMENTALS: DETERRENCE, FORCE, AND PACIFISM

The eruption of concern and protest in the wake of the 1979 dual-track decision was widely interpreted as a watershed, a reversal of the post-1945 consensus on Western defense and security policy.[11] But if there was widespread belief that the INF debate represented a reversal, the source of change was attributed to a variety of causes. For some, the doubts that appeared both in polls and in protests were largely a short-term affair, a reaction to events that, once played out, would see the re-emergence of consensus. For example, Josef Joffe attributed the rise and eclipse of the peace movements to a generational cycle in which successive age cohorts of Europeans are required to come to grips with the painful paradox of stability achieved through nuclear deterrence.[12] One might also see the anti-nuclear mood as part of the malaise brought on in the 1980s by the abrupt reversal of prosperity, employment, and growth in social spending. However gloomy, the implicit prediction of these observations was that political polarization and "Europessimism" might be cured with the return of even modest prosperity.

As we saw in the preceding chapter, there was also speculation about long-term forces that could erode the security consensus. Theorists had been arguing for over a decade that the utility and domestic acceptability of military force had been called into question by a number of developments: the emergence of strategic parity and the "stalemate" effects of mutual assured destruction; the effect of the Vietnam War on calculations of the cost and acceptability of military force as an instrument of policy; and the emergence of important non-security issues – primarily but not exclusively economic – that had lowered the public priority of national security and placed pressure on the attention and resources of governments.[13]

The surveys presented in Chapter 3 showed that none of these views is entirely correct. Although the state of the military balance and the emergence of parity had certainly made security policy more widely debated among élites and within public opinion, this did not mean that military force had been totally rejected. Moreover, there was soon evidence that military force still enjoyed domestic support. There were deployments of British or French forces to Africa, the Indian Ocean, the Middle East, and – of course – the South Atlantic. In the latter case, the reaction of the British public hardly indicated that military force had become an anachronism in the public mind.[14]

But had these expeditions been the exceptions, acceptable to public opinion precisely because they were limited, quick, relatively low-cost affairs conducted largely at sea? Broader opinion surveys suggest not, for they show that before and after the turbulent period of public debate beginning with the INF decision in 1979, European opinion remained strongly committed to key components of postwar security policy. Indeed, surveys indicate that fundamental attitudes toward military force have changed very little since the 1960s and 1970s.

In the Netherlands, for example, a loud domestic debate over NATO's nuclear strategy had begun in 1977 in reaction to the possible deployment of the "neutron bomb". Fueled by the INF decision, protest culminated in 1981 and 1982, when thousands of people participated in demonstrations against NATO's INF decision. According to surveys, majorities of the Dutch population agreed with the slogan of the anti-nuclear Inter-Church Council (IKV): "Free the world of nuclear weapons, and let it begin with the Netherlands". Moreover, depending on the poll, as many as 50 to 60 per cent of the Dutch population opposed the INF deployment.[15] Writing in 1981, Walter Laqueur identified the Netherlands as the most advanced case of European pacifism and neutralism.[16]

Yet despite this public outcry, opinion surveys demonstrated surprisingly little change in the public's attitudes on fundamental issues of national security. For example, although the Dutch have a history of debating the role of the armed forces in a democratic political order, surveys showed very little change in the pragmatic acceptance of military force that had characterized attitudes since the Second World War. Throughout the 1960s and 1970s, well over 80 per cent of the Dutch accepted their armed forces as "necessary" or "a necessary evil". At the peak of peace movement activity in 1982, this acceptance stood at 82 per cent. After dipping very slightly during 1983 and 1984, it returned to earlier levels in 1985. In addition, in a survey conducted throughout the 1970s and 1980s, there were only minor fluctuations in the percentage of the Dutch who believed that "a military counterbalance is necessary . . . to offset the power of Russia". Even during the INF episode, it remained at 60 to 70 per cent.

Finally, despite the apparent sympathy in Holland for nuclear disarmament, opinion surveys also showed a surprising degree of appreciation for nuclear deterrence. In 1982, over 60 per cent of the Dutch population believed that the absence of war between NATO and the Warsaw Pact was "mainly or somewhat due to the existence of nuclear weapons". The figure had not changed when the survey was repeated in 1985. Despite the desire to "free the Netherlands of nuclear weapons", a number of surveys also showed a pragmatic side to Dutch thinking. Strong majorities believed that unilateral disarmament was not yet possible and that disarmament would have to be achieved in a way that was consistent with NATO commitments.[17]

The West German case is similar. Just as the Dutch have a long tradition of skepticism toward military institutions, post-war West Germany experienced profound ambivalence about military force. After the devastation of the Second World War, there was little sentiment for rearmament or alliance. In fact, rearmament, conscription, and accession to NATO were initially opposed by majorities of the population. Although these steps were eventually accepted, West Germans have conducted a forty-year debate over such issues as leadership and tradition within the armed forces and the relationship of the armed forces to democratic institutions.[18]

Given this ambivalent history, it is all the more surprising that West Germans' acceptance of military institutions survived the vociferous security debates of the 1980s. The percentage of West Germans who had a "good opinion" of the Bundeswehr increased from 62 per cent in 1964 to 74 per cent in 1980 despite repeated controversies about military tradition and ceremony. In addition, 70 to 80 per cent believed that the Bundeswehr was "important to the country" during the 1970s and 1980s, a decided increase over levels of the 1960s. Perhaps most telling, the acceptance of the Bundeswehr is not diluted when questions place military institutions in a broader context. For example, one question posed by the West German Ministry of Defense asked West Germans to weigh military efforts against the goal of détente: "Do you think that through the Bundeswehr an effective détente policy . . . is disturbed . . . or do you think that the existence of the Bundeswehr makes peace more secure?" During the actual détente period in the 1970s, 70 per cent of the population believed that the Bundeswehr "makes peace more secure", and in 1978, this figure rose to 90 per cent along with a more general rise in West German perceptions of threat. Most surprising, the intense debate over INF hardly affected these sentiments. In 1984, 87 per cent of West Germans still thought that the "Bundeswehr makes peace more secure". These figures are all the more surprising when one considers the high priority that West Germans attach to détente (presumably the reason that the Defense Ministry chose to monitor these sentiments).[19]

Finally, like the Dutch, West Germans continue to accept nuclear deterrence. For example, one survey question asked West Germans if "an attack from the East is best deterred when the West itself is sufficiently armed?". Although the question is not ideal for gauging the public's support for specific policies (what is "sufficiently"?), it does offer the "peace through strength" argument that was so heavily criticized by the peace movement. The responses show very little change. In 1976, 72 per cent agreed, and the percentage fluctuated little during the INF controversy, standing at 68 per cent at the end of 1981. Moreover, the Ministry of Defense put opinions of *nuclear* deterrence to a very severe test in 1984, just after the actual INF deployment. Describing a conversation between an opponent and a supporter of nuclear deterrence, the Ministry asked respondents which of two views they supported. A first statement was that "We live here on a powder keg. The use of nuclear weapons would be so terrible that we should immediately get rid of them." The second view was that "Nuclear weapons have never been used in the last three decades exactly because their use would be so terrible. Without nuclear deterrence, the danger of a conventional war in Europe would be much higher." The responses to this question surprised even the Ministry: 61 per cent of the population chose the view that nuclear weapons are an effective deterrent.[20]

Paradoxically, British and French attitudes on issues of nuclear deterrence are similar to those on the continent. Although it is often argued that the British and French have to some extent been immunized from "Hollanditis" by the presence of a native finger on the trigger of their nuclear forces, the polls indicate that in these two countries the same pattern prevails. There is a general nervousness about nuclear weapons, but it is tempered by support for their deterrent value. In Britain, for example, there is the same basic desire for disarmament that exists in Holland and West Germany. Indeed, in 1982 over 60 per cent of the British said that they would support a proposal for a freeze in the production and deployment of nuclear weapons, and 40 to 50 per cent of the British claimed to agree with demonstrations against nuclear weapons.[21] Yet, as shown in Table 4.1, this sentiment did not translate into support for a uni-

Table 4.1 Support of the British Public for an Independent Nuclear Force

	Favor (%)	Oppose (%)	Don't know (%)	Net support (%)
1958	59	28	14	+31
1959	50	30	20	+20
1961	59	26	16	+33
1962	64	22	14	+42
1967	69	19	12	+50
1979	65	20	15	+45
1980	66	25	9	+42
1981	64	27	9	+36
1982	65	26	9	+39
1983	71	23	6	+48
1984	71	20	9	+51
1985	68	23	9	+45
* 11/1986	66	27	7	+39
1/1987	55	34	11	+21
* 4/1987	67	25	8	+42

NOTE: With minor variations, the question reads: "It has been suggested that Britain should give up relying on nuclear weapons for defence whatever other countries decide. Do you think that this is a good idea [oppose] or a bad idea [favor]?" In 1958, the question refers to the British "hydrogen bomb"; in 1967, it asks if "we should give up the bomb and rely on the US?". When more than one survey is available in one year, the average for that year is shown. In November 1986 and April 1987 the question included the phrase "as long as the Soviet Union has them".

SOURCES: Surveys by Social Surveys Ltd (Gallup), Marplan, and NOP, as reproduced in Oksana Dackiw, "Defense Policy and Public Opinion: The British Campaign for Nuclear Disarmament, 1945–1985", doctoral dissertation, Department of Political Science, Columbia University, 1986, Chapter 4. Figures for 1986 and 1987 provided by Social Surveys Ltd (British Gallup).

lateral dismantling of the British nuclear deterrent. Indeed, public support for the British nuclear force has been very stable, averaging over 65 per cent since the 1960s.[22]

Because of the strong French consensus surrounding the independent *force de frappe* and the absence of a viable peace movement in France, the French are sometimes seen as the last true believers in nuclear deterrence, unaffected by the pacifist ills that afflict other countries. The polls tell a different story. Despite the French government's loud criticism of "pacifist" movements in other countries and its strong endorsement of the INF deployment, the French public was just as sympathetic to disarmament proposals as were citizens of other countries. For example, over 50 per cent of the public opposed the INF deployment, and a similar majority confessed to feel sympathy for pacifist demonstrations.[23]

None the less, like other Europeans, the French are willing to suppress a basic sympathy for disarmament in the name of deterrence (Table 4.2). The first question in Table 4.2 shows answers to a straightforward question asking if France "should have its own atomic striking force". Opinions on this question were closely divided during the 1960s, but support for the *force de frappe* improved strikingly during the late 1970s and into the 1980s, perhaps a response to the fact that the French parties of the Left abandoned their opposition to the *force de frappe*. In the second question shown in Table 4.2, respondents were asked if a country such as France "could assure its defense without a *force de frappe*?". As the Table shows, this Gaullist formulation usually elicits a more favorable response, and like the first question, support increased greatly during the 1980s. In separate polls that specifically mention the Gaullist orthodoxy of security through the independent nuclear force, huge majorities endorse the *force*. For example, 75 per cent agree that "By having the nuclear force, France demonstrates to the world its independent spirit."[24] It is therefore unsurprising that the French appear to appreciate the paradoxical utility of nuclear deterrence. Asked in 1985 if the French *force de frappe* "protects France from potential aggression because of the risk that an attacking country would run" or if "the force serves no purpose because if it is used, we risk getting blown off the map", majorities in 1984 and 1985 chose the former response.[25]

Admittedly, in both Britain and France there is some ambivalence about the national deterrents. In both countries, support for national nuclear forces drops when the budgetary cost is mentioned in survey questions.[26] Yet one could argue that these currents are not new. The sensitivity of public opinion to defense spending more generally is well established but, as I shall argue in Chapter 6, it is more likely to be aroused by economic and budgetary conditions than by changes in strategy or weapons deployments.

European public opinion reveals a clear profile on issues of military force and deterrence. Although citizens of all countries do show sympathy for the goal of disarmament, support for military institutions and for policies of deterrence are also high. Although the INF

Table 4.2   Support of the French Public for an Independent Nuclear Force

	Favor (%)	Oppose (%)	Don't know (%)	Net support (%)
Question 1				
1956	27	51	22	−24
1959	37	38	25	− 1
1962	39	27	34	+12
1963	37	37	27	0
1964	39	49	12	−10
1970	39	45	16	− 6
1977	49	38	13	+11
1980	50	35	15	+15
1981	72	15	13	+57
1983	66	20	14	+46
Question 2				
1965	49	32	19	+17
1978	55	25	20	+30
1981	63	20	17	+43
1982	67	19	14	+48
1983	67	20	13	+47
1984	72	14	14	+58
1985	68	17	15	+51

NOTES:
Question 1. In 1956 and 1959, the question asked "would it be desirable or undesirable for France to construct its own atomic bombs?". From 1962 to 1970 and in 1981, the question read "Do you feel that France should have [continue to have] its own atomic striking force [nuclear defense/deterrent force]?" In 1977, 1980 and 1983, the question asked if opinions of the French nuclear forces were "positive/negative" or "favorable/unfavorable".

Question 2. In 1965, the question stated: "[Do you agree or disagree] that a power such as France cannot be assured of its defense unless it has its own atomic arms?" From 1978 to 1985, the question asked "Can a country such as France assure its defense without a nuclear deterrent force?"

SOURCES: George Gallup, Jr, *The Gallup International Public Opinion Polls: France, 1945–1975*, 2 vols (New York: Random House, 1975) pp. 200, 262, 263, 325, 388, 403, 417, 478 and 783; "Opinion et Défense en 1985", *Armées d'aujourd'hui*, no. 04 (October 1985) p. 15; and Renate Fritsch-Bournazel, "France: Attachment to a Nonbinding Relationship", in Gregory Flynn and Hans Rattinger (eds), *The Public and Atlantic Defense* (Totowa, N.J.: Rowman and Allanheld 1985) p. 84.

debate suggested a groundswell of opposition to security policies, surveys indicate that military force and deterrence continue to enjoy broad support in European public opinion.

NUCLEAR WEAPONS AND THE FEAR OF WAR

None of this is meant to say that there is no popular questioning of security policy in Western Europe. Rather, the variety of surveys on such fundamental issues as deterrence and military institutions gives pause to the assumption that recent controversies within the Alliance are part of a secular reversal in fundamental attitudes towards national security. This is important, for it suggests that there remains a more substantial base of domestic consensus than would be indicated by recent references to pacifism.

However, it will come as no surprise that this consensus is over-layed by a deep ambivalence about nuclear weapons that transcends the specific issue of INF deployment. In fact, three broad sets of concern were evident during the early 1980s. The first was a dramatic rise in the fear of war and in the judgment that the United States was putting European interests at risk as it adopted an increasingly strident tone in its dealings with the Soviet Union. The subjects of disagreement are familiar: the lack of an agreed response to the Soviet invasion of Afghanistan; disappointment over the failure to ratify the SALT II Treaty; confusion and disagreement about out-of-area contingencies; the growing restlessness with the failure to begin INF negotiations; and the entire series of arguments surrounding political and economic relations with the East, especially after the imposition of martial law in Poland.[27]

European opinion registered a sharp increase in fear during this period. Between 1977 and 1981, estimates of the probability of "world war" increased dramatically in Europe. In the four countries studied here, only 20 to 30 per cent of the population considered a war probable in 1977, but the percentage doubled in every country by 1981.[28] Moreover, just as European leaders attempted to brake the deterioration in East–West relations by warning the United States of the dangers of overreaction, public opinion in Europe took on a profoundly skeptical tone toward American foreign policy. For example, asked in 1980 and 1981 whether their countries should "back the United States against the Soviet Union [or] do everything possible to stay out of arguments between the United States and the Soviet

Union", majorities in all countries but West Germany chose to "stay out of arguments".[29]

These were not simply the responses of frightened or cautious allies, for the polls reveal quite specific complaints. We saw in Chapter 3 that, although Europeans preferred military parity by wide margins, during the early 1980s the view was widespread that the United States was seeking superiority. In addition, in surveys sponsored by the American government, the general image of the United States showed its most precipitous decline since the 1950s. Favorable images of the United States had outnumbered unfavorable images by as much as 80 percentage points in 1978, but by 1981 this figure had been cut by half or more in all countries except France, where the American rating has historically been low in any case. In Britain, favorable ratings outnumbered unfavorable ratings by 63 percentage points in 1981, but it dropped to 20 points in 1984. The drop in other countries was equally dramatic. In West Germany, the US image fell from 81 points favorable in 1978 to 37 points in 1984. In France it fell from 49 points to 18, and from 62 to 19 points in the Netherlands.[30]

Nor does it seem that Europeans were reacting to more general feelings about American society or to the increasing troubles in transatlantic economic relations, for more specific polls revealed a chasm of doubt about the direction of American foreign policy. For example, since 1960 the British Gallup organization has offered a question on "confidence in the ability of the United States to deal wisely with present world problems". As shown in Figure 4.1, British confidence in American policy has fluctuated, but it began dropping sharply in 1979, and the 1980s yielded negative confidence ratings that are lower than any yet seen. Other British polls confirm the depth of alienation, as in figures showing that the Reagan Presidency is rated far more negatively than the Carter period.[31]

Similar results were found on the continent. In West Germany net confidence in American foreign policy was at 68 percentage points in 1960 and remained positive in 1980. By 1983, it had dropped to *negative* 24 per cent, and it remained negative through 1986. There was a similar level of disenchantment in other countries, especially in 1981 and 1982.[32]

Yet, despite the obvious estrangement revealed by these surveys, the frequently cited fears of "anti-Americanism", "equidistance" and "neutralism" in European opinion were exaggerated. One reason is that these "image" and "net confidence" scores fluctuate considerably. They have dropped before, especially during the

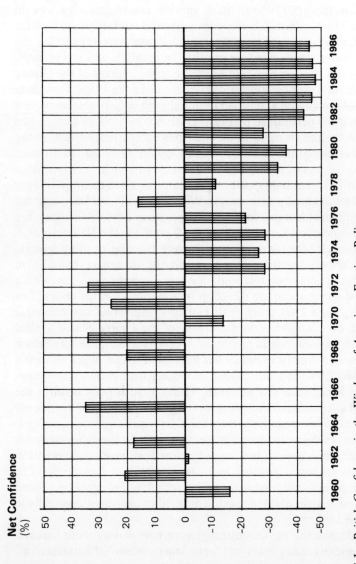

Figure 4.1 British Confidence in the Wisdom of American Foreign Policy

SOURCE: Oksana Dackiw, "Defense Policy and Public Opinion: The Campaign for Nuclear Disarmament, 1945–1985", doctoral dissertation, Columbia University, 1986, ch. 7.

Vietnam War and at the height of the Watergate scandal, but they recovered fairly quickly. The variability of these opinions in the past indicates that Europeans are certainly capable of harsh judgments about American policy and American politics in the short term. None the less, the fact that they improved also indicates that this was not the result of a secular change in their assessment of the United States. Further, we shall see in Chapter 5 that, although the commitment to the NATO Alliance also dropped during 1981 and 1982, it remained well over 50 per cent in most countries, and as the tensions of the early 1980s receded, it quickly returned to earlier levels. Moreover, despite their disenchantment with the United States, Europeans were even *more* negative in their evaluations of the Soviet Union in the wake of the invasion of Afghanistan and the imposition of martial law in Poland. Talk of "equidistance" notwithstanding, Europeans apparently distinguished between temporary assessments of American policy and the deeper interests and values of their countries. In 1982, for example, when net confidence in American foreign policy had actually turned negative in most countries, majorities of 50 to 80 per cent of Europeans expressed the judgment that their countries' "basic interests" were in agreement with those of the United States. Equally large majorities felt that European and Soviet interests were not in agreement. Finally, in an interesting question asked in 1982 and 1985, majorities as high as 70 per cent claimed that their values were similar to American values. When the same question was asked of the consistency of European and Soviet values, only small minorities found them similar.[33]

The evidence therefore indicates that European sentiment in the early 1980s did not represent a fundamental change in attitudes towards nuclear weapons, the Alliance, or the United States. It was a fearful and critical response to the crisis atmosphere of the early 1980s and the militant tone of American foreign policy. Although the 1979 INF decision was clearly an Alliance responsibility, by 1981 the international situation had changed dramatically, and in the event operational control of the missiles would be in the hands of a senior partner whose outlook and behavior were now under challenge by leaders and public alike. As one Dutch politician of the Labour Party observed in 1983: "Both the strategic and political environments in which the initial [INF] decision was taken have altered substantially, to the extent that if the questions that drove the original decision were reconsidered, then I am sure that the answers today would be very different."[34] At least as concerns American handling of East–West relations in the early 1980s, the polls suggested that the public agreed.

This interpretation is reinforced by a second set of concerns, revealed in those polls on the INF deployment that were repeated continuously after NATO's decision. In the Netherlands, opinions on the deployment were closely divided, but in 27 identical soundings on the issue between 1981 and 1985, the peak of outright opposition occurred in 1982. Opposition declined in 1983 and 1984 as negotiations proceeded and the general climate of East–West relations improved.[35] The same pattern was evident in Britain, where nine identical polls on the deployment showed a peak in opposition in 1982, followed by a decline until the actual deployment approached in late 1983.[36] In additional polls in Britain and in West Germany, unconditional opposition to INF deployment peaked in late 1981 or early 1982, but it subsided in both countries during 1982. Conversely, support for parallel deployment *and* negotiation rose as the negotiations got underway in late 1981 and early 1982. A series of USIA surveys between 1981 and 1984 revealed that the percentage of the public who thought that INF would "make a Soviet attack more likely" reached its peak in 1982 before declining until actual deployment approached in late 1983.[37] Overall, then, when identical surveys are tracked over time, the peak of opposition to INF occurs in late 1981 or early 1982.

It may be that governments' justification of the deployment during the heated debates of 1981 and 1982 explains the subsequent improvement in the public's attitude toward the Pershing and Cruise missiles. None the less, opinions also seem to represent a more general barometer of East–West tension, for they closely follow the rise and fall of the fear of war between 1981 and 1984. Of course, the beginning of the INF negotiations in 1982 was itself part of this improved climate, but the close correspondence of the INF polls with more general fears about East–West relations and American foreign policy suggest that the INF deployment had become symbolic not just of the specific desire for arms control, but also of broader dangers perceived by Europeans. What Josef Joffe has said with regard to the peace movement applies to public opinion as well: "The peace movement of the 1980s could not have flourished without the decline in moderation that accompanied the frightening surge in the quantity and quality of nuclear weapons. Conversely, the movement would not have receded as quickly without the calming moderation in the tone and discourse of international politics by the mid 1980s."[38]

These sentiments were sensitized by a third set of concerns: the near-unanimous aversion of Europeans to the use of nuclear weapons in any but a retaliatory role. Table 4.3 summarizes these opinions: in every country, unconditional opposition to *any* use of nuclear weapons is fairly high, and in no country does more than a quarter of the public support NATO's current policy of reserving the option to use nuclear weapons first.

These sentiments could hardly have been calmed by the now-famous statements of American officials on the possibility of limited nuclear engagements, horizontal escalation, and sustainability of forces in prolonged conflict. None the less, the evidence indicates that "anti-use" opinions were not *created* by those statements. Public rejection of the use of nuclear weapons preceded the Reagan administration by many years. In the Netherlands, opposition to the performance of "nuclear tasks" by Dutch forces was high and essentially the same in 1975 and 1980. In West German polls before the INF decision, huge majorities were prepared to defend the national territory, but only tiny minorities favored using nuclear weapons to do so.[39] Finally, according to one opinion analyst in the American government, large majorities in all European countries opposed first-use of nuclear weapons in surveys as far back as 1955 and 1963: "opposition to the use of nuclear weapons . . . is nothing new in Western European thinking but a matter of long standing".[40]

To the extent that the Reagan Administration's statements or the INF deployment itself were related to anti-nuclear sentiments, they acted more as catalyst than as cause. This is hardly surprising. It is difficult to imagine large percentages of poll respondents in favor of unleashing nuclear weapons under any but the most desperate circumstances, and surveys are purely hypothetical. Of course, this recognition does not relieve the Alliance of dealing with public concerns, for the issue is likely to remain on the public agenda. The INF debate, in addition to arousing the public's attention, stimulated yet another energetic discussion of the role of nuclear weapons in NATO strategy. That discussion has focused attention on such questions as whether, when, and in what numbers NATO should use nuclear weapons.[41] Moreover, the double-zero INF Treaty has once again raised the issue of tactical (battlefield) nuclear weapons. With the United States and the Soviet Union now agreed to remove all medium- and short-range nuclear systems from Europe, strategists and policy-makers are re-examining the deterrent and defensive role of these tactical-range nuclear weapons. General Bernard Rogers,

Table 4.3   Public Opinions on the Use of Nuclear Weapons

"There are different opinions about the use of nuclear weapons in
Europe by NATO. Which of the following opinions is closest to yor own?"

	Under no circumstances (%)	Only if USSR uses first (%)	Only if overwhelmed conventionally (%)	Don't know (%)
FRANCE				
July 1981	44	32	17	7
October 1981	39	32	14	15
April 1982	37	31	22	10
October 1983	27	52	8	13
BRITAIN				
July 1981	24	47	19	10
October 1981	31	41	24	5
April 1982	22	51	21	5
July 1982	30	45	19	6
October 1983	24	61	8	7
May 1984	24	51	18	7
WEST GERMANY				
July 1981	29	37	17	17
October 1981	38	28	16	17
April 1982	34	36	19	11
July 1982	38	33	16	13
October 1983	31	42	4	23
May 1984	44	42	11	2
NETHERLANDS				
July 1981	36	32	19	13
October 1981	50	31	11	8
July 1982	37	32	16	15
October 1983	42	36	4	18
May 1984	36	30	16	17

NOTE: The full responses to the question are as follows: "NATO should not
use nuclear weapons of any kind under any circumstances"; "NATO should
use nuclear weapons only if the USSR uses them first in attacking Western
Europe"; "NATO should use nuclear weapons to defend itself if a Soviet
attack by conventional forces threatens to overwhelm NATO forces".

SOURCES: Office of Research, USIA, *West European Opinion on Key Security Issues, 1981–1982*, Report R–10–1982 (Washington, D.C.: June 1982)
Table 25, and *West Europeans Still Predominantly Oppose INF: Some Doubt*

the Supreme Commander of NATO's forces, has already voiced his skepticism of the double zero solution on the grounds that the resulting reliance on tactical-range systems "would guarantee that West Germany was the battlefield in a nuclear exchange".[42] In such a context, it is difficult to maintain the separation of nuclear deterrence, which the public accepts, and nuclear defense, the consequences of which the public woud prefer not to contemplate.

MORE ON INF

The surveys presented in the previous section suggest that European reactions to NATO's most recent nuclear modernization were influenced more by the political context of the decision than by the military implications of INF deployment and arms control. Public evaluation of the consequences of change in the military balance had not shifted dramatically, and nervousness about the state of East –West relations had reached extremely high levels. Long-held reservations about using nuclear weapons were also sensitized as defenders and critics of INF publicly rehearsed the deterrent and defensive role of nuclear weapons in NATO strategy.

None the less, despite widespread concern, it would be erroneous to conclude that European public opinion had rejected nuclear weapons entirely. We have already seen that nuclear deterrence was endorsed by public opinion even during the INF debate. Although the INF deployment certainly divided public opinion, survey experts have pointed out that these responses were greatly influenced by the wording of the question.[43] However, rather than criticize the apparent lack of depth and consistency in the public's views, perhaps we should turn vice to virtue and ask if the variety of questions and responses collected over the past several years yields any systematic pattern in the public's sentiments. The answer is clear. Judging from responses to a myriad of questions on the INF deployment, public opinion is influenced by sensitivity to Soviet deployments; by the desire to see deployments accompanied by arms control negotiations;

Table 4.3 – cont.

US Commitment to Negotiation, Report M–9/19/84 (Washington, D.C.: September 1984) Table 2; and Stockholm International Peace Research Institute, *The Arms Race and Arms Control, 1984* (London and Philadelphia, Penn.: Taylor and Francis, 1984) p. 19.

and by the desire to see deployments held to equal levels on both sides.

Sensitivity to Soviet force levels was illustrated in a 1981 poll conducted in seven European countries. The survey asked half the respondents simply if "you favor or oppose having new nuclear missiles that can reach the Soviet Union". The second half of the sample was asked this same question, but it was prefaced by the observation that "the Russians have about 450 warheads on new medium range missiles . . . while NATO has no such missiles". In the second version (including mention of Soviet warheads), opposition to INF deployment averaged 11 per cent less than in the version without the "Russian" preface.[44] Even starker differences emerged in a number of West German polls in the Fall of 1983. Surveys mentioning INF as a "counterweight" to Soviet missiles or as necessary to "remain strong *vis-à-vis* the Soviet Union" brought majority support for INF. Other questions that omitted mention of the Soviets but did mention negotiations brought majorities opposing deployment and favoring negotiation.[45]

In fact, the positive value placed on the negotiating track of the 1979 decision is one of the clearest findings of recent opinion surveys. Table 4.4 summarizes opposition to INF deployment in two *separate* surveys commissioned in 1981 and 1982. The first set of responses come from a simple "favor/oppose" question that included mention of 450 Soviet warheads. The second set of answers were in response to a question that did not mention Soviet warheads but *did* allow respondents to choose from among responses ranging from unconditional opposition, to "deploy while negotiating", to unconditional support. It is interesting to note that the mention of arms control options is apparently an even stronger consideration than is mention of Soviet capabilities. Even fewer respondents opposed deployment unconditionally when it was considered against negotiating options than had opposed it when Soviet deployments were mentioned. Put another way, the prospect of negotiations seemed to defuse opposition to the new INF deployments even more than ominous warnings about Soviet capabilities. As the full responses show (see Table 4.5), support for some variant of "deploy/negotiate" was usually the plurality view – in some cases the majority – when the question included these choices.

In summary, the survey data indicate that the overall political climate was a major factor underlying the drift of support and opposition to INF. The surveys cited in this section show that sensi-

Table 4.4 Opposition to the INF Deployment: Two Survey Questions

	Question 1: Oppose when Soviet warheads mentioned (%)	Question 2: Oppose when arms negotiations mentioned (%)
FRANCE		
July 1981	32	29
October 1981	36	33
April 1982	40	33
BRITAIN		
July 1981	29	22
October 1981	35	32
April 1982	37	28
WEST GERMANY		
July 1981	29	26
October 1981	33	32
April 1982	39	29
NETHERLANDS		
July 1981	51	38
October 1981	56	47

NOTES: The table shows responses to two separate questions. The first contains the following preface: "Well, as you may know, the Russians have about 450 nuclear warheads on new medium-range missiles aimed at Western Europe, while NATO has no such missiles". The second does not contain the warhead reference, but it offers the choice between opposition to INF and a number of "deploy/negotiate" options. Figures do not add to 100 per cent because other responses (favor INF, don't know) are not shown here.

SOURCE: Office of Research, USIA, *West European Opinion on Key Security Issues, 1981–1982*, Tables 42 and 43.

tivity to Soviet deployments is also an important factor. In the tense atmosphere of the 1980s perhaps it should come as little surprise that a third pattern – toleration of balanced deployment when tied to negotiations – was also apparent. These motivations were captured in a survey conducted just as the first NATO deployments approached in late 1983. Asked how NATO should resolve the INF issue, pluralities in all countries except Italy and Spain chose to "introduce just enough nuclear weapons to create a balance between East and West until an acceptable agreement can be found".[46]

Table 4.5   Opinions of the INF Deployment

"There are many different opinions on how to deal with the issue of stationing of these new nuclear missiles that could reach the Soviet Union. Listed on this card are different opinions about these new nuclear missiles. Which of these opinions is closest to your own?"

	Oppose uncondition ally (%)	Accept with arms talks (%)	Accept uncondition ally (%)	Don't know (%)
FRANCE				
July 1981	29	39	11	21
October 1981	34	37	11	17
February 1982	30	31	11	28
April 1982	33	44	12	11
*Average 1981/82	32	38	11	19
BRITAIN				
March 1981	31	39	15	15
July 1981	22	50	17	11
October 1981	32	45	15	8
December 1981	36	43	13	8
February 1982	36	41	12	10
April 1982	28	53	12	7
*Average 1981/82	31	45	14	10
WEST GERMANY				
March 1981	40	46	9	5
July 1981	26	45	12	17
October 1981	32	44	6	18
December 1981	40	39	3	17
January 1982	47	45	6	2
February 1982	39	41	9	12
April 1982	29	49	9	13
*Average 1981/82	36	45	8	12
NETHERLANDS				
March 1981	39	31	8	21
July 1981	38	42	9	11
October 1981	47	39	7	8
December 1981	52	40	5	3
*Average 1981	44	38	7	11

NOTE: The full responses to the question are as follows: "Oppose unconditionally"; "Accept only if arms talks with USSR have failed"; "Accept only if there are arms talks with the USSR at the same time"; "Accept without first insisting on arms talks".

SHOT IN THE FOOT: THE "LESSONS" OF INF

Public opinion surveys in Western Europe indicate that continuing efforts to negotiate nuclear arms control will be important to the preservation of the security policy consensus. To judge from public opinion, this is less because the public rejects nuclear weapons *per se* than because of what the weapons represent. At times of high tension in East–West relations, the arms control process becomes a symbol of conflict management, a rein on the actions of the United States and the Soviet Union. Indeed, the ultimate irony of the INF debate is that NATO's 1979 decision was born of the European fear of arms control collusion, only to be buffeted by fears of a superpower collision that threatened to end all hope of negotiation.

In the immediate aftermath of the INF decision, it appeared that the fear of collision remained most salient, and for this reason Europeans warmly welcomed the resumption of US–Soviet arms control talks in 1985. However, as negotiations progressed – from the Reagan–Gorbachev summit of 1985 through the Reykjavik summit of 1986 and the breakthrough to an INF agreement in late 1987 – the fear of arms control collusion once again came to the fore. European governments were particularly nervous after the Reykjavik summit, for President Reagan's apparent willingness to consider the total elimination of both strategic and intermediate nuclear forces brought European fears of decoupling to the surface once again.[47] These fears receded somewhat when both Reagan and Gorbachev retreated from their more ambitious proposals, but they reappeared with full force in April 1987, when Secretary Schultz received a renewed Soviet offer to negotiate a "zero solution" to the INF issue in Europe. Within days, it became clear that the United States was very interested in an agreement based on the zero solution, but it was also evident that Europeans were not totally enthusiastic.[48]

There ensued a familiar debate within NATO. Europeans believed that Gorbachev's proposal would undermine what had been accomplished by the INF deployment. NATO would be left with no missiles capable of reaching Soviet territory, and initially it seemed

---

Table 4.5 – cont.

The two responses involving "arms talks [continue/fail]" have been combined in the column labelled "accept with arms talks".

SOURCE: Office of Research, USIA, *West European Opinion Key Security Issues, 1981–1982*, Table 43.

that the Alliance might find it necessary to build up INF forces of shorter range to match the SS-22 and SS-23 missiles that the Soviets had deployed in response to NATO's modernization. When Gorbachev made it clear that he could be persuaded to eliminate these latter weapons as well, NATO was back to dealing with the persistent dilemma of flexible response: could NATO deter Soviet conventional forces with its remaining battlefield nuclear weapons, the use of which would destroy what NATO was trying to defend? If not, how credible was the ultimate back-up – the American strategic guarantee – in a world yet characterized by mutually assured destruction? Within the space of several weeks after Shultz' Moscow visit in April 1987, journalists, politicians, and strategists rehearsed these and other arguments that had surrounded flexible response since its adoption.[49]

The role of public opinion was important in these developments. Indeed, press reports indicated that the governments of the Alliance responded to the arms control diplomacy of the mid 1980s largely on the basis of the expected (or feared) public reaction. On both sides of the Atlantic officials went through two stages of worry. After the resumption of negotiations in early 1985, the general concern was that the Soviet Union could take advantage of the anti-nuclear neuralgia that Western publics had displayed during the INF debate. There was also the feeling that in democracies, negotiation simply feeds the public appetite for continued détente. As Gorbachev moved briskly to establish contact with the West, there was much consternation at the possible public relations effects of his peace, charm, and reform offensives. As one West German daily put it: "The political intent of [Gorbachev's] dual strategy is self-evident: above all, the Kremlin wants to score points among the European public so that the latter will put pressure on its own government and on the Americans. The way the Soviets figure it, this would make the price they will have to pay for a new agreement in Geneva correspondingly lower."[50]

A second set of concerns was the reaction of the public to specific negotiating positions. For example, former US Secretary of Defense James Schlesinger pointed to public opinion in his criticism of President Reagan's performance at the Reykjavik summit:

the publics and much of the press in Europe have been excited by the promise of major arms control agreements, and particularly the elimination of the Soviet intermediate-range threat directed against Western Europe. They have been persuaded that the elimination of the dreaded SS-20 threat would have taken place had it not been for the American obstinacy about SDI. While the Soviets will remain unsuccessful in the near term in changing the attitudes of governments, they have been given a fertile field to sow in the battle for public opinion.[51]

The success of the Schultz visit in early 1987 demonstrated that lack of progress on SDI would not prevent the United States and the Soviet Union from nearing agreement on the INF issue. None the less, public opinion remained a source of caution. Although many European governments had doubts about the "decoupling" effect of a "double-zero" solution that would eliminate both medium-range and short-range INF forces, they reportedly suppressed these feelings because they feared a negative public reaction. According to one news report, Prime Minister Thatcher and Chancellor Kohl felt caught between obligations to their publics and their fears that a zero agreement would weaken the American commitment to Europe. For the public, the zero agreement would be a "breathtaking event that would hearten publics grown cynical about arms control".[52] Other news reports indicated that elements of the West German government were wary of the zero option for medium-range forces, and in any case they wanted NATO to preserve the right to deploy short-range forces rather than negotiate a zero agreement for them as well. However, the German government deliberately kept these feelings from the public. One official who discussed them openly received a reprimand from the Chancellor.[53]

European governments, it seems, were operating under the apparent "lessons" of the INF controversy. Given the level of public worry that had been evinced in the intense nuclear debate of the early 1980s, governments were not inclined to stand in the way of apparent progress in negotiations, for this would contradict the public's desire for arms control and play into the hands of Gorbachev's "charm" offensive. Further, despite the fact that they had serious doubts about the details of the proposed agreement, European leaders suppressed these doubts (at least publicly) for fear of creating a public backlash. In the end, the negotiated solution to the INF issue is the "double-zero" option eliminating both medium- and short-range INF – precisely the outcome of least appeal to European governments, but one which they felt compelled to accept. The most immediate alternatives, a solution at greater than zero INF or a build-up of short-range systems, were options that few governments felt able to risk with public opinion.

It is among the most startling of the many ironies of the entire INF affair that these "lessons" are probably misguided. Leaving aside strategic arguments surrounding the INF Agreement, there is good reason to believe that estimates of the public reaction to the arms negotiations were off the mark. As I have argued in detail above, the more exaggerated concerns about the public's rejection of deterrence and nuclear weapons were dispelled in numerous surveys. In addition, despite the repeated attempts of the Soviet government to play on the fears of Europeans, the Soviet image throughout the INF affair remained extremely negative.

In fact, arms control euphoria may be a myth. During the 1970s, opinion surveys inquiring of the SALT agreements showed that Europeans were hardly utopian about the potential results of arms control negotiations. It is true that both SALT Treaties were welcomed by large majorities in France, Britain, and West Germany, and substantial if lesser percentages felt that SALT would contribute to deterrence and peace. But few thought that SALT would end the arms race, and in some West German polls up to half the respondents were either uninformed about SALT II or did not think that it had much effect on peace or the arms race.[54] In fact, West German expectations of the *results* of détente more generally have always been cautious. Although huge majorities during the 1970s favored efforts to continue negotiations with the Soviets, 50 to 60 per cent of the public also thought that the Soviets used détente to "further their power" and that the Soviets profited most from improvements in relations.[55]

Opinions on a potential INF agreement were also cautious. Certainly, continued negotiation of the INF issue was a high priority in European opinion throughout the debate of the early 1980s. None the less, in no country did more than one-third of the public think that the negotiations would soon succeed. In surveys on SALT and on INF, European respondents were markedly suspicious about Soviet sincerity and reliability in negotiations. Between 1981 and 1984, a period when American foreign policy was under severe attack in Western Europe, Europeans none the less believed on balance that the United States was making "a sincere effort" in arms control negotiations. Except in the Netherlands, no more than one-third believed that the Soviets were making a sincere effort. In 1984, 60 to 80 per cent doubted that the Soviets would "keep their word" in arms control agreements. Near-unanimous percentages (80 to 90 per cent) agreed that verification procedures were necessary "to check that the Soviets are keeping the agreement". In 1981 and 1982 surveys matching the President with Soviet leaders (a tough test given Reagan's negative image at the time), Reagan enjoyed an advantage in the relative sincerity ascribed to arms control initiatives. At the end of 1985, Reagan continued to lead Gorbachev in a European poll asking "who is more serious about reaching an arms control agreement?".[56]

It was only in 1986 and 1987 that President Reagan's "sincerity advantage" began to slip. Even so, it was not so much that the American image or Reagan's image began to decline. Quite the opposite, the President's confidence deficit of the early 1980s had improved somewhat (although it was still negative). But under Gorbachev, the Soviet image had improved even more. Under Gorbachev, the distinctly negative ratings of Soviet foreign policy have been ameliorated, although they remain more negative than those for American foreign policy.[57] Gorbachev, it seems, is closing the East–West confidence gap. In British and German polls in 1987, Gorbachev was considered even more believable than Reagan on arms control.[58]

American observers have used these and other polls to resurrect arguments about "equidistance" – a European tendency to place the United States and the Soviet Union on the same moral plane.[59] These arguments are without basis in the polls. One reason has already been discussed: this type of survey on image, confidence, and sincerity is highly variable. They therefore do not reflect deep-seated sentiments, let alone secular trends. Equally important, we have seen that, whatever the readings of the "image" polls in Europe, direct questions about values and national interests indicate little affinity for the Soviet Union.

What does seem apparent is that the recent poll readings reflect the political fortunes of the two leaders. President Reagan had a tough time of it during 1986 and 1987. Europeans did not have to look far to find criticism of his policies or his decision-making style. The Reykjavik summit and the Iran/Contra revelations produced a near-constant stream of negative commentary. Gorbachev, in contrast, has enjoyed the positive limelight. His domestic reforms captured a fascination in the West. His "zero option" on INF was warmly greeted. In the East–West popularity contest, Gorbachev was speaking the language of *glasnost* while the US Congress investigated the activities of Presidential agents acting without authority. In this context, it does not seem surprising that, for the moment at least, Soviet trust and "sincerity" ratings should show an upswing.

But this does not mean that European attitudes towards arms control have been transformed. Paradoxically, one way to demonstrate this point is to cite *American* polls. Americans, presumably more hardline and unaffected by "equidistance", had this to say about Gorbachev in 1985: more likely to ease tensions (61 per cent); more likely to want an arms control agreement with the US (58 per cent); and "more attractive" than other "Russian" leaders (58 per cent). In the Spring of 1987, a survey for the *New York Times* found that Gorbachev was viewed more favorably than Wall Street investors, the CIA, Richard Nixon, and the Reverend Jerry Falwell. These reactions occurred despite the fact that the American public continued to distrust the Soviets generally.[60]

In fact, despite the common image of the American population as being comparatively hardline on issues of arms control and East–West relations, it actually resembles European opinion surveys. American polls are similar to the European polls in revealing a populace quite anxious to control nuclear weapons and supportive of US–Soviet negotiations – but cautious about the expected results of negotiation with a difficult partner. Americans favor arms control negotiations as a necessary element of conflict management, but they appear to be under no illusions about the difficulties of the arms control process. Like Europeans, they simply want to keep trying.[61]

Thus, despite the visibility of European concerns about nuclear weapons, there is nothing to suggest that they want "arms control at any price". Although Gorbachev had obviously put the West in a difficult position with his "double zero" solution, there is little in the polls to suggest that the public would have revolted at a counterproposal that reflected official European worries about decoupling and the balance of conventional forces. The pattern of opinion from the early 1980s suggests that European governments underestimated the degree to which public sentiments were consistent with official views. As Paul Nitze observed himself during the initial round of INF negotiations, the European public was never wedded to the "zero option". It was prepared to accept equal levels above zero. Moreover, just as European governments express concern about putative Soviet superiority in particular classes of weapons, the polls suggested that the public was sensitive to Soviet force levels and to the argument that *balance* – rather than elimination – was the desired outcome of arms control. Presumably the same set of concerns applies to the conventional force balance that will become crucial after the implementation of the double-zero solution to INF. Finally, the persistent worry of European governments that the public would become frightened or enraged at the failure to reach agreement (especially if the West was seen as the culprit) was simply not borne out during the 1980s. Public concern about arms control actually declined by 1982. Subsequently, both polls and protests registered decreases in concern, despite the fact that no real agreements were reached in any negotiation. Indeed, with the announcement of SDI in 1983, the prospects for successful arms control dropped decidedly, if temporarily. The public reaction in Europe was muted (more on this below). Even after Reykjavik, where SDI was the stumbling block to agreement in other areas, the negative public reaction feared by Schlesinger never erupted.

Thus, European governments appear to have overestimated the likelihood of public backlash in the absence of arms control agreements. None the less, a final paradox is that the negotiations have yielded the one outcome that *is* likely to rekindle public unrest. The United States and the Soviet Union will now eliminate both medium- and short-range INF systems. The NATO Alliance has agreed to this solution.[62] Systems of very short-range – so-called tactical or battlefield nuclear weapons – will not be affected. As a result, journalists, strategists, and government planners have already begun yet another debate over flexible response. The debate has refocused attention on the questions of how soon and where NATO would use tactical-range nuclear weapons to counter a Soviet conventional assault.[63]

This subject will strike a nerve in the public, for on the question of the *use* of nuclear weapons, public attitudes have been negative for many years. Talk of using nuclear weapons probably contributed as much to the eruption of public concern about INF as did deployment of the weapons themselves. In this context, General Rogers's recent comment that the double-zero solution could leave Germany a "nuclear battlefield" is hardly propitious for public relations. Strategists and government officials may be uncomfortably resigned to the uncertainties surrounding flexible response; the public is not, at least when the discussion involves scenarios for the use of nuclear weapons (as noted above, the public *does* seem to accept nuclear deterrence). Should the double zero INF agreement bring a public laundering of the uncertainties of flexible response, the public reaction could be negative.[64]

The ultimate irony of the INF episode is therefore that a misreading of public opinion may have boxed NATO into precisely the position that is most likely to stir public unease. Of course, a public uproar on the scale of the INF controversy remains a conditional probability – not a certainty. Many of the factors that contributed to public unease during the early 1980s may not be present as the decade comes to a close. The fears caused by the crisis conditions of the early 1980s were a crucial variable in the outbreak of public worry in 1981 and 1982. A "dual track" approach to East–West relations, modelled on the Harmel formula of strength and negotiation, could therefore be sufficient to dampen debates that arise over flexible response. Similarly, to the extent that European fears were directed at the belligerent tone of American foreign policy, continued negotiation and the preservation of the Reagan–Gorbachev détente will do much to reassure the public. Finally, it may very well be that the recent outcome of the INF negotiations has transformed the politics of arms control. European governments cannot have failed to notice that both the Reykjavik summit and the zero solution seemed to have been calculated to slow the erosion in President Reagan's domestic standing.[65] The result may be that attention will shift from the apparent breakdown of the European *domestic* consensus to faults in the *transatlantic* relationship.

CONCLUDING COMMENTS: THE FUTURE POLITICS OF ARMS CONTROL

At the symbolic level, recent arms control negotiations do much to satisfy a basic European desire to see a moderation of tension and arms competition. The permanence of this positive tone will depend on a number of factors, and to judge from the pattern of past surveys, the future state of East–West relations is clearly the most important. Although much would depend on the circumstances, should events lead to a major reversal of the current trend toward détente, one can predict that Europeans – leaders and public alike – will once again reach for the reins of negotiation. Arms control would again become the crucial symbol of desires to calm the waters. The opposite fear – that successful negotiations might neglect or ignore Europeans interests – seems less salient at present, at least within the public. Given the desire for relaxation and the public's limited knowledge of particular weapons systems, the details of potential treaties seem less important than continuation of the process itself. To paraphrase Jane Sharp, the cohesion of the Alliance on arms control issues appears to be more a function of political confidence than of military hardware.[66]

There are potential exceptions to this proposition. As noted above, public opinion could be aroused once again by a lengthy debate about the use of tactical nuclear weapons for deterrence and defense. But perhaps the most significant potential problem is President Reagan's strategic defense initiative (SDI). This is not the place to rehearse the growing list of arguments for and against SDI. That has been done at great length by experts in the field.[67] None the less, the impact of SDI on European perceptions deserves comment. There is, of course, the double fear of abandonment: SDI may lead the United States either to abandon European defense altogether or to (finally) shift the brunt of that defense to the conventional level. The latter prospect is especially troubling to West Germans for reasons of geography, but given the cost of conventional weapons, it cannot be appealing to any European nation. In the case of France and Britain, there is the additional complication that unconstrained defenses would call into question their independent nuclear forces, which serve important political purposes and allow savings in conventional forces. For these reasons of doctrine, it is no surprise that European governments are decidedly skeptical of SDI and would hardly object to an arms agreement that banned deployment.[68]

In addition, opinion surveys reveal some broader perceptions that may reinforce European opposition to SDI. First, the systems will be a new departure, and it is widely perceived as an area in which the United States enjoys a wide advantage. SDI therefore challenges the opinion of many Europeans who see the current strategic balance as essentially equal and prefer that it stay that way. Nor is this concern confined to public opinion. In 1984, West German Defense Minister Wörner (a conservative) remarked that "It would be intolerable . . . for one of the two superpowers to gain a one-sided lead in setting up such a system. The superpower with the advantage would then have absolute superiority and the other power would basically have to submit. The strategic balance would then be upset."[69] Finally, deployment of SDI in the absence of negotiated limits would represent a severe blow for Europeans, for the abrogation of the 1972 ABM Treaty would bring the military implications mentioned above, and it would signal a major reversal of the arms control process that they value in political terms. For these reasons, Europeans have stuck to the position that, while research on SDI is acceptable and perhaps even desirable, deployment must not be envisioned in such a way as to put the ABM Treaty in danger.[70]

Beyond these obvious concerns surrounding SDI, much depends on the details and outcome of the negotiating process. It is idle to speculate on those details, but a more general point deserves comment. The political debate about SDI has been driven not by public opinion, but by the arguments of governmental leaders and strategic experts. When President Reagan announced the SDI in March 1983, criticism emerged almost immediately from government chancellories in Europe – vigorous in the French case, more subtle in the case of West Germany and Britain.[71] Yet, almost two years later, a staff team from the Congressional Research Service travelled to Europe to study reactions to SDI, and they found that "as of February 1985 SDI has not yet become an important public issue".[72] Of course, it was not long before the pollsters had queried the public for their views on SDI, but the responses – largely negative – should probably be read as an echo rather than as a stimulus. Significantly, large percentages of respondents chose the "don't know" response in questions on Star Wars. In addition, in 1986 54 per cent of the British and 51 per cent of the French supported *research* on SDI – precisely the position taken by their governments.[73]

This interpretation matches dominant scholarly models – only recently reconsidered – that see public opinion on complex policy issues as a reflection of the cues provided by governmental leaders, party élites and the media.[74] Scholars will no doubt debate the accuracy of this model, but it has obvious implications for the politics of arms control. Most of the issues are technical and largely unfamiliar to all but sophisticated strategic analysts. Few are experts on such issues as cruise missiles, battlefield weapons, or the targeting prerogatives of the NATO commander. In such a context, the public's views – and thus the political context of arms control – are likely to reflect the political and expert debates of the coming months and years. To judge from the recent literature, three issues will be of potential salience.

The first is the treatment of British and French nuclear forces in future arms control agreements. As in prior SALT accords, these forces were excluded from the INF Agreement and, by and large, political debate on the issue has been low-key to non-existent.[75] None the less, if these forces become the object of disagreement or breakdown in future negotiations on long-range systems, they may create political fissures within Europe in much the same way that a stalemate on SDI could create transatlantic difficulties. Significantly, the American government is attentive to the issue. In 1983 it conducted a poll in West Germany asking whether British and French forces should be included in the INF talks. The results indicate the potential for friction. Inclusion of British and French forces was favored by 58 per cent of SPD followers, 72 per cent of the FDP and 48 per cent of the CDU; among the "attentive public" of those with higher education, the figure is 60 per cent.[76] These figures obviously do not mean that an intra-European squabble will erupt. They do suggest the potential for differences should the issue become prominent.

The second issue of potential controversy is already apparent: the call for NATO to move toward a policy of no-first-use (NFU) of nuclear weapons. Once again, the issue has been framed by experts (although perhaps in response to vocal public concerns). As we have seen, this is an issue on which there is a very broad consensus within all European publics. There is great receptiveness to any initiative that would reduce the probability that nuclear weapons would be used first. Although the NFU debate seems to have lapsed as SDI and other issues come to the fore, it is likely to be resurrected by the renewed attention to battlefield nuclear weapons that will result from the double-zero INF agreement. The problem, of course, is that neither governments nor experts agree on the military desirability of NFU. The political problem of confidence in deterrence (and the American guarantee) is also a major source of doubt. Even modest proposals for reduction, repositioning, or replacement of battlefield nuclear systems are offered cautiously, for they might symbolize a decoupling of the American deterrent or a shift to the conventional emphasis that is troubling to Europeans on budgetary and geographical grounds. The paradox appears once again: to modernize nuclear weapons is to stimulate European fears of an arms race, but to reduce their role or remove them is to provoke the fear of abandonment.[77]

None the less, the dilemma may not be as severe as is often supposed. To be sure, a sudden blanket declaration of no-first-use would be unsettling – for allied governments, if not for the public. However, more modest steps to replace vulnerable or obsolescent systems or to reconfigure dual nuclear/conventional forces would not only be acceptable to the public, they might also be a positive contribution to consolidating the domestic calm that has accompanied the resumption of arms control talks.[78]

Of course, it may have been the source more than the content of NFU proposals that most unsettled allied governments. It is troubling for Europeans to hear fundamental assumptions called into question by Americans who were once responsible for their articulation. It may be that Europeans are inured, if not immune, to the openness and robustness of American strategic debates, inside and outside government. None the less, the past decade has brought what must seem to Europeans like a barrage of official and unofficial surprises and reversals, to say nothing of the disappointment at occasional inaction. Once again the list is long and acrimonious: from energy policy and the neutron bomb to SALT II ratification, currency management, and consultation on trade embargoes.

As Stanley Hoffmann has observed, confusion and disappointment is neither new nor surprising in an alliance of democratic societies whose institutions are diverse and subject to mutual misunderstanding.[79] Yet recognition of the difficulty gives all the more reason to foresee its effects, and there are already signs that better transatlantic communication will be necessary as arms control negotiations move forward.

For example, it is now commonplace in the American press to describe the bureaucratic battles and problems of coordination that accompany the formulation of American negotiating positions. Moreover, even before the Iran/Contra debacle, the issue of Presidential knowledge, competence, and control had become a familiar theme. In the early 1980s there were already ample signs that Europeans were concerned about the lack of coherence in Washington. Reviewing Strobe Talbott's account of the START and INF negotiations, Lawrence Freedman observed that his major concern was not with questions of strategy or weapons: "The strategic disability revealed by this book . . . has nothing to do with the balances of power or the loyalty of allies or the combat readiness of the armed forces. The picture presented here is of a shambles of a government."[80]

These were harsh words, but it seems unlikely that intervening years have brought much improvement. The decision-making process that led to the SDI announcement was roundly criticized. The Congressional team studying European reactions to SDI brought home a clear message: "Virtually every official of an allied government interviewed complained that the Reagan administration had failed to consult his government before the President announced his plans. . . . West European leaders have spent three decades persuading their people that deterrence is the cornerstone of NATO defense policy. Suddenly . . . officials of the Reagan administration announced that nuclear weapons are 'immoral'."[81] Europeans were further worried by the decision to abandon compliance with SALT II, and of course the Iran/Contra episode has cast a heavy shadow on judgments of American decision-making. Finally, Europeans were deeply distressed by the apparent lack of preparation for the Reykjavik summit and by what James Schlesinger calls the "breathtaking" discussions held there: "The Europeans, needless to say, were vastly disturbed to discover that such revolutionary changes in the Western security system affecting Europe could be proposed and negotiated without any prior consultation. But they were perhaps even more disturbed by the sudden realization that the American negotiators apparently proceeded at Reykjavik without the slightest understanding of the basis of the system of Western security. . . . Their confidence in American leadership is significantly weakened."[82]

Schlesinger's words echo European sentiments that were already evident during the transatlantic squabbles of the early 1980s. In interviews with more than a hundred European politicians, civil servants, and strategists in 1981 and 1982, William Domke and his colleagues found that the consistency and reliability of the United States had become a fundamental worry for European leaders – as it is with public opinion. The twists and turns of American policy were seen not just as the result of a tendency to overreact or to "wash the slate clean" after every election. Rather, the problems appeared structural, as revealed by the complexity of legislative staffs and the seeming inability of the executive to coordinate its policies. Moreover, American policy in (and toward) Europe had become the prisoner of domestic politics. Major changes and reversals could not be precluded as Presidents and Congress used foreign policy to gain tactical political advantage.[83]

In summary, both public and élite opinion in the early 1980s had turned decidedly skeptical about the substance and process of American foreign policy. A major question for NATO is whether the alliance itself will survive this erosion of confidence.

5 The Three Pillars of Western Security: Public Opinion and the NATO Alliance

> Recent discussion of the Atlantic relationship has been preoccupied with the 'disarray' of the Atlantic Alliance. Pessimism about its future is the current mood. Indeed, if the standard of comparison is the Alliance in its early years, or the expectations of orthodox Alliance doctrine, the state of the Alliance is disheartening.

Words such as these are now commonplace in discussions of the Western Alliance. Since the late 1970s, the Alliance has been bedevilled by a series of disputes and controversies that have at times called its very existence into question. The neutron weapons controversy in 1978 was merely a prelude. In 1979, the hostage situation in Iran, followed by the Soviet invasion of Afghanistan, led to a transatlantic debate over "out-of-area" operations. Soviet pressure and martial law in Poland produced a bitter dispute over the pipeline embargo and the wider question of economic sanctions as an instrument of East–West competition. As economies deteriorated in the wake of the oil shock of 1979, the perennial choice between "guns and butter" plagued all Alliance governments, and the difficulty was exacerbated by divergent budget priorities in the United States and Western Europe and by severe disagreement in trade relations and monetary affairs. Finally, all these disagreements occurred against the backdrop of the intense nuclear debate described in the preceding chapter. In the year of its thirtieth anniversary, NATO faced dispute and controversy in virtually every aspect of its operation.

The purpose of this chapter is to examine the impact of these events on public support for the NATO Alliance. In the following two sections, I provide a brief overview of the three "pillars" of security, economic, and political interests that have bound the members of the Alliance, and I discuss recent strains in each of these pillars. Following this review, I present historical polls which show that support for NATO in European public opinion is surprisingly high. Even when offered alternatives, European opinion chooses NATO. However, later sections of the chapter reveal that the stability of attachment to NATO is not matched when the question turns to transatlantic economic and political cooperation. In addition, there are partisan and generational differences in support for NATO. I conclude the chapter with a discussion of how these complications will affect the cohesion of the Alliance.

THE THREE PILLARS OF WESTERN SECURITY

NATO has a long history of recurring "crises". In fact, the words cited at the outset of this chapter were published not during the turmoil of the 1980s but in 1966, as the opening passage of Harold Van B. Cleveland's *Atlantic Idea and its European Rivals*.[1] At that time NATO faced a similar plethora of problems. President de Gaulle, irritated by American defense and economic policy, had withdrawn French forces from NATO's integrated command. A severe recession had hit Europe, in some countries interrupting an unbroken record of economic growth that began in the 1950s. The American commitment in Vietnam and the growing strain on the dollar exacerbated transatlantic discord. For their part, the United States pressed Europeans to offset the foreign exchange costs of American forces in Europe. In the nuclear realm, the question of "control sharing" was soon to be joined by the question of how European interests would be treated in any Soviet–American arms control negotiation. As Cleveland's words make clear, in the late 1960s the Alliance faced a dismal future.

Why did NATO survive this and other crises? The dominant interpretation is structural. That is, for many students of the Alliance, three "pillars" of common interest in security, economic, and political affairs go far in explaining the resilience of the Alliance in the face of near-permanent transatlantic controversy.[2] In the security realm, Europe and the United States have been bound by common interests and by a lack of alternatives to the NATO Alliance. For the United States, containment of the Soviet Union was at first most urgent in Europe. Later the European commitment became part of a global pattern. For Europeans, geography combined with internal weakness to make the Atlantic connection a *sine qua non* of security and even survival. Further, failing a truly unified European defense force that would include a nuclear deterrent for *all* of Europe (es-

pecially for West Germany), the Atlantic connection remained the
only alternative that seemed both feasible and politically acceptable.
Despite near-constant wrangling across the Atlantic – and even within
Europe – NATO remained the cornerstone of European defense. In
the words of one influential analyst, "The Alliance endures not
because it is perfect, but because it serves the interests of its members
better than the feasible alternatives."[3]

Economic interests are equally important. Initially, the Marshall
Plan and the Bretton Woods system provided the basis for post-war
recovery and the construction of a global economic system that would
supersede the economic nationalism and rivalry that had contributed
to the failures of the inter-war period. As the transatlantic economy
grew, the benefits of the new system were clear, for all Western
economies experienced an unprecedented increase in growth and
citizen welfare. For Europeans as for Americans, economic interdependence had produced one of the great success stories of history.

The third pillar of the Alliance was less tangible, but presumably
no less important, for politically the Western community was more
than a like-minded bastion in the ideologically charged atmosphere
of the Cold War. Americans, after all, drew their political heritage,
first from the philosophical ideas of the European enlightenment,
later from European immigrants who reinforced the American connection to the Old World. The liberal democratic values of the
Alliance were thus rooted in almost two hundred years of common
experience. Moreover, as the European recovery – political as well as
economic – got underway, the peculiar American model of egali-
tarian individualism offered an attraction to Europeans who were
weary of their own experience, certainly with the horrors of fascism,
but also with patterns of tradition and class that were seen in stark
contrast to the American dream of upward mobility. As Van Cleveland had noted in 1966, the Atlantic Alliance was far more than a
traditional military pact. It was a nascent "community" in the
broader sense, a group of societies bound by national interests to be
sure, but a community whose members were attracted by common
values as well.

THE ALLIANCE UNDER STRAIN

If the troubles of recent years now seem particularly severe, it is
above all because each of these pillars of the Alliance have come

under strain. Preceding chapters of this book have documented the security debates in great detail. Not only was NATO forced to deal with a number of difficult decisions, on nuclear weapons as on "out-of area" problems and East–West trade. More important, the very wisdom and reliability of the dominant Alliance partner had been called into question. Especially in reaction to domestic and transatlantic quarrels on the issue of nuclear strategy and arms control, there were calls both by strategists and by politicians for a stronger "European" approach as an alternative to dependence on an unpredictable (or disagreeable) United States. Pieter Dankert, President of the European Parliament and a prominent politician of the Dutch Labour Party, called for Europe to take more responsibility for its own defense: "A more unified European approach could restore the mutual confidence and respect that is essential if the Atlantic relationship is to survive. A more unified approach could also help Europe to act as a moderating influence in the current stand-off between the superpowers."[4] Even Helmut Schmidt, whose concern for coupling had motivated his 1977 speech that stimulated NATO's 1979 decision on INF systems, later argued that Europe (and especially France and Germany) had to collaborate more on defense issues, given the unpredictability of American behavior and the need to protect European interests in arms control.[5] In both academic and political circles, interest in a stronger "European pillar" was a prominent feature of the literature of the 1980s.[6]

The interest in a more "Europeanist" approach to security seemed to indicate that the special set of circumstances that had bound the Western nations had been superseded by a search for better alternatives. In the economic field controversy was equally severe. As the oil shocks of 1973 and 1979 worked their effects, both the intent and the impact of American economic policies came under fire in Europe. In the early 1980s the related issues of the American budget deficit, interest rates, and the strength of the dollar were at the top of Europeans' list of complaints. The investment needed to pave the transition to a post-industrial, "high-technology" economy was hindered by the flight of capital to the United States. Third World markets, crucial to European exports, had been shrunk by the debt crisis as the developing countries reduced imports to preserve funds for debt servicing. Finally, the very success of post-war economic policies had produced problems, for in agriculture and other areas, the states of the developed world, fully recovered and now in possession of surplus capacity, were competing for global markets at a time of recession and growing capacity among the "newly industrialized countries". In every sphere of economic policy – trade, monetary affairs, and aid – the United States and Western Europe found themselves in disagreement and often in bitter controversy.

These disputes aggravated a simmering divergence in the third pillar of the Alliance, the ties of common political values. For Europeans, perhaps the disenchantment had begun with the Vietnam War or the outbreak of racial unrest in the United States during the 1960s. The United States, admired in the immediate post-war period as a partner and as a model in political and social terms, was now seen by many as overextended and even brutal in its military policies, and the domestic disharmony of American society came as a harsh disappointment to those who had seen the United States as the land of upward mobility. Moreover, the primacy of market and individual in American economic and social policies clashed with European notions of cultural preservation and social solidarity. European governments had also moved to consolidate their budgets in the face of declining revenues and currency instability, but the American model of budget cuts and *laissez-faire* seemed to them a rather drastic approach.

As the 1980s progressed, the Atlantic community developed an entirely new field of debate, this time over superior styles of political economy and the proper balance between individual and governmental responsibility. In the opinion of many Americans, the European economies had become incurably clogged by "Eurosclerosis" – the accumulation of taxes, spending, and regulation that support the welfare state. Exacerbated by disputes in the trade and monetary sectors, the American critique was both harsh and frequently stated. In Stanley Hoffmann's words, "There is a kind of global indictment of Western Europe's behavior, beliefs, and evolution. . . . Americans, it is well known, do not like losers, and today, Western Europe looks like one."[7]

As the decade of the 1980s reached its midpoint, the Western Alliance had come under strain in each of the "pillars" that had supported it for over thirty years. Although earlier crises had passed, this time the weight of disagreement seemed overwhelming. Moreover, as disagreement mounted, there was growing concern that the domestic base of support for the Alliance had been eroded, not only by the conflicts in interest and perspective described above, but also by the social and political changes of the post-war period. Reports of neutralism and pacifism in European public opinion seemed to confirm a prediction made by Anton DePorte in 1979. Although he remained convinced that external constraints and common interests made an alternative to NATO unlikely, he cautioned that *domestic* change might threaten the Alliance in the future: "A new challenge, not yet in focus, is the prospect that economic difficulties and political realignments within advanced countries may call into question their internal stability and the relations between them."[8]

THE NATO ALLIANCE: FAUTE DE MIEUX?

This fear was apparently unfounded. Despite the acrimony that characterized transatlantic relations during the 1980s, the commitment of European public opinion to the NATO Alliance remains astonishingly high. The broadest evidence of this commitment comes in a standard USIA question that has been posed in Western Europe since 1967 (Table 5.1). With the unsurprising exception of the French, public opinion in Europe has remained firm in the belief that the NATO Alliance is "essential" to European security. Although there was a drop in the attachment to NATO during the peak of the INF controversy in 1981 and 1982, it returned to earlier levels by 1984 (this is most easily read from the final column of Table 5.1, "net support for NATO", which subtracts the "NATO not essential" percentage from the "NATO essential" percentage). Moreover, endorsement of NATO remained quite strong even in the two countries that experienced the most intense debate over the INF deployment: West Germany and the Netherlands. Despite a period of protest and bitter exchanges on a wide variety of security issues and a noticeable drop in Europeans' confidence in the wisdom of American foreign policy, Europeans' attachment to the security pillar of the transatlantic community emerged as strong as before.

The two Dutch surveys reproduced in Table 5.1 also reveal the importance of question wording, and they suggest care in interpreting the meaning of this type of survey. In the first survey, the Dutch are asked if NATO is "necessary for peace" in Europe. Responses to this question show declines in the late 1960s, early 1970s, and again in the early 1980s. Each of these periods was characterized by debate in Dutch politics about détente and about American foreign policy. In the earlier periods, there were calls for a stronger détente policy within the Alliance, and the American role in Vietnam was strongly criticized. In the 1980s, of course, the controversy centered around the INF deployment, but there was once again harsh criticism of the

Table 5.1 Is NATO Essential to European Security?

	NATO is essential (%)	NATO is not essential (%)	Don't know (%)	Net support for NATO (%)
FRANCE				
1967	34	30	36	+ 4
1969	47	37	16	+10
1971	54	35	11	+19
1973	42	34	25	+ 8
1976	42	35	23	+ 7
1977	44	29	27	+15
1978	39	35	26	+ 4
1980	44	34	23	+10
1982	34	25	40	+ 9
1987	48	19	32	+29
BRITAIN				
1967	59	15	26	+44
1969	68	15	17	+53
1971	81	12	7	+69
1976	69	15	16	+54
1977	73	8	19	+65
1978	70	10	20	+60
1980	79	13	8	+66
1981	70	15	15	+55
1982	65	25	10	+40
1984	76	12	12	+64
1985	76	13	11	+63
1987	72	16	12	+56
WEST GERMANY				
1967	67	17	16	+50
1969	76	13	11	+63
1971	84	11	5	+73
1973	73	13	14	+60
1976	85	10	5	+75
1977	79	7	14	+72
1978	84	5	11	+79
1980	88	8	4	+80
1981	62	20	19	+42
1982	66	18	16	+48
1983	86	12	2	+74
1984	87	10	3	+77
1987	70	15	15	+55

NETHERLANDS

1967	85	7	8	+78
1968	83	15	2	+68
1969	65	13	22	+52
1970	66	14	20	+52
1971	71	12	17	+59
1972	65	16	19	+49
1973	65	17	18	+48
1974	76	9	15	+67
1975	77	9	14	+68
1976	81	9	10	+72
1977	75	11	14	+64
1978	76	9	15	+67
1979	79	9	12	+70
1980	79	14	7	+65
1981	64	18	18	+46
1982	64	15	21	+49
1983	64	15	21	+49
1984	61	21	18	+40

	Remain in NATO	Withdraw	Don't know	Net support for NATO
1969	65	13	22	+52
1971	71	12	17	+59
1972	65	16	19	+49
1974	76	9	15	+67
1979	76	12	12	+64
1980	76	14	10	+62
1981	78	14	8	+64
1982	76	13	11	+63
1983	76	15	9	+61
1984	77	15	9	+62
1985	76	15	10	+61
1987	75	8	17	+67

NOTES: The question on "NATO essential" asks "Some people say that NATO is still essential to our country's security. Others say NATO is no longer essential to our country's security. Which view is closer to your own?" The 1967 wording was slightly different; it says "Some people say that the Soviet Union does not pose a serious military threat and that there is therefore not much need for NATO . . . others say that NATO is still essential". In 1973, the question asked if NATO was "still important" rather than "still essential".

In the Netherlands, the "NATO necessary" question asks: "Some people think NATO is necessary for peace in Europe. Others do not think so. What do you think: is NATO necessary or not?" The "remain/withdraw" question asks: "The Netherlands is a member of NATO. What's your opinion: Should our country remain a member in NATO or withdraw?"

"Net support" is calculated by subtracting opposition to NATO from support for NATO.

hardline tone of American policy. I shall return to this relationship between judgments of the United States and views of the Alliance, but here it is useful to point out that, at least in the 1980s, the erosion of the Dutch belief that "NATO is necessary for peace" was not accompanied by a decline in support for remaining in NATO (the second Dutch question in Table 5.1). Quite the opposite: between 1980 and 1985, support for NATO membership remained very stable. Although the Dutch were apparently sensitive to the effect of NATO policies on "peace in Europe", they none the less continued to support membership of the Alliance itself.

Moreover, these readings occurred despite the apparent growth of Europeanist sentiment in the security field. In the early 1980s, there was, in fact, a noticeable increase in the percentage of Europeans who felt that security policy decisions should be taken by the "European Community acting together . . . [rather than] by each country separately". In 1978 the "Europeanists" in responses to this question averaged about 50 per cent, with little variation among the countries studied here. By 1984, the percentage had increased to 57 per cent in Britain, 68 per cent in France, 60 per cent in West Germany, and 64 per cent in the Netherlands.[9] Like the strategists and politicians who spoke increasingly of the need for a stronger European pillar in defense, European public opinion seemed attracted to the possibility of expanding the Community to the security field.

Table 5.1 – cont.

SOURCES: Through 1981, "NATO Essential" is from Kenneth Adler and Douglas Wertman, "West European Security Concerns for the 1980s: Is NATO in Trouble?", paper prepared for delivery to the Annual Meeting of the American Association of Public Opinion Research, Buck Hill Falls, Pa, May 1981. For later years, the responses are from the following reports of the Office of Research, United States Information Agency: *July 1982 NATO Summit Follow-up*, (Washington, D.C.: Machine-Readable Branch, National Archives and Record Service, Study numbers I8229, I8230 and I8235); *NATO and Burden-Sharing* (Office of Research, Report n–9/11/84–c); *Differences in Some Foreign Policy Views Between Supporters of the Major West German Parties* (Office of Research, Report N–11/7/83). Data for 1987 were provided by USIA.

For the Netherlands, the "NATO is necessary question" is from Hendrik J. C. Rebel, "Public Attitudes in the Netherlands toward NATO, Peace and Security Affairs", (The Hague: Ministry van Defensie, n.d.). The question on remaining in NATO is from Netherlands Institute for Public Opinion (NIPO), Reports 1648, A–407/42, 2023, and 2112. Figures after 1982 were furnished by Professor Philip Everts of the University of Leiden (surveys by NIPO).

Yet this may be one of those cases where a "good thing" that is mentioned hypothetically in a survey question should be treated with caution. In fact, European public opinion has long been favorable to the general idea of European integration (including defense integration), but policy coordination and institutionalization have obviously not always resulted.[10] I have already mentioned some of the complications in the security field: the problem of a European nuclear deterrent; competing national interests *within* Europe; and the delicate issue of how to include a non-nuclear West Germany in any European defense community. These problems have together resulted in continuing dependence on the Atlantic connection and the American nuclear deterrent. Although NATO has had its share of problems, as in DePorte's analysis, it has also been the most feasible of the alternatives. The attachment may be *faute de mieux*, but it has held none the less.

The continuing appeal of the NATO option is clearly revealed when surveys offer alternatives to NATO (Table 5.2). These surveys require close study. The response options have varied over the years, but the surveys always offer Europeans the choice of an "independent European command" or a "European command allied to the United States" versus the status quo option of the NATO Alliance "as it now stands". Except for the French, among whom opinions are extremely fragmented, a clear plurality of Europeans generally choose the status quo of "NATO as it now stands". Perhaps not surprisingly, it is the West Germans – whose options are most limited – who show the strongest attachment to NATO. For a non-nuclear West Germany, it appears, there is no alternative to the Atlantic connection.

The first 1987 survey in Table 5.2 is puzzling in some respects. On the one hand, the percentages who choose NATO are consistent with past figures on this option. On the other hand, both the "independent" national defense option and the "independent European" option are much higher in the 1987 survey. Have these sentiments truly grown, perhaps in response to recent discussion of European collaboration (or frustration at having to collaborate at all)?

A close examination of the survey suggests not. In the first place, the wording of the question is different. It uses the phrase "West European countries" rather than the phrase "our country" that was used in the earlier surveys. This presumption of unity to European actions no doubt colors the responses. As suggested above, there *is* warm sentiment in Europe for furthering unity in the Community. Secondly, the percentages in the 1987 survey are actually in line with

Table 5.2   The Alternatives to NATO

	April 1979 (%)	March 1980 (%)	April 1980 (%)	Oct. 1980 (%)	Dec. 1982 (%)	Jan. 1987 (%)	Nov. 1987 (%)
FRANCE							
1. NATO as it now stands	21	10	12	10	–	26	20
2. European command allied to USA	–	26	28	16	–	–	43
3. Independent European command	24	18	14	9	–	35	10
4. Independent national defense effort	24	17	16	24	–	20	9
5. Accommodate Soviets	–	6	6	7	–	–	–
6. Don't know	22	23	25	35	–	20	18
BRITAIN							
1. NATO as it now stands	57	44	46	43	42	41	46
2. European command allied to USA	–	17	22	24	20	–	28
3. Independent European command	8	9	8	5	10	23	7
4. Independent national defense effort	16	13	11	13	11	26	10
5. Accommodate Soviets	–	4	3	5	5	–	–
6. Don't know	16	13	10	11	12	10	9
WEST GERMANY							
1. NATO as it now stands	55	50	47	57	60	54	45
2. European command allied to USA	–	27	19	18	22	–	28
3. Independent European command	11	5	9	3	8	19	6
4. Independent							

national defense effort	8	3	4	10	2	25	11
5. Accommodate Soviets	–	2	4	2	4	–	–
6. Don't know	17	14	17	11	4	2	10

NETHERLANDS

1. NATO as it now stands	61	–	37	49	–	–	–
2. European command allied to USA	–	–	30	17	–	–	–
3. Independent European command	5	–	7	7	–	–	–
4. Independent national defense effort	15	–	4	10	–	–	–
5. Accommodate Soviets	–	–	10	11	–	–	–
6. Don't know	11	–	13	7	–	–	–

NOTE: Except for January 1987, the question reads: "Which one of the courses listed on this card seems to you the best way to provide for the security of our country?" The full response categories are as follows:

1. Continue in the NATO Alliance among the countries of Western Europe and the United States and Canada;
2. Establish within NATO a unified West European Defense Force under European command, but allied to the United States;
3. Establish an independent West European Defense Force under European command, but not allied to the United States;
4. Rely on our own nation's defense forces without belonging to any military alliance; in 1979 the response is "Do not participate in any alliance – take a completely neutral position". In 1980 the "independent defense" responses are combined with a second response, "Withdraw our military forces from NATO but otherwise remain in NATO for things such as policy consultation";
5. Reduce our emphasis on military defense and rely on greater accommodation of the Soviet Union.

In 1979, a sixth response (European non-military alliance) was offered, but it attracted very small percentage responses.

In January 1987, the question read: "Most Western European countries are linked to the USA for their defense in NATO. Do you think the Western European countries should maintain their military links with the US through NATO, create a common European defense independent of the US and NATO, or should each European country be fully responsible for its own defense?"

the total for the two options in the earlier surveys that mention "Europe". Finally, it is useful to note that the first 1987 survey offered only three response options, whereas the earlier surveys offered as many as six. The latest survey therefore "forces" respondents to choose in a way that the earlier surveys do not. Especially in light of the stability of the "NATO" choice across this variety of survey wordings, the data in Table 5.2 suggest that the choice of NATO from among the hypothetical alternatives has remained clear in the minds of respondents. What is more, compared to the very early years of NATO, public support for the Alliance has actually grown. During the 1950s, when the future of the European system was not yet clear, only 20 to 30 per cent of Europeans chose NATO over other alternatives.[11]

Admittedly, the surveys in Table 5.2 are complicated (perhaps favoring the most familiar responses), and some of the options are purely hypothetical. None the less, the same attachment to NATO is found in other surveys as well, including some that put opinions to a severe test. For example, since 1966 the West Germany Ministry of Defense has posed a question which begins by conceding that the Alliance is "often debated" and asks further if West Germany should remain in the Alliance as it currently exists or if it should strive for a "looser" association. The percentage of West Germans choosing the status quo in this question rarely drops below 70. In 1986, after several years of intense security debates, it stood at 75 per cent.[12] In the Netherlands, where the INF deployment and American foreign policy were criticized very heavily (and generally opposed by about 50 per cent of the public), only 27 per cent in 1982 were willing to leave NATO, "even if the Alliance holds on to nuclear weapons".[13]

Thus, despite several years of near-constant transatlantic controversy and despite the apparent growth of sentiment to pursue alternative security arrangements, European public opinion remains

---

Table 5.2 – cont.

SOURCES: J.-R. Rabier, *et al.*, *Eurobarometer 11: April 1979* (Ann Arbor, Mich.: ICPSR Study 7752, 1981); Office of Research, United States Information Agency, *Multi-Regional Security Survey* (Washington, D.C.: Machine-Readable Branch, National Archives and Record Service) Study nos. I8007, 18010, 18005; Rabier, *Eurobarometer 14: October 1980* (Ann Arbor, Mich.: ICPSR Study 7958, 1983); Social Surveys Ltd, *Gallup Political Index*, no. 259, March 1982; and *The Guardian*, 16 February 1987. Figures for November 1987 provided by USIA.

strongly behind the NATO Alliance as the framework of European security. Moreover, surveys which confront respondents with the status quo of NATO membership versus a number of alternatives produce a distinct preference for NATO. Surveys revealing the hypothetical attractiveness of neutralism or a European option may reflect an abstract affinity, but they do not consider the limits to choice. Although the figures in all countries do not match the West German attachment to the Alliance, certainly they suggest the continuing relevance of DePorte's argument that the reasons for NATO's durability lie in the lack of feasible substitutes.

The alternative explanation is that this commitment is merely symbolic (reflecting political affinities as much as alliance politics), and from the perspective of the United States, it may even be disconcerting. After all, continuing membership in the Alliance does not guarantee agreement on all policy issues. Indeed, one might even argue that membership is the minimum condition of "free riding". It may also be a source of frustration for Americans that Europeans remain attached to NATO in part because a unified European defense effort has remained a distant goal.[14]

To some extent, the response to such criticism depends on one's expectations. For alliance "minimalists" it is sufficient that membership in the Alliance enjoys support, for this commitment provides the troops and equipment that serve the Alliance's central purpose of deterrence and defense. The polls are telling on this point, both because the question of membership is continually posed (frequently under the sponsorship of the American government) and because support for membership reaches levels rarely seen in public opinion surveys on any political issue. Nor can the question be viewed as merely symbolic, for European governments often justify their policies domestically with the argument that NATO commitments must be met. Membership in NATO has been neither self-evident nor cost-free in European eyes, a fact that further underscores the depth of commitment found in these surveys.

Finally, it is well to recall that this commitment underwent a very severe test during the 1980s. As we saw in the preceding chapter, faith in the dominant Alliance partner declined precipitously in 1981 and 1982. The INF issue focused the costs of Alliance membership quite explicitly. Throughout this debate, the issue of "independence versus alliance" lurked in the background, as in British discussions of "the finger on the nuclear trigger" and in German debates about the negative effect of the deployment on *Ostpolitik*. Commitment to membership in NATO may very well be a minimum condition, but that commitment was broadly questioned in the early 1980s. NATO may indeed be favored *faute de mieux*, but the result is that the security pillar of the Atlantic Community has endured the bitter debates of the 1980s with a strong base of support in public opinion.

TIES THAT DIVIDE: ECONOMICS AND WELFARE

The same cannot be said for the public's acceptance of transatlantic economic and political collaboration. Figure 5.1 shows the declining enthusiasm of the British public for economic and foreign policy collaboration. The survey question shown in the figure asked if "Britain should work more closely, less closely, or as at present" with the United States. In the figure, I show a "net approval" score for collaboration with the US, which I calculated by subtracting the percentage who oppose collaboration from the sum of those who approve of collaborating "more closely" and "as at present". The drop in support for transatlantic cooperation is evident in the 1984 poll, and the figures for 1986 show a particularly severe erosion. In 1986, support for cooperation barely exceeds opposition (the latter is not shown in the figure, but it has grown to about 40 per cent). This is in stark contrast to opinions of NATO, where support exceeds opposition by as much as 70 percentage points.

Although historical polls on these subjects are not available in other countries, surveys from the period following the economic shocks in 1979 and 1980 also reveal far less enthusiasm for Atlantic cooperation in economic or foreign policy than was the case for cooperation in the security field. Table 5.3 summarizes responses to two questions on these subjects. These surveys are similar to the "alliance alternative" questions discussed above. They ask respondents to state which framework is best for their country's economic and foreign policy interests: an Atlantic connection; a common European approach; or an independent, national approach. The table shows that Atlantic cooperation in the economic and foreign policy fields is rarely a substantial or even a plurality view. In 1980, when recession had begun to set in and economic issues disturbed Atlantic relations, the highest support for Atlantic economic collaboration was the 22 per cent of West Germans. Clearly, European opinions are more favorable to a European economic approach or an independent national stance.

Atlantic collaboration in foreign policy is even less popular. Except

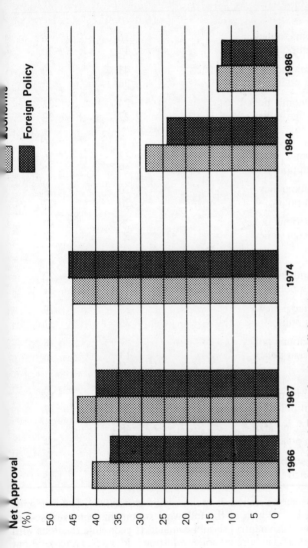

Net Approval
(%)

Foreign Policy

Figure 5.1 British Approval of Transatlantic Collaboration

NOTE: The question reads: "Do you think that Britain should work more closely or less closely with the United States than it is at present on questions of foreign policy [economic policy]." The graphic shows the difference between those who say "more closely . . . [or] as at present" and those who say "less closely".

SOURCE: Ivor Crewe, "Why the British Don't Like Us Anymore", *Public Opinion* 9/6 (March/April 1987) p. 54.

Table 5.3   The Coordination of Economic and Foreign Policy

	April 1980 (%)	Oct. 1980 (%)
FRANCE		
Atlantic economic policy	16	6
Atlantic foreign policy	12	10
An EC economic policy	43	29
An EC foreign policy	36	30
A national economic policy	24	21
A national foreign policy	27	22
BRITAIN		
Atlantic economic policy	33	16
Atlantic foreign policy	20	17
An EC economic policy	20	14
An EC foreign policy	20	17
A national economic policy	38	40
A national foreign policy	35	37
WEST GERMANY		
Atlantic economic policy	33	22
Atlantic foreign policy	25	31
An EC economic policy	35	29
An EC foreign policy	25	31
A national economic policy	17	18
A national foreign policy	13	16
NETHERLANDS		
Atlantic economic policy	25	18
Atlantic foreign policy	25	27
An EC economic policy	48	33
An EC foreign policy	33	34
A national economic policy	17	17
A national foreign policy	22	18

NOTES: The Table shows responses to *two separate questions*. The economic policy question asks: "Which of the following statements comes closest to your views of how [our country] should conduct its economic relations with the rest of the world?" The foreign policy question is identical and asks about "the conduct of [our] foreign policy".

Not all response categories are shown. The foreign policy question includes the option of a "pan-European" foreign policy involving Western Europe, Eastern Europe, and the Soviet Union. In October 1980 the question includes the option of a "trilateral" economic policy.

in West Germany, the strongest sentiment in 1980 was divided between a preference for an EC approach or an independent, national foreign policy. In a 1982 poll (not shown in Table 5.3), respondents were asked what was best for their nation's interests: to coordinate foreign policy with the United States or to conduct foreign policy without giving special consideration to American interests. Majorities in Britain and France chose the "independent" response. It was only in West Germany that a majority favored cooperation with the United States.[15]

In summary, the polls show clearly that European opinion is far less enamored of the Atlantic connection when the question moves beyond the security pillar of NATO. Indeed, on some questions involving economic policy, the polls reveal outright suspicion and mistrust of American intentions. Finally, together with the polls on the wisdom of American policy presented in Chapter 4, these polls on foreign policy coordination confirm that Europeans are skeptical, to say the least, of tying their broader foreign policies to those of the United States.

Does this signal a crumbling of the economic and political pillars of the Alliance? Such a conclusion seems premature. One reason is that these currents are not new. Distance – and even ideological conflict – have been present in the economic and political relations of the Western Alliance almost from the beginning. As Grosser's history of the relationship reminds us, the origins of the economic relationship were not altogether smooth. Ideologically, the views of the working-class Left and the "aristocratic" Right were joined in a healthy skepticism of the American style of capitalism. After his visit to Detroit in 1928, for example, Ernest Bevin observed, "A hard cruel city. . . . No culture. . . . No one talks to you except in dollars and mass production."[16] Later years may have seen a contentment with American economics and perhaps even an attraction, but the global economic problems that first emerged in the late 1960s may have resurrected rather than created the European feeling that in economics, American policies were not entirely compatible with European interests and political economic values. Consider Hoffmann's characterization of European reactions to the economic changes of

---

Table 5.3 – cont.

SOURCES: J.-R. Rabier, *et al.*, *Eurobarometer 13: April 1980* and *Eurobarometer 14: October 1980* (Ann Arbor, Mich.: ICPSR Study nos. 7957 and 7958).

the 1980s: "European élites are torn between a technological 'discourse' that stresses the need to climb aboard the train of the new technologies . . . and a cultural tradition that still despises the disenchanted world of profits, production, money, and merchandise, still dreams of art, prowess, the life of the mind for the mind's sake, and criticism of society rather than prosaic adjustment to and marginal reforms of it."[17] The implicit critique of the unfettered style of American capitalism is evident in this view.

Nor does it seem that a skeptical public is the only source of the problem. One could hardly argue that public opinion has forced its critical sentiments on more Atlanticist government officials. From de Gaulle's attack on American monetary policy to Helmut Schmidt's frustration with just about *all* aspects of American economic policy, it is European officials who have led the way in the questioning of American policy. Indeed, when Domke and his colleagues interviewed European officials during the Alliance crisis of the early 1980s, respondents in all European countries were quick to characterize the problem as one of economic policy rather than security policy. A new definition of security was needed that would take *economic* factors into consideration. There was also a need for a "new division of labor" in which the costs of (American) budget and monetary policy would be recognized as a source of European difficulty.[18]

Thus, although it is clear that the economic pillar of the Alliance is under strain, it is not entirely clear that this strain is altogether new, and certainly it is difficult to argue that public opinion has been a driving source of the discontent. Yet the strain is no less important for that, for it may represent an even more difficult problem for the Alliance than issues of security have been. One reason is that economic debates seem to have transcended the mere assertion of national interests. As in the 1940s and early 1950s, once again the transatlantic debate is focused on the competing values that underlie economic and budgetary policy. For many Americans, European economic problems result not from American interest rates or budget deficits but from the mistaken policies of welfare states that have clogged the arteries of economic growth with taxes, spending, and regulation. Americans are calling on Europeans not simply to harmonize global economic policies, but to reform domestic policies of primary political and economic importance.

To Europeans, these criticisms seem both dangerous and insincere. The danger arises from the fact that the European welfare states represent far more than short-term bargains with interest groups or others whose electoral support is required. Rather, it serves to support the (historically unique) social consensus of the post-war period, a consensus that could be threatened by an all-out attack on systems of social protection. Moreover, Europeans are capable of a cultural critique of their own, as in the observation (most often made in private) that American policies may have produced economic growth, but they have also left entire communities in which it is unsafe to walk. Finally, European doubts as to the sincerity of American criticisms can be read from the polls as well. In 1979 – *before* the recession and economic disagreements of the 1980s – an average of 50 per cent of Europeans thought that the United States seeks "unfair advantage" or "domination" in its economic dealings with Europe. A similar majority believed that the United States gave "little or no consideration" to European views on issues of economic well-being.[19]

For the NATO Alliance, perhaps the most inauspicious aspect of this economic debate is the prospect that it will become linked to the security pillar that has so far managed to survive repeated controversies. For Europeans, American security policy is itself an economic problem, for aside from questioning the American military build-up on security grounds, defense spending is seen as the source of the budget deficits that have complicated European economic policy. Further, on some issues, security and economic issues may be linked in particularly divisive ways. For example, an official of the European Community observed in 1985 that the American SDI is troublesome on economic as well as security grounds: the ultimate cost of SDI, he argued, could ultimately equal the total current debt of the Third World; it will aggravate the American budget deficit; and it will soak up the investment needed if the transition to a post-industrial economy is to be made.[20]

The American response is direct. The defense budget, after all, is devoted in great part to European security, so that critiques of the deficit seem inopportune at best. Moreover, the American commitment is necessary in part because Europeans themselves have been unwilling or unable to provide for their own defense. Finally, the American commitment to Europe is seen by some as a subsidy to the European welfare states that are already treated with derision on ideological and economic grounds. For example, in a speech that was otherwise animated by a strong endorsement of the Alliance, David Aaron none the less noted that domestic political currents in the

United States might bring a linkage of the NATO and welfare issues: "At a time when the average German worker gets seven and a half weeks vacation a year, and the average American only two and a half, increasing the economic burden on American workers to keep NATO sacrosanct won't wash. The NATO commitment has become a hidden entitlement program that in the Graham–Ruddman era will not escape the most careful scrutiny."[21]

In summary, although economic and political differences have always characterized the transatlantic relationship, they appear to have grown more fundamental. These differences now threaten to spill into the security area. Paradoxically, although recent commentary on the "crisis in NATO" focused on security issues, public opinion surveys suggest that it is on issues of public political economy that the two sides of the Atlantic now diverge most widely. The most visible debates have been about deterrence and nuclear weapons, but perhaps the most threatening development for the future of the Alliance is the possibility that security issues will become linked to a transatlantic debate about the proper relationship of citizen and state. NATO has survived its crisis on the INF issue. The question for the future seems to be whether it will survive a shouting match about the proper path to economic growth and social justice.

ALLIANCE POLITICS AND DOMESTIC POLITICS: WHO ARE THE ATLANTICISTS?

The surveys presented in this and earlier chapters would suggest that the primary line of domestic polarization in matters of alliance coordination will be the partisan leanings of the respondents. Overall, public opinion is far more critical on questions of the economic and political utility of the transatlantic alliance than on the security "pillar" that underlies defense collaboration. As we noted above, even in the formative years of the transatlantic relationship, ideological debates over the nature of economic policy and the utility of economic collaboration were heard. The historical antipathy of the European Left *and* Right to the materialist and individualist emphasis of American capitalism were one source of this division, as was the fear (especially on the Left) that the Atlantic connection could tie Europeans to a "conservative combine" that would include not just Americans, but also serve the interests of conservative interests in Europe. The unprecedented economic growth of the 1950s and 1960s may have muted these differences, but the 1970s and 1980s brought economic problems and divisions to the fore once again, and this time there has been a direct opposition of the American style of economic reform and a European critique that questions the motives, interests, and values that underlie American reform. Finally, all of this is overlayed by economic and budgetary debates *within* European societies. These debates have repolarized partisan conflicts that were once assumed to have gone the way of the "end of ideology", and they reinforce (in some cases they are directly tied to) the transatlantic debate.

Even in the security realm, partisan approaches are not without their relevance. We have seen in previous chapters that the public's views of security issues are conditioned by their party associations. I have attributed this correspondence to the "cue giving" function of political parties as well as to the historical tradition of ideological conflict about the utility of military force as an instrument of national policy. On such issues as the military balance and its implications, the views of Left and Right are distinct, a cleavage that could influence issues of military alliance as well. In addition, the Alliance issue raises the question of collaboration with the United States, and here the economic arguments of the last decade have surely worked an effect.

However convincing these hypotheses, students of international relations might question them, for when the debate turns to alliance politics, both national tradition and external factors could override domestic divisions. The most obvious example is France, where the Gaullist principle of independence remains a near-religion for all French parties. A less exaggerated version of the same attitude may color the opinions of the British, who also possess a national deterrent and for whom global interests remain important.

In the Netherlands and West Germany, external constraint may very well accomplish a similar "levelling" of domestic cleavage on Alliance issues. For the Dutch, there is certainly a tradition of partisan conflict on security issues, but the commitment to NATO is derived from a careful reading of national interests. Thus, although NATO itself has been overtly contested in the Netherlands (especially in the Labour Party), the Alliance commitment has won out, for the options available to the Netherlands outside of NATO are quite limited. The Dutch are also concerned about two additional factors: maintaining influence within the Western community and in East–West relations; and insuring that there is a stable environment for the continued integration of West Germany in the Western community. For West Germany, these concerns are themselves one reason to repeat the pledge of allegiance to NATO. This consideration is further reinforced by Germany's nonnuclear status and dependence on the United States for its security. It is precisely when security issues are most contested that the critics (especially in the SPD) are most vocal in protesting their loyalty to NATO.

To summarize, on the question of NATO and alternatives to the Alliance, the existence of ideological conflict – present historically and exacerbated by recent transatlantic disputes in political economy – may be overridden. Yet a final theoretical perspective is also relevant. The young members of the successor generation, although obviously affected by the economic and ideological debates of the recent past, may be less influenced by national traditions and external constraints. For young West Germans, perhaps the burdens of the past and dependence on the United States are less convincing.[22] The same might be said for the successor generation in other countries, although the direction of generational change is not self-evident. For example, although the French successor generation may be less convinced of Gaullist orthodoxy, is it more likely that they would develop a more "Atlanticist" policy (in fact following the drift of recent French policy), or would they be more attuned to a European or neutralist alternative in defense?

NATIONAL TRADITION AND DOMESTIC CLEAVAGE

An overview of these competing influences on European opinion is set out in Table 5.4, which displays a combined generational and partisan breakdown of the "NATO is essential" question discussed earlier (the "difference" column summarizes the gap between respondents with higher and lower education). These generational views of NATO mirror the overall profile of national traditions. British, West German, and Dutch respondents of all age and educational levels match the high level of the overall population's support for NATO, while French respondents reveal their well-known detachment (although it is hardly overwhelming in this question). As concerns the young educated, the French and Dutch successor generations are noticeably less enthusiastic about NATO than are their cohorts with lesser educational attainments. In Britain and West Germany there are no generational differences to speak of, at least at the level of the overall population.

Table 5.4 *Percentage Responding "NATO is Essential", by Age,*
Education, and Political Party Affiliation (October 1980)

	Under 35 Education			Over 35 Education		
	Lower (%)	Higher (%)	Difference (%)	Lower (%)	Higher (%)	Difference (%)
FRANCE						
Total population	**56**	**44**	**−12**	**60**	**55**	**− 5**
Ecologistes	41	31	−10	55	*	*
PCF	54	26	−28	19	*	*
Socialist	65	28	−37	63	55	− 8
UDF (Giscard)	92	66	−26	68	45	−23
Gaullist (RPR)	35	93	+58	62	70	+ 8
n =	78	98		220	47	
BRITAIN						
Total population	**84**	**84**	**0**	**86**	**87**	**+ 1**
Labour	77	77	0	76	87	+11
Liberal	83	91	+ 8	87	88	+ 1
Conservative	94	94	0	97	100	+ 3
n =	200	61		360	28	
WEST GERMANY						
Total population	**94**	**89**	**− 5**	**92**	**90**	**− 2**
Greens	50	86	+36	56	40	−16
Social Democrats	95	94	− 1	94	96	+ 2
Free Democrats	100	94	− 6	96	94	− 2
CDU/CSU	93	90	− 3	92	94	+ 1
n =	233	63		394	115	
NETHERLANDS						
Total population	**68**	**56**	**−12**	**77**	**84**	**+ 7**
PvdA (Labour)	70	48	−22	60	68	+ 8
D '66	64	49	−15	65	77	+12
CDA	78	66	−12	89	92	+ 3
VVD	76	86	+10	98	91	− 7
n =	126	112		254	98	

NOTES: Unless otherwise noted, in this and following tables, higher education is defined as age nineteen or older on completion of full-time education. Political party affiliation is intended vote "if an election were held tomorrow". Figures for total population include affiliates of parties not listed separately.

The breakdown by party affiliation reveals four different profiles.[23] In West Germany there are near-identical levels of support for NATO among all major parties and generations; all parties but the Greens are above the 90 per cent level. Astonishly, even young, educated followers of the Green party think "NATO is essential". In Britain similarly high levels of support for NATO exist among followers of all parties, but the parties do differ in emphasis. Within all generations, Tory followers are more enamored of NATO than are Labour or Liberal followers.

Dutch and French respondents are doubly divided: by generation and by party affiliation. In the Netherlands, every generational grouping is polarized according to partisan views. Among the older Dutch, this cleavage occurs at very high levels of support for NATO. Among the young, however, the division is more close, and among the young educated it is very deep indeed. While 70 to 80 per cent of young, educated members of the Center-Right parties (CDA and VVD) are supportive of NATO, the figure drops to less than fifty per cent among young, educated identifiers of the Center-Left (PvdA and D'66). The Netherlands therefore typifies the "glacier-type" coexistence of generational change and traditional polarization: it has a classic "successor generation" – concentrated in the Center-Left – who are most skeptical of established policy, but the remaining sectors of society are also polarized along traditional partisan lines.

The French, as always, are different – and very complicated.[24] Not surprisingly, members of the Ecologist and Communist parties (especially young, educated members) are very skeptical of NATO. Socialists and UDF members display the more Atlanticist orientation that characterizes French policy of the early 1980s, but the successor generation within these parties is much less so (but note that older, educated Socialists and UDF members are also less "Atlanticist" than their cohorts). Ironically, at least in this question, only Gaullists show much affinity for NATO. Thus, in its particular way, France resembles the Netherlands: there is a successor generation, concentrated in the Center-Left, that is proportionately most skeptical of NATO, but other sectors of society are also divided by the differing alliance affinities of political parties.

Table 5.4 – cont.

The difference column subtracts the views of those with lower education from those with higher education.

SOURCE: Rabier *et al.*, *Eurobarometer 14: October 1980*.

Taken together, the responses to this "NATO is essential" question suggest the relevance of national alliance traditions as well as political polarization *within* those traditions. Clearly, the French overall are the least enthusiastic about NATO, while the West Germans, British, and Dutch show strong support. But there are competing sentiments within these national orientations, especially in the Netherlands and France. In both of these countries, the successor generation of young, educated partisans of the Center and Left are decidedly less supportive of NATO. And in Britain, the parties do differ in levels of support for NATO, albeit at much higher levels than in France and Holland.

What would the skeptics prefer? In part, the answer to this question depends on how respondents interpret the "NATO is essential" question. Obviously, they may simply read it for what it asks: the utility of the Alliance in the pursuit of national security. Yet this is a very abstract question, for it raises the additional query: essential compared to what?

Answers to this latter question, broken down by generation and level of education, are shown in Table 5.5. To construct this table, I averaged the responses to questions on NATO and alternatives to NATO that were shown earlier in Table 5.2.[25] There are some clear patterns in this comparison. Certainly national tradition is even more strongly evident when respondents can compare NATO to alternative frameworks. For example, about forty per cent of the French were willing to say that "NATO is essential", but here no more than one quarter of *any* French population group favor NATO. Support for NATO is also less in other countries when compared to other alternatives, but it remains high (always a majority or more), none the less.

The most striking pattern is the impact of higher education: the more highly educated differ from their cohorts in all countries, but the pattern of cleavage varies according to country and generation. First, the educated respondents of both generations are less "isolationist". They are less likely to choose the "national" option of no alliance (this is most easily read from the "difference" column, which shows the difference between those with higher and lower education). However, the consequent preferences of the educated "élites" differ between generations. Notice that in all countries the older, educated generation translates its disdain for independence into greater support for NATO. In other words, the older educated differ from their age cohorts most noticeably in their greater propensity to choose "NATO as it now stands".

Table 5.5   Average of Responses to Alliance Questions by Age Group and
Level of Education (1979–80)

	Under 35 Education			Over 35 Education		
	Lower (%)	Higher (%)	Difference (%)	Lower (%)	Higher (%)	Difference (%)
FRANCE						
National defense	33	25	− 8	31	18	−13
European alliance	40	46	+ 6	48	52	+ 4
Accommodate Soviets	11	15	+ 4	8	9	+ 1
NATO as it now stands	19	19	0	17	24	+ 7
BRITAIN						
National defense	18	10	− 8	15	10	− 5
European alliance	24	29	+ 5	25	25	0
Accommodate Soviets	6	10	+ 4	4	5	+ 1
NATO as it now stands	54	53	− 1	56	60	+ 4
WEST GERMANY						
National defense	9	8	− 1	8	6	− 2
European alliance	27	31	+ 4	29	23	− 6
Accommodate Soviets	2	8	+ 6	2	5	+ 3
NATO as it now stands	63	55	− 8	62	68	+ 6
NETHERLANDS						
National defense	15	17	+ 2	12	5	− 7
European alliance	18	22	+ 4	20	19	− 1
Accommodate Soviets	5	10	+ 6	4	5	+ 1
NATO as it now stands	62	50	−12	63	71	+ 8

NOTES: The table shows the average for each response category from surveys in April
1979, March 1980, and October 1980. Full responses to the surveys are displayed in
Table 5.2. The two response categories involving a "European command" (numbers 2
and 3 in Table 5.2) have been combined in this table. In October 1980 the "Gaullist"
option has been combined with the "national defense" option. Since the March 1980
survey is not available for the Netherlands, the averages are for two surveys only.

The difference column subtracts the views of those with lower education from those
with higher education.

SOURCE: Rabier, et al., Eurobarometer 11: April 1979 and Eurobarometer 14: October
1980; and Office of Research, United States Information Agency, Multi-regional
Security Survey.

Among the younger educated, there are two patterns. In France
and Britain the lesser "isolationism" of the younger successor generation translates into marginally higher support for a European alliance or for "accommodating the Soviets", but these differences are
quite small. Nor does the level of education noticeably divide the
young in their preference for NATO. In the Netherlands and West
Germany, however, the crucial cleavage is indeed in the rejection of
"NATO as it now stands" among the young educated and the

resulting difference this produces in their preference for "accommodating the Soviets". In the latter two countries, the successor generation is markedly less enamored of NATO and markedly more sensitive to the détente orientation suggested by the "accommodate" option.

To summarize, what these patterns suggest is that the older, educated élite in all countries, when faced with the choice, are less enthusiastic about an independent approach and more attracted to the Atlantic connection in security. Although the young educated are also less isolationist, in no country does the successor generation show this greater affinity for NATO. Indeed, reading across the table, a notable cleavage is the distance between the young and older educated "élites" in their support for NATO – visible in all countries but especially clear in West Germany and Holland. NATO, it appears, does have a problem with the successor generation, especially when one considers that it is the active and articulate "élites" that are most negative in their views.

There is an important caveat to this conclusion, however. In the first place, these cleavages should not distract attention from the glass half-full. There remains a consensus for NATO "as it now stands" in all countries and generations (excepting once again the French). Moreover, a close examination of the options listed in Table 5.5 reveals a choice that is somewhat false: is it fair or realistic to suggest that security must be secured *either* through NATO or through the "détente" approach of accommodating the Soviets?

The obvious objection is that the NATO Alliance does not define its choices in this manner. Since 1967 NATO has based its policy on the Harmel formula of complementarity of military strength and détente with the East. Paradoxically, then, the affinity of the Dutch and West German successor generations for "accommodating the Soviets" can be read as support for official Alliance doctrine. In any case, these considerations make clear that the "NATO and alternatives" question is not merely tapping respondents' views of the proper alliance framework. It seems also to sensitize respondents to the broader question of what mix of policies the Alliance should pursue. Nor does it seem surprising that the young educated would be most sensitive to "accommodating" the Soviets. This "détente generation" grew to maturity at a time when this policy dominated the agenda, especially in the Netherlands and West Germany.

Based on the party breakdowns to the "NATO essential" question, these generational differences are presumably concentrated in young members of parties of the Center-Left. Table 5.6 shows that this is indeed the case, at least in the Netherlands and West Germany. Table 5.6 is different from those presented elsewhere in this book. It shows generational differences by party affiliation – but only for those response categories to the question on "NATO and the alternatives" that most divide the generations. I list the Netherlands and West Germany first in this table because the combined impact of generation and partisan affiliation is most clear in these countries. The Dutch successor generation is doubly divided. Young, educated members of the Left (PvdA) and Center (D'66) are much less attached to the NATO option and far more attracted to the "détente" option of "accommodating the Soviets" (once again, these differences are most clearly seen in the "difference" column, which subtracts the views of the lesser educated from the those of the higher educated of each party). This pattern does not characterize older Dutch respondents, but they *are* clearly polarized in their warmth for NATO along the Left–Right spectrum of parties. In the Netherlands NATO is contentious in a number of ways.

In West Germany, attachment to NATO is fairly uniform, but the successor generation of Social Democrats and Free Democrats stands out (if in a minority) as the group most sensitive to the "accommodate" option. In France there is also a successor generation phenomenon, but it does not involve the "accommodate" option (which few French of any party or generation select), but the NATO versus European options. The French successor generation of the Center-Left is less supportive of NATO and more attracted to the European option. Not surprisingly, many Gaullists choose the "no alliance" option (not shown in the table), but among young, educated Gaullists, the table shows a preference for NATO rather than the European option. The younger French "élite", then, appeared to be moving in different directions. For the Center-Left the European option was preferred, but for the Right (Gaullists) the Atlantic connection appeared more important.[26]

We show only the "NATO" responses in Britain, for the British are in fact fairly uniform in their responses among categories. As was the case with the "NATO essential" question, here there is no evidence of generational conflict. The primary line of division is within generations, from stronger support for NATO among Tories to lesser support among Labour supporters.[27]

Britain is therefore unique among the countries presented here, for they show none of the questioning of NATO that characterizes the

Table 5.6 *Alternatives to NATO: Selected Responses by Age, Level of Education, and Party Affiliation (October 1980)*

	Under 35 Education			Over 35 Education		
	Lower	Higher	Difference	Lower	Higher	Difference
WEST GERMANY						
Prefer "NATO as it now stands"						
Social Democrats	62	63	+ 1	69	71	+ 2
Free Democrats	68	50	−18	62	71	+ 9
CDU/CSU	63	85	+22	62	70	+12
Prefer "Accommodate Soviets"						
Social Democrats	0	11	+11	1	2	+ 1
Free Democrats	0	13	+13	0	0	0
CDU/CSU	1	0	− 1	1	0	− 1
NETHERLANDS						
Prefer "NATO as it now stands"						
PvdA (Labour)	58	23	−35	40	60	+20
D'66	46	40	− 6	51	66	+15
Christian Democrats	63	58	− 5	69	60	− 9
Liberals (VVD)	65	70	+ 5	70	72	+ 2
Prefer "Accommodate Soviets"						
PvdA (Labour)	9	32	+23	14	15	+ 1
D'66	6	14	+ 8	2	12	+10
Christian Democrats	2	6	+ 4	5	6	+ 1
Liberals (VVD)	0	4	+ 4	2	0	− 2
FRANCE						
Prefer "A European Command"						
PCF	16	26	+10	19	*	*
Socialists	38	52	+14	44	57	+13
UDF	22	41	+19	48	*	*
Gaullists	43	27	−16	27	*	*
BRITAIN						
Prefer "NATO as it now stands"						
Labour	36	39	+ 3	42	88	+46
Liberal	43	42	− 1	56	55	− 1
Conservative	54	68	+14	55	42	−13

NOTES: The table shows the response categories for which there is the most noticeable difference among parties and generations. The complete responses to this survey are presented in Table 5.2.

The difference column subtracts the views of those with lower education from those with higher education.

SOURCE: Rabier *et al.*, *Eurobarometer 14: October 1980.*

successor generations of other countries. In France, West Germany, and the Netherlands, the successor generation is skeptical of NATO, and in the latter two countries they react more positively than others when the "accommodate Soviets" option is offered. However, in Britain and the Netherlands the traditional doubts of the older Left about NATO also show through, for they are less attracted to the NATO option than are parties of the Right. Whether these divisions signal a portent of weakness for the Alliance is discussed in the final section of this chapter. However, it remains to ask if these questions on NATO are not really a measure of trust in the United States.

THE NATO ALLIANCE AND THE UNITED STATES

To this point, I have shown that European views of the NATO Alliance reflect a mixture of national tradition and domestic cleavage. Across countries, the views of national sub-groups reproduce each country's traditional security alignment: detached in the case of France; and a solid Atlanticist commitment in West Germany, Britain, the Netherlands. *Within* these traditions, there is none the less evidence of conflict. In all countries but Britain the successor generation is less enamored of NATO, and in many countries the Left and the Right of all generations are divided in their support for NATO. Yet the glass is also half-full, for except in France, almost all sub-groups of the population still support NATO by a majority.

These surveys from the early 1980s raise two additional questions. This was a time of intense and often bitter debate on a number of issues facing NATO. Is it not possible that the degree of polarization in public opinion has eased as the international climate has become less contentious? Secondly, the trend surveys on NATO showed a downturn in 1981 and 1982 before improving in later years. This negative "blip" in support for NATO parallels the dramatic negative turn in the general image of the United States that was documented in Chapter 4. This raises the second question: is the domestic polarization revealed in the NATO surveys of the early 1980s merely a reflection of disenchantment with the United States? Put another way, do the domestic divisions revealed in these surveys merely reproduce general differences in trust in the United States or confidence in its policies?

Let us examine the second question first, for if views of NATO are indeed a reflection of trust in the United States, then predictions about improvement in the degree of domestic polarization can be inferred from views of the United States. I have already noted that overall population trends in support for NATO are similar to the trend in overall images of the United States. Here the question is whether domestic divisions in views of the United States affect assessments of NATO and the tendency to choose alternative security frameworks when the choice is offered in survey questions. I analyzed this question statistically, as shown in Table 5.7. The table shows the results of multiple regression analysis performed on the 1979 and 1980 questions on "NATO and the alternatives", where the response choices ranged from national independence or accomodating the Soviets to "NATO as it now stands". The variables listed at the top of the table were presented in percentage form earlier in this chapter: ideology (here measured using the familiar Left–Right self-placement scale); successor generation (here using a unique "dummy" variable to single out the impact of the young educated); and "views of the USA", as measured in *Eurobarometer* questions on the general image of the United States.[28]

The results of this analysis strongly confirm the importance of the American image to assessments of the NATO Alliance. In every country the American image is strongly (and significantly) correlated with views of NATO and alternatives to NATO.[29] In addition, the ideology of respondents on the Left–Right scale is also strongly correlated with views of NATO. Consistently, those on the political Right are more "Atlanticist" than are those on the Left.[30] Finally, in West Germany and the Netherlands the "successor generation" does have a significant negative influence; even after (statistically) controlling for respondents' ideology and views of the United States, young, educated West Germans and Dutch are more skeptical of NATO.

There is therefore strong evidence – both from historical trends in the American image and in these statistical analyses from 1979 and 1980 – that assessments of NATO in survey questions are a "stalking horse" for more general judgments of the United States, judgments which are in turn influenced by ideological differences. The impact of the views of the Dutch and West German successor generations, seen earlier in the survey percentages, is also confirmed in this statistical analysis. This returns us to the first question posed at the outset of this section: has the improvement in the international climate since the early 1980s resulted in a lessening of domestic polarization in opinions of the NATO Alliance?

Table 5.7   Regression Analysis of Support for NATO

	Ideology	Variable Image of USA	Successor generation	R^2
FRANCE				
1979	.19*	−.19*	.03	.09
1980	.11*	−.19*	.02	.06
GREAT BRITAIN				
1979	.17*	−.15*	−.02	.06
1980	.15*	−.13*	.02	.04
WEST GERMANY				
1979	.07	−.28*	−.05	.09
1980	.13*	−.16*	−.07*	.06
NETHERLANDS				
1979	.25*	−.25*	−.11*	.17
1980	.22*	−.26*	−.13*	.17

NOTES: The table shows standardized regression coefficients (beta weights) from a multiple regression of ideology, image of the United States, and a "successor generation" variable on the "NATO and alternatives" questions displayed earlier in Table 5.2. Coefficients marked with a "*" are twice as large as their standard errors.

Ideology is measured on a left-right scale; a positive sign indicates that those toward the right of the ideological spectrum are more supportive of NATO. The US image is measured from good to poor; a negative sign indicates that those who hold a poor image of the United States are generally less supportive of NATO. A negative sign for "successor generation" indicates that the young, university educated are generally less supportive of NATO. See note 28 for additional information about these variables.

SOURCE: Rabier *et al.*, *Eurobarometer 11* and *Eurobarometer 14*.

It is difficult to answer this question with any finality, for the detailed breakdowns required to analyze it are not possible: the "NATO and alternatives" question is not included in any recent survey available from archives. However, an indirect judgment is possible by reversing the direction of inference: if views of NATO do indeed reflect judgments of the United States, then we would deduce that polarization on the NATO question was less *in the past*, before the bitter squabbles of the early 1980s that produced the downward drift of confidence in the United States. Figure 5.2 provides some

Gap Between German Parties on "NATO Is Essential"
CDU/CSU minus SPD (%)

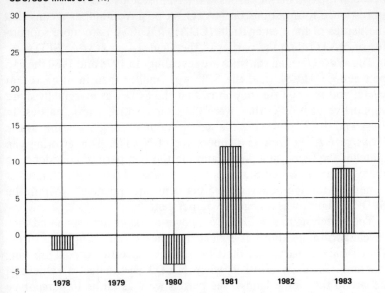

Gap Between Dutch Parties on "Remain in NATO"
CDA minus PvdA (%)

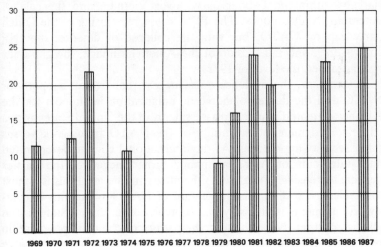

Figure 5.2   Party Views of the NATO Alliance

SOURCE: See Table 5.1.

evidence that this is indeed the case. The figure shows the gap between the two major parties in the Netherlands and West Germany in response to questions on NATO. A positive number means that the parties of the Center-Right (CDA; CDU/CSU) are more support-ive of NATO than the parties of the Center-Left (PvdA; SPD).

The West German statistics are revealing. In 1978 and 1980 the gap between CDU/CSU and the SPD was smaller than in more recent years, and in any case they show that the SPD was marginally more supportive of NATO than were the Conservative Union parties. In 1981 and 1983, however, the gap grew much larger, as the SPD's views of NATO grew less supportive of NATO. This growing gap matches the increasing polarization in the two parties' confidence in the wisdom of United States policy. In 1983 CDU/CSU estimates of American foreign policy were 5 per cent "net positive". Within the SPD the figure was a negative 52 per cent.[31]

The Dutch figures in Figure 5.2 cover a longer time span and they reveal two things. First, it is clear that the differing emphases of the Dutch Labour party and the Christian Democratic Appeal are long standing. As early as 1969 (when NATO was in fact a subject of debate in the Netherlands), the parties were as far as 10 percentage points apart in their attachment to NATO, and the gap grew to over twenty percentage points during the early 1970s and the debate (largely within the Labour party) over Vietnam and the role of détente in NATO policy. The 1970s saw some closing of the Dutch party gap on NATO, but with the collapse of détente, the INF controversy, and the erosion of the American image, the gap once again reached the level of 1972.

In summary, the evidence does suggest that overall support for NATO and the degree of domestic polarization in support for the Alliance is related as much to assessments of the United States as to a strategic judgment of the utility of the NATO framework versus other security approaches. As the international climate deteriorated and judgments of American policy turned negative, the parties became increasingly polarized. Of course, on one level this is almost self-evident: the distinguishing feature of NATO versus other secur-ity arrangements is precisely that it involves the United States as an alliance partner. None the less, the pattern of changing polarization over time does suggest that the relationship is not purely one of ideological difference. Parties of the Left in the Netherlands and West Germany have at times of lesser controversy been less divided from the Center-Right on this issue. The real divide, it seems, is due not to an absolute rejection of the American partner on ideological grounds, but to a rejection of the direction of East–West relations and American policy during the tense years of the early 1980s.

If correct, this relationship has much to say about the possibility of improvement in the degree of domestic polarization on Alliance issues. On one level, recent events have probably done little to close the domestic gaps that were opened in the early 1980s. The data presented in Chapter 4 showed that through 1986 the American image (and confidence in American foreign policy) had not regained its earlier levels. Perhaps this has been offset by the general softening of the East–West climate, culminating in the resumption of arms control negotiations in 1985, the Reykjavik summit of 1986, and the signing of the INF Agreement in 1987.

However, a quick reading of domestic politics in Europe suggests that the divisions revealed in this chapter remain. Especially in Britain and West Germany the debates of the early 1980s created deep fissures in party politics. In Britain the antinuclear policy of the Labour Party stands in stark contrast to the Tories. In West Germany the Social Democrats have developed an alternative security policy based on the "security partnership" concept that might have been predicted from the détente sensitivity shown in West German survey responses. And in all European countries the policies of the United States remain a subject of domestic debate, especially in the wake of the Iran/Contra scandal. Economic relations also remain strained. We must therefore ask whether these divisions now threaten the cohesion of the Alliance.

SUMMARY AND IMPLICATIONS: PUBLIC OPINION AND THE FUTURE OF NATO

The state of public opinion on the NATO Alliance is clear. Whether the question is the historical evolution of attitudes or the degree of domestic polarization in recent years, alliance with the United States is preferred by a 2:1 margin in almost all countries and within almost all sub-groups of the population. To be sure, there are some significant signs of domestic polarization. In France, West Germany, and the Netherlands, the successor generations are less supportive of NATO. In Britain support for NATO is high among all generations and parties, although there is less enthusiasm for the Alliance among Labour supporters of all ages.

The major question for this concluding section is whether these signs of polarization will have an impact on the cohesion of the Alliance. Such an assessment depends on expectations. At the level of the continuing existence of NATO and the continued adherence of the member states, there seems little reason to predict that much will change. One reason is that, more so than the other issues discussed in this book, the sentiments described in this chapter are based on hypothetical alternatives. That is, pollsters frequently ask citizens what type of hypothetical alliance they would prefer. In some cases there is sentiment (always a minority) that alternatives to NATO should be pursued. However, a major reason for the endurance of NATO in its present form has been the lack of success of proposals for alternative security arrangements. The major alternative, a European defense community, has foundered on numerous problems, but the "German problem" has been primary. For many Europeans, the American presence in Europe has served not only to deter the Soviets – it also stabilizes the *Western* balance and reassures the partners of West Germany. In Joffe's words, the United States are Europe's "pacifiers" as well as defenders.[32]

As time passes these concerns may fade in importance, but a second major obstacle remains: Reykjavik notwithstanding, the Soviets are likely to remain a nuclear power. European security will therefore continue to depend on nuclear deterrence. Of course, the central element of a European deterrent would have to be the forces of Britain and France, and it is here that uncertainties remain. British forces are committed to NATO if necessary, but French policy still insists on the independence of French nuclear decisions. Although recent years have brought much discussion of "extending" France's deterrent (especially in the context of Franco-German security collaboration), France remains hesitant to commit itself to more than consultation. Proposals for extending the French deterrent and for strengthening and coupling French and West German conventional forces are met with detailed objections – primarily involving the uncertainties of French policy.[33] Although there has been increasing consultation on Franco-German (and Anglo-French) nuclear collaboration, for the moment it seems unlikely that the nonnuclear states of Western Europe will substitute this consultation for the American nuclear deterrent. Presumably it is precisely this reasoning that undergirds the majorities of poll respondents who remain committed to "NATO as it now stands". Not surprisingly, the West Germans show the strongest sentiment in this regard.

Despite apparent sentiment for an alternative to NATO, the current alliance structure remains the framework that is both consistent with external constraints and supported by internal consensus. Of course, this does not mean that all will be smooth within NATO. Quite the opposite. The evolution of European public opinion indicates that there is much that could trouble policy harmonization within the Alliance. Both in this and the previous chapter, I have documented the sensitivity of European opinion to American policy. Especially in Holland and West Germany opinions of the Alliance are sensitive to the state of East–West relations. The successor generation of Dutch and West Germans condition their support of NATO on the continuation of some détente along with deterrence. In Britain and France opinions of American policy have also declined, and these are a strong conditioning factor in commitment to the Alliance. Thus, to the extent that external events or changes in American policy once again raise the issue of the balance of strength and détente in Western policy, the Alliance could become a focal point of contention.

Finally, discontent in Atlantic relations is increasingly fueled by disagreement in other policy areas. Europeans have always been less enamored of transatlantic policy collaboration in economics and foreign policy – they prefer to "go it alone" or to collaborate within the European community. Moreover, unlike the alternatives to NATO, the alternatives to Atlantic collaboration in these fields are not hypothetical. On foreign policy matters there is the Community institution of European Political Cooperation that has already caused some disagreement between the United States and Europe. And of course, it is in the economic realm that Europe offers its most institutionalized challenge to the United States. Especially in the latter sphere, there is every sign that contention will remain or increase. The Venice Summit in 1987 showed that macroeconomic coordination remains a sore point in the West. Recent disputes over agricultural trade is an another example. Other controversies, perhaps involving the EC's move toward full market integration, are just over the horizon. Given trends in global markets and production capabilities, it seems certain that the United States and the European Community will remain competitors. Given their level of interdependence, it also seems certain that they will be challenged to harmonize their fiscal and monetary policies.

As we have seen, the domestic base of support for cooperation in these fields is not nearly as high as in the security field. What is more, the domestic consequences of economic adjustment may make collaboration even more difficult. On both sides of the Atlantic, economic and budgetary problems have brought a resurgence of ideological conflict over such issues as subsidies, welfare spending, and the relative priorities of "guns and butter". These domestic debates have been joined to a transatlantic quarrel, as Americans argue for more guns and less "Eurosclerosis". Since European views of security issues are already polarized along ideological lines, these debates about economic and welfare policy are likely to complicate NATO issues.

Paradoxically, it may even be that NATO is now poised for change despite the fact that it has weathered its crisis in the security field and despite the fact that the domestic consensus surrounding the Alliance appears to have held. One sign of change is that European statesmen now talk almost routinely of the inevitability of a restructuring within the Alliance. The need to strengthen the European pillar is the most frequent focus of these remarks. Given what has been said above, the reasons for this renewed discussion should come as little surprise: Europeans are not jumping for change in NATO because they prefer it; they are searching for alternatives because they have been pushed by the United States.

This American push is not unrelated to security issues. Just after the apparent resolution of the INF issue with the beginning of deployments in 1983, a series of American decisions have resurrected traditional European concerns about the decoupling of the American security guarantee. The SDI initiative is the most obvious, as it challenged Europeans' attachment to nuclear deterrence; raised the prospect of an isolated, "fortress" America; and called into question the future of independent European nuclear forces. The apparent abandonment of the SALT II Treaty and the challenge to the ABM Treaty raised doubts about the future viability of negotiated arms control. Finally, the Reykjavik summit and the recent movement toward a "zero option" resolution of the INF question rolled all of these fears into one.

Yet none of these concerns seem entirely new. Indeed, the concern for coupling is as old as the Alliance itself, but it has never pushed Europeans to a serious search for an alternative to the Alliance. Rather, the seriousness of current European initiatives seem to have their origin in the fear that budgetary and economic disagreements will result in a real shift in American commitment. Given the pressures on the American budget and the simmering disputes on economic, trade, and even welfare issues, a reduction in the American troop commitment to Europe now seems likely. As a result, the options that formerly seemed unpopular or unworkable must now seem necessary.

We seem now to be witnessing a second round of interest in the strengthening of the European pillar. A first round, initiated during the INF controversy, arose from the intense – if different – concerns of the French and West Germans. In France, there was concern that the peace movements could lead to instability as West Germany drifted away from the Alliance. In West Germany, a firmer French commitment offered the prospect (as in Helmut Schmidt's proposal) of strengthening conventional deterrence while at the same time providing some insurance (or insulation) from the uncertainties of American strategic policy. Despite initial objections to the desirability or feasibility of such plans, interest has intensified in the last year. President Mitterrand has reportedly invited Helmut Schmidt on two occasions to explain his plan for a strengthening of conventional deterrence on the basis of Franco-German collaboration. The French and British have committed themselves to stronger consultation on nuclear matters.

Whether this collaboration will overcome the obstacles that have hindered a European Defense Community in the past remains unclear. Certainly, one should not expect the rapid evolution of a totally independent Europe in the nuclear field. Yet it seems likely that Europe will take more responsibility for conventional defense, probably on the basis of Franco-German collaboration. Although a US–European alliance in NATO is likely to remain, the "balance of responsibility" may shift toward the West European pillar of the Alliance. This evolution raises many questions, but perhaps the most important is whether the problems of the Alliance will be much different with a stronger "European pillar". One possibility is that disagreements that were formerly transatlantic will become intra-European squabbles. Chief among these is the adequacy of conventional defense and the likely expense of any European effort to take up the slack left by a reduction in American troops. To choose just one example, French defense budgets have recently favored nuclear rather than conventional forces, and on present plans they are likely to continue in this direction.[34] How does this square with German desires to lower the nuclear threshold?

As discussion of these issues become more prominent, the role of public opinion will certainly remain salient. This chapter has shown that a stronger European option may find a tolerant public reaction. The European option has always been second in the public's list of preferences, and support for the European Community more broadly has always been strong. What has changed is that these options, long relegated to the status of purely hypothetical possibilities, have now become the focus of very real decisions. The attention to the changes of 1992 give added impetus. Given the reactiveness of public opinion to the state of discussion at the leadership level, one should not be surprised to find opinion moving toward support for a stronger European pillar. As one noted analyst of public opinion recently observed: "Crucial to this scenario is the state of the élite consensus in the key European states, especially France and the Federal Republic. If major European political and military leaders agree on the need to coordinate closely on defense, then the publics will follow."[35] Finally, public opinion will play a major role in another way, for the ability of European governments to finance conventional forces, either to replace American reductions or to reduce reliance on nuclear weapons, will depend on public support for defense spending.

6 Old Politics and New Politics: The Public and Defense Spending

Lack of public support for defense spending is potentially the most severe constraint on security policy that will face West European governments in the 1990s. It is true that European governments have always been obliged to balance defense spending with the competing priorities of economic growth and social consensus. None the less, several developments have combined recently to make this task even more difficult. The oil-price shock of 1979 and the subsequent recession were the most obvious problems, as they led to conservative budgetary policies designed to reduce government deficits in an era of volatile credit and currency markets. The fear of "Eurosclerosis" added to the mood of restraint.

Yet even as they attempt to limit civilian spending, European governments remain under pressure to increase defense budgets. Doubts about the American commitment are one source of this pressure. In addition, demographic changes may increase the cost of defense personnel as recruiters compete in a shrinking manpower pool. Inflation in the price of weapons is a further problem. Finally, the recent INF Treaty and criticisms of NATO's nuclear strategy have produced widespread calls to increase expensive conventional forces.

This chapter examines the state of domestic consensus on these difficult issues of defense spending. Although it is generally a less visible political issue than the questions of deterrence and arms control discussed in previous chapters, in the final analysis it is the politics of defense spending that will determine how European governments make the strategic choices of the next decade. At a more theoretical level, opinions of defense spending provide a useful opportunity to evaluate alternative explanations for change and cleavage in public opinion because they lead naturally to two compelling – if different – perspectives: *generational change*, which emphasizes the differing experience and educational achievements of younger age cohorts and the resulting differences in their values and policy views; and a *welfare politics* perspective, which recognizes that the modern welfare state now constitutes a substantial priority for the older, established members of society, a priority that may conflict with any budgetary tradeoff in favor of defense spending.

These theoretical perspectives are not merely of academic interest. As policymakers seek to discover the basis of consensus on security matters, it is crucial to ascertain whether public attitudes toward defense spending are governed by frequently cited generational differences or by the traditional self-interest of budgetary politics. Does criticism of defense spending come mostly from the younger and better educated members of the successor generation or from the older members of the "successful" generation?

RECENT TRENDS IN SUPPORT FOR DEFENSE SPENDING

Before turning to these competing perspectives, it is useful to review historical trends in public opinions of defense spending, for these suggest that budgetary politics rather than security considerations dominate public evaluations of the defense budget. Examining the familiar question which asks whether the defense budget should be increased, decreased, or remain the same (Table 6.1), there is somewhat of a surprise. Despite the economic gloom and partial détente of the 1970s, the public's desire to *decrease* defense spending actually declined during the decade. Indeed, in every country the percentage who thought that defense spending should be decreased was lower in 1979 than it had been a decade or more earlier.

There is also a strain of ambivalence in these surveys. The decline in the desire to cut defense spending was not matched by support for the increases envisioned under NATO commitments. Only in Great Britain was such a pattern in evidence. In France, West Germany, and the Netherlands, the declining percentage favoring cuts was accompanied by a rise in the percentage who favored keeping defense spending at current levels. In any case, by 1981 the period of declining opposition to defense was reversed. In Great Britain there was a slight rise in the percentage favoring cuts in 1979, 1981, and 1982. After a surge in support for increases after the Falklands War in 1982, support for defense spending collapsed by 1985 to levels that matched historical lows. In West Germany the percentage favoring

Table 6.1   *Should Defense Spending be Decreased, Kept the Same, or Increased?*

	Decrease (%)	Keep same (%)	Increase (%)	Don't know (%)
FRANCE				
1968	38	47	5	10
1971	39	38	7	16
1972	51	32	7	10
1979	23	43	13	21
1980	22	50	15	13
1981	24	49	15	11
1982	24	55	16	5
1985	16	41	12	31
BRITAIN				
1961	46	28	10	16
1965	43	28	8	21
1968	37	24	16	23
1971	26	40	16	18
1972	20	38	32	10
1975	36	27	19	18
1976	24	23	33	20
1977	24	25	31	20
1978	17	23	37	24
1979	28	29	25	19
1980	19	31	29	21
1981	22	34	35	9
1982	27	25	40	8
1983	46	34	12	8
1985	53	29	10	8
1986	54	27	10	8
WEST GERMANY				
1967	41	37	8	14
1968	27	35	16	22
1969	31	36	16	17
1971	38	46	12	4
1972	38	38	11	13
1973	35	39	10	17
1974	34	42	9	15
1975	38	42	10	11
1976	27	47	13	13
1977	27	50	12	11
1978	27	58	11	4
1979	27	59	10	3
1980	22	58	17	3
1981	34	52	14	1

1982	34	54	10	1
1983	35	52	12	2
1984	39	50	9	1
1985	36	42	7	15
1986	42	49	7	1
1987	45	47	6	2
NETHERLANDS				
1970	47	25	10	18
1971	51	34	10	5
1975	40	33	10	17
1978	32	33	13	23
1980	31	51	10	8
1981	36	35	11	17
1984	29	49	8	14

NOTES: In Britain and West Germany the question asked if defense spending is "too much, just right, or too little?" Responses to this question are listed as "decrease, keep same, or increase." In Britain the defense question appears in a battery of questions about other spending programs (education, health). In West Germany the question is prefaced by the remark that "security costs money". The Dutch question in 1980 referred to "defense spending in support of NATO".

SOURCES: *Britain* Social Surveys Ltd (Gallup), *The Gallup International Public Opinion Polls, Great Britain* 2 vols, (New York: Random House, 1975) pp. 580, 800, 1011; and *Gallup Political Index*, nos 185, 199, 207, 216, 232, and 235. Data for 1971/2 are from Kenneth Adler and Douglas Wertman, "West European Security Concerns for the Eighties: Is NATO in Trouble?", Paper prepared for delivery to the Annual Meeting of the American Association of Public Opinion Research, Buck Hill Falls, Pa, May 1981. Data for 1981 are from *Political, Social and Economic Review*, 34 (December 1981) p. 23; survey by NOP for *The Observer*. Data for 1985 and 1986 provided to the author by Social Surveys Ltd.

France 1968–80: Adler and Wertman, "Is NATO in Trouble?", Table 5; 1981/2: Office of Research, United States Information Agency, *West European Public Opinion on Key Security Issues 1981/1982*, Report R–10–82 (Washington, D.C.: June 1982) Table 21, and *1985 Post-Geneva Survey [Contractor's Reports]* (Washington, D.C.: mimeographed).

Netherlands 1970/1: Netherlands Institute of Public Opinion (NIPO), Report 1486; 1975/8: Werkgroep Kontinu-Onderzoek FSW-A, *Dutch Continuous Survey* (Amsterdam: Steinmetz Archive, 1972–) Waves 9 and 17; 1981/1982: USIA, *Key Security Issues*, Table 21; and 1984: Office of Research, USIA, *NATO and Burden-Sharing*, Report M–9/11/84 (Washington, D.C.: 11 September 1984) Table 12.

West Germany Press and Information Office, Federal Ministry of Defense, *Meinungsbild zur Wehrpolitischen Lage [Sicherheitspolitik]*, yearly surveys provided by Ministry of Defense; surveys by EMNID. The 1985 figures are from USIA, *1985 Post-Geneva Survey*.

cuts increased from 1981 to 1987. In France public opinion remained essentially the same from 1979 to 1982; the only other change was a puzzling increase in "don't knows" in the 1985 survey. In the Netherlands opinion moved to the position that defense spending should be kept stable.

The more recent surveys are significant, for the 1980s were a time of very high international tensions. Yet public attitudes toward defense spending either reversed their generally tolerant trend (Great Britain, West Germany) or remained essentially what they had been for the preceding years. Obviously, the crisis atmosphere of the late 1970s and early 1980s did not lead European publics to conclude that more spending for defense was necessary.

What explains this pattern? Had this question been posed five years ago, a popular answer would have been that the defense budget was part of a more general wave of public rebellion on security issues. For example, in 1981 Feld and Wildgen characterized the lack of support for increased defense spending in West Germany as "a manifestation of a strong pacifist and neutralist attitude among many Germans, especially the youth".[1] This observation was far off the mark. The opinion surveys presented in previous chapters show that public opinion in all West European countries continues to support the essentials of post-Second World War security policy: membership in NATO and alliance with the United States; retention of standing military forces; and even under some circumstances the maintenance of nuclear weapons as part of NATO's deterrence strategy.

The trends in support for defense spending indicate that economic circumstances and government fiscal policy – rather than security considerations – are the driving forces underlying public opinions of the defense budget. During the 1970s European governments maintained a uniformly expansionist budgetary policy. There were healthy real increases in both defense *and* civilian spending in all the countries surveyed here. It was only during the recession that began in 1981 that a "guns–butter" trade-off was implied, if not always implemented, by the emphasis on civilian spending restraint at a time of increasing international tensions and defense commitments. Although no government (with the exception of the Dutch) actually cut total civilian spending, there was a noticeable decline in growth rates and some cuts in specific programs. And in contrast to the recession of 1974/5, when public spending was expanded in the classic Keynesian fashion, in the 1980s spending has been constrained. In the recession of 1974/5, for example, French social security spending was increased by over 10 per cent in real terms, while in 1979/81 its growth was reduced to 6 per cent. A similar retrenchment took place in other countries as well (in West Germany, social security spending increased by 11 per cent in 1974/5 and by 3 per cent in 1979/81; in the Netherlands, the figures were 9 per cent and 3 per cent; and in Britain 6 per cent and 4 per cent).[2] The expansionist fiscal policies of the 1970s gave the public little reason to criticize defense spending. It was only in the recession of the early 1980s that a shift in budget priorities took place.

The importance of budgetary considerations is reinforced by another finding of the polls. In almost every available European survey since the 1950s, defense spending has ranked last in the public's priorities. During the Korean War, for example, European publics were asked if they favored "building up military forces at this time". The question evinced plurality support in France (46 per cent) and West Germany (45 per cent) and an overwhelming majority in Great Britain (79 per cent). None the less, when asked further whether it was more important to "rearm according to plan, or to improve the standard of living", improvement of living standards was preferred by 60 per cent of the French and 71 per cent of West Germans. Only in Britain did a plurality (46 per cent) favor rearmament over improvement in living standards.[3]

Even in Britain the defense budget has been listed as the preferred target of government spending cuts since the Korean War, and similar priorities also characterize French, Dutch, and German surveys since the 1960s and 1970s (see Table 6.2). In addition, "most important problem" surveys during the post-Second World War period have shown that, with the exception of extreme crisis periods, defense issues are a much less salient concern of the public than are economic and social problems. These priorities continued even during the intense debate over the INF missile deployments.[4]

This preference for domestic programs does not contradict the trends set out earlier in Table 6.1, for those surveys did not directly pose a choice among spending priorities. Yet this summarizes much of the experience of the 1970s: public opinion always placed civilian programs first, but budget policy never really challenged these popular sentiments. Given growth in both guns *and* butter, there was no need to choose. With the recent shift to tighter budgets, the public has responded, not with a new-found hostility to defense spending, but with a long-held preference for social and other civilian programs.

Table 6.2   The Public's Spending Priorities

Which Government Spending Program Should be Cut First?

	Defense (%)	Health or Social (%)	Education (%)
BRITAIN			
1952	54	27	–
1953	35	6	9
1955	32	4	4
1963	29	1	5
1980	30	49	4
1983	50	26	–
1983	58	32	–
FRANCE			
1963	42	4	0
1966	64	7	3
1969	53	5	7
1983	81	5	–
WEST GERMANY			
1975	76	–	–
1976	58	3	12
1977	55	–	–
1980	44	6	16
1983	67	15	–

Which Government Programs Should be Increased First?

	Defense (%)	Health or Social (%)	Education (%)
NETHERLANDS			
1967	0	49	15
1971	2	49	5
1976	5	79	–
1983	27	54	–

NOTES: In all countries, the choice of spending programs to cut varies greatly. Programs combined under "health and social" include health, social, housing, and public assistance. Other choices are not shown (foreign aid, civil servant salaries). In Britain the question generally asks, "If government spending has to be reduced, which is the first on this list you would cut down on?" In France the question reads, "on which of the following areas does the State spend too much?" West German questions contain the preface that the "State must economize" and ask "in which areas should the government cut back first?". In the Netherlands one question contains the preference that "government revenue is growing", while others simply ask respondents to rank government spending programs. The 1983 question for all countries

The margin of preference for social programs is revealed in surveys which do pose the "guns or butter" trade-off directly. When asked in 1980 and 1981 if defense spending should be increased even if it would mean a cut in social spending or an increase in taxes, support for increased defense spending, already low, declined even further (Table 6.3). Once again, only in Britain was there any substantial toleration for trade-offs – a pattern that holds in the 1983 question that tested willingness to finance increased defense spending through higher taxes alone. None the less, even in Britain the willingness to support a "defense/welfare" trade-off declined during the rough economic years of the early 1980s. In 1981, a British survey showed that 30 per cent believed that defense spending should be the first program to be cut if necessary, while 44 per cent thought that social security should be the first program cut. By 1983, the percentages had reversed: 50 per cent thought that defense should be cut and only 26 per cent favored cutting social security.[5]

In summary, the dominance of "bread and butter" priorities in current public opinion surveys should come as little surprise – it has been evident since the early 1950s. For specialists in security matters, the defense budget represents strategic choice. For public opinion, it is a competitor for budgetary resources. Surveys from all four countries generalize an observation about British politics that was made by Harold and Margaret Sprout in 1968. The Sprouts argued that the maturation of working-class democracy, together with the relative decline in British military power and the emergence of strategic nuclear stalemate, had brought a shift in popular attitudes: "The weight of the evidence known to us suggests that Britons these

---

Table 6.2 – cont.

asks respondents if they support or oppose "reducing defense expenditure and using some of this money for social services, health and education".

SOURCES: For Britain and France, *The Gallup International Public Opinion Polls, Great Britain [France]*, at years noted. For West Germany, Adler and Wertman, "Is Europe in Trouble?", Table 6, and Martin and Sylvia Greiffenhagen, *Ein Schwiereges Vaterland* (Munich: List Verlag, 1979) p. 406. For the Netherlands: Interuniversity Consortium for Political and Social Research, *Dutch Election Study 1971* (Ann Arbor, Mich.: 1975) p. 44; Werkgroep nationaal verkiezingsonderzoek, *De Nederlandse Kiezer '72* (Alphen aan den Rijn: Samson Uitgeverij, 1973) p. 273; and Werkgroep Kontinu-Onderzoek, *Dutch Continuous Survey*, Wave 13. Figures for 1983 for all countries are from the Atlantic Institute-Louis Harris Poll, "Industrial Democracies and World Economic Tensions" (Paris: 1 April 1983) p. 9.

Table 6.3   Guns, Butter, and Taxes

Percentage still favoring an increase in defense spending even if it would mean:		
A cut in social spending or a tax increase		A tax increase
1980 (%)	1981 (%)	1983 (%)
France	8	4	28
Britain	34	17	46
West Germany	13	13	19
Netherlands	–	8	–

NOTES: 1980 and 1981: Asked only of those responding "increase" to a prior question on defense spending: "Do you think [your country] should spend more for military purposes even though taxes might go up or social services might decline as a result? Or do you think we should not increase military spending under those conditions?" 1983: "Some people think that to better assure the defense of the Western nations, it is necessary to increase the defense budget in our countries. Would you accept an increase in the defense budget even if that would mean additional taxes?" "Don't know" included in calculation of percentages.

SOURCES: Office of Research, United States Information Agency, *Multiregional Security Survey, Questions and Responses* (Washington, D.C.: April 1980) p. 5, and *Alliance/Security Survey: Questionnaire and Results* (Washington, D.C.: March/April 1981) p. 16; and Institut International de Géopolitique, *Guerre et Paix, Quelles Guerres? Quelles Paix?* (Paris: April/May 1983); survey by Louis Harris.

days are more concerned about taxes, pay, new cars, better schools, and a host of other problems close at hand, than about Russia, China, communism, Vietnam, de Gaulle or the H-bomb."[6]

The dominance of social priorities is not confined to Britain. None the less, despite the generality of this evidence, the precise implications of these domestic constraints remain largely unexplored. Although labels such as "pacifism" and "neutralism" have given way to more searching political and social analyses, the constraints of the modern welfare state have not yet been related to the politics of defense policy.

THE SUCCESSOR GENERATION AND THE SUCCESSFUL GENERATION

Theories of generational change provide a logical starting point for attempts to understand societal cleavages on defense spending, for the experience of the "successor generation" described in previous chapters would suggest that the young are likely to be less enthusiastic about the defense budget. In the first place, the changes in the international environment described both by theorists of international politics and by theorists of generational change occurred during the crucial period of adult socialization of the post-1945 "détente" generation. Growing to maturity in the 1960s and early 1970s, the younger generation escaped the antagonisms of World War and Cold War, but they did experience the relaxation of tensions that resulted in the arms control agreements and other negotiated settlements of the early 1970s. As discussed in previous chapters, the higher educational attainments of the successor generation could reinforce this tendency to see the international environment as less threatening. And if the successor generation feel more secure than their elders, would they not also be less inclined to support the defense budgets designed to meet threats to national security?

The value changes described by Inglehart are also relevant. "Postmaterial" values such as self-expression and self-fulfillment are not unrelated to the emphasis on individual dignity and social security that has animated the expansion of the post-Second World War welfare state. The successor generation may be less attuned to the unqualified goal of economic growth as the fountain of social reform, but this does not preclude the belief that the state must place a high priority on maintaining the social security and quality of life of its citizens.

In short, theories of generational change provide a useful perspective for the study of European opinions on defense spending, for they call attention to the consequences of social and political changes which, when seen in conjunction with changes in the security environment over the last decade, would suggest a disproportional skepticism of the young toward traditional security policies and the defense spending that supports those policies.

Nevertheless, as an explanation of opinions of defense spending, an undivided focus on the young is not completely convincing. We have already seen that 60 to 90 per cent of the populations of France, Britain, Germany, and the Netherlands oppose increasing defense if social services would be cut as a result – proportions that could hardly be confined to the young. Moreover, the beneficiaries of the most extensive public spending programs (social security and health care) are primarily the older, more established members of society. Forty to fifty per cent of government spending is devoted to these two programs in the countries studied here.[7] Thus, the lion's share of public spending in the modern welfare state goes to those who are or have been the "successful" generation of wage earners in the post-war European *Wirtschaftswunder*. If the younger generation were socialized during a period of declining tensions, strategic stalemate, and arms control, the older generation had become accustomed to unprecedented growth in the scope and generosity of government-mandated income support.

The political significance of this welfare expansion is fundamental. As Harold and Margaret Sprout observed in their study of British budgetary politics, the welfare state represents an historical transition from the priority of state and national security to needs and demands that had been denied budgetary favor before extension of the franchise. Applying the Sprouts' analysis to French politics and defense policy, Edward Morse argued that the post-war broadening of the electorate and the resulting shift to domestic priorities had already begun to constrain defense programs. In the United States, Samuel Huntington argued that the "welfare shift" resulting from the demands of newly mobilized interests in the 1960s and 1970s could constrain resources at times of security crises.[8]

These analyses are crucial, for they point to a dimension of the welfare state that goes beyond its immediate budgetary impact. In Western Europe the welfare state has been far more than a short-term material reward for electoral or other political advantage. It is part of a broader reconciliation of social classes and political interests in the democratic consensus of the post-Second World War period, a consensus that is historically unique in many European countries.

Ironically, the modern welfare state may also contain the seeds of discord. As both Peter Flora and Hugh Heclo have argued, the post-war expansion of social security was financed largely on the "individualistic" principle of social insurance, that is, on the premise of some individual contribution in return for benefits.[9] Although we normally associate welfare policy with social solidarity, increasingly it is an individual rather than a social contract.[10] What is more, the emphasis on "earned" benefits makes any retrenchment based on solidaristic principles increasingly difficult. Can governments cut what workers have financed through their contributions? Social security, originally designed to reconcile the principles of individual and community responsibility, has become the largest program of the government budget, and given the earned nature of many benefits, it will be politically difficult to control.

The welfare state, therefore, poses a threefold constraint: it is the largest component of government spending; it is of fundamental importance to social stability and political consensus; and its benefits are increasingly perceived as earned. At a time of budgetary scarcity, the post-war "successful" generation may represent a larger source of opposition to the defense budget than the younger, successor generation.

THE NEW POLITICS AND THE OLD POLITICS

At first glance, theories of generational change and welfare politics offer contrasting views of conflict in the politics of defense spending. For theorists of generational change, the young are more likely to oppose defense spending because their experience has not included the bitterness of the Cold War and because their value priorities in general stress "quality of life" goals rather than traditional goals such as national security. Students of the welfare state, in contrast, would see opposition to defense spending as equally if not more severe among the older members of society who are accustomed to growth in social benefits that could be threatened in times of budget austerity and growing security challenges.

However, in present circumstances these differences should not be exaggerated. In the first place, Inglehart and other students of generational change have emphasized that the transition to "post-material" society is a slow, gradual process rather than an abrupt transformation. The image is one of a glacier process in which generational value change overlays the traditional class and party orientations of industrial society. At present, post-materialists remain a minority in all advanced, industrial democracies by an average ratio of one to two.[11] Thus, theorists of generational change are the first to concede that there remains a substantial residue of the "old" material and class cleavages that are consistent with the successful generation argument presented here.

There is an additional qualification. Welfare constraints presumably arise from budgetary self-interest rather than principle. The older generations who benefit from social programs are presumably more attuned to the "Cold War" axioms and military preparedness, *unless these latter priorities conflict with social priorities*. Thus, the successful generation of the modern welfare state would oppose defense spending most prominently – perhaps only – at times of economic and budget scarcity. Of course, if the successful generation argument is most relevant at times of austerity, its contemporary policy significance is no less for that. The immediate future promises little relief from the difficult task of reconciling defense spending, social priorities, and fiscal restraint.

Finally, Inglehart's own recent work indicates that the two strata of the post-industrial glacier process may be joined in a broader alignment along the Left-Right ideological spectrum. In a study of European opinion in 1979, he found that opinions on both "old", traditional issues (public ownership, income equality) and "new" issues (abortion, nuclear energy) were very strongly related to ideology.[12] This finding is of considerable interest because theories of generational change would suggest that this correlation would gradually break down as new, generational value cleavages supplant traditional class and ideological alignments.

Inglehart argues that the continuing relevance of ideological views reflects a basic need in a world of complex and changing political issues:

> the Left-Right dimension, as a political concept, is a higher level abstraction used to summarize one's stand on the important political issues of the day. It serves the function of organizing and simplifying a complex political reality, providing an overall orientation toward a potentially limitless number of issues, political parties and social groups . . . to speak of Left and Right is always an oversimplification – but an extremely useful one.[13]

Although values and issues may change as both society and the political agenda evolve, citizens' opinions of political issues can be related to a more fundamental worldview, a view governed by familiar ideological attitudes towards social change and the role of government.

The continuing relevance of ideological polarization may provide a bridge between generational and welfare cleavages in public opinion on defense spending. I have already noted that some of the values and interests of younger and older Europeans on welfare issues are compatible. In addition, the successor generation and the traditional Left share a skepticism of military force (although the young may be more intensely skeptical). The views of both groups could thus be similarly structured by ideological debates and party programs on defense and welfare policy issues. Secondly, defense issues are among the most complex and difficult of public issues, and even the most educated members of society are likely to seek some guidance as defense issues arise in public debate. As I have observed throughout this book, European citizens seeking cues on defense issues will find a strong tradition of party conflict.

In fact, perhaps this explains one of the most surprising findings in Inglehart's recent study, the fact that in 1979 opinions of defense spending were *more strongly correlated with ideology* than were opinions on any other public issue ("old" or "new"). In Inglehart's view, this correlation results from the fact that the Vietnam War transformed the politics of national security:

> domestic opposition to one's own defense establishment took on new overtones during the war in Vietnam. Opposition to the war came to be motivated much less by traditional reasons (above all, opposition to heavy government expenditures and higher taxes) than by a postmaterialist concern for the impact of the war on the purported *enemy*. Though the defense issue is ancient, both the motivations and the social bases that underlie it have changed. . . . Opposition to the war became a major postmaterialist cause, linked with humanitarian (rather than economic) concerns, as well as opposition to the hierarchical authority patterns of industrial society.[14]

There is much to the notion that Vietnam affected popular attitudes towards national security. However, Inglehart's explanation overstates the historical novelty of ideological conflict on security issues – at least in the European context. In Europe, ideological conflict on national security far predates Vietnam. Although one might argue that the Vietnam War raised these debates in a new context, they were hardly new to Europeans. We must also remember that defense spending is an issue of *budgetary* as well as security politics, something on which ideologues and political parties have a familiar basis for debate, especially in the recent climate of halting economic growth and budgetary retrenchment.

Thus, Inglehart's recent findings are of interest, not so much for their novelty, but for the demonstration that an undivided focus on generational change may overlook the continuities of traditional political conflict. If the recent interest in generational change indicates a tendency to turn from one set of generalizations to another, a review of scholarly work on public opinion, generational change, and welfare politics indicates that a more complex analysis will be needed to comprehend the social and political cleavages that structure the public's views of defense spending.

THE EVIDENCE: PUBLIC OPINION AND DEFENSE SPENDING

The surveys described in previous chapters have demonstrated that there is rarely one "true" opinion profile. Depending on question wording, the country surveyed, or the date of the survey, opinions may vary from majorities in one direction to majorities in the other. In the case of public opinions of defense spending, we have already seen one obvious consequence of question wording: opinions are much less supportive when popular social priorities are mentioned in the survey question.

Fortunately, the recent interest in the public's views on defense issues has contributed to a proliferation in the number of available opinion surveys. Despite some variation in wording, it is now possible to conduct detailed analyses of opinions on defense spending using surveys made available in the European Community's *Eurobarometer* series and in the USIA (United States Information Agency) opinion surveys on European security issues. Between 1979 and 1983, for example, the *Eurobarometer* survey asked Europeans bluntly if they agreed or disagreed that "Western Europe should make a stronger effort to provide adequate military defense". This question does have some weaknesses. First, it mentions "stronger effort" and "adequate defense" without clarifying the meaning of these terms. Secondly, it mentions "Western Europe", a community that evokes varying degrees of warmth in different countries. None the less, the survey is a rare opportunity, for it was posed identically in all countries over a four-year span, and it does focus on the symbolic issue of military strength for which generational experience and budgetary interest should be salient influences.

Responses of European publics to this "strengthen defense" question are displayed in Table 6.4. There is generally strong support for strengthening defense – an overwhelming majority in Britain and lesser majorities in West Germany and France. Although majorities of the Dutch did support strengthening defense through 1981, by 1983 that percentage had turned to a slim majority against. However, the level of support for strengthening defense evolved differently in each country between 1979 and 1983. Only in Britain is support both high and stable. In France, opinions in 1979 actually showed a slim majority *against* strengthening defense. Support increased drastically during the crisis atmosphere of 1981, but it declined once again in 1983. Dutch and West German opinion did not react to the tensions of the early 1980s at all, as support for strengthening defense re-

Table 6.4   Should Europe Strengthen Defense?

"*Western Europe should make a stronger effort to provide adequate military defense*"

	Agree (%)	Disagree (%)	Net support (%)	Don't know (%)	n
FRANCE					
April 1979	47	53	– 6	29	1146
October 1981	67	33	+34	20	1006
April 1983	57	43	+14	25	1011
BRITAIN					
April 1979	78	22	+56	17	1008
October 1981	72	28	+44	15	1088
April 1983	71	29	+42	15	1027
WEST GERMANY					
April 1979	64	36	+28	16	1003
October 1981	64	36	+28	16	962
April 1983	51	50	+ 1	13	1049
NETHERLANDS					
April 1979	57	43	+ 6	11	991
October 1981	53	48	+ 5	13	1011
April 1983	38	62	–24	10	998

NOTES: "Don't knows" are shown for information only; they are not included in calculation of percentages.

SOURCE: Computed from: J.-R. Rabier *et al.*, *Eurobarometer*, nos 11, 16 and 19 (Ann Arbor, Mich.: Interuniversity Consortium for Political and Social Research, Study nos 7752, 9022, and 8152).

mained largely the same from 1979 to 1981, with significant declines by 1983. In summary, these opinion surveys on "strengthening defense" seem to match the evolution of European governmental reaction to security problems: consistent firmness in Britain; a dramatic shift toward concern in France; and cautious to skeptical reactions in West Germany and the Netherlands.

Figure 6.1. shows the same surveys, now broken down by the two major age groups. Since each country reveals a somewhat different pattern of age differences, it is useful to examine each in turn.

The *British* provide the most clear and consistent picture. The

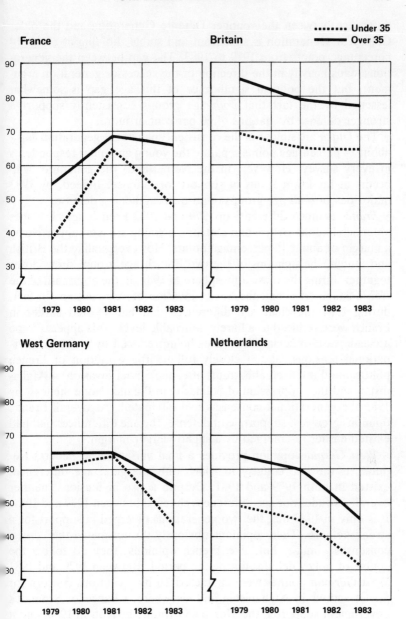

Figure 6.1   Percentage who Agree in "Strong Defense", by Age Group

SOURCE: See Table 6.4.

difference between the younger Détente Generation and the older Cold War Generation is significant and stable, holding at about 14 percentage points from 1979 to 1983. The gap between the generations leans heavily in the direction of the successor generation argument, but the political significance of this age gap is somewhat lessened by the fact that *both* age groups consistently support a stronger defense by margins of 60 per cent or more.

The *Dutch* are similar in the consistent span of the generation gap – about 14 percentage points separate the young and older respondents in every survey. However, in the Netherlands the generation gap occurs at far lower levels of support for defense. Indeed, by 1983 majorities of *both* age groups oppose strengthening defense.

France is much different. In 1979 and 1983 French age cleavages are much like the British and Dutch: the young are less supportive by a margin of about 16 percentage points. However, unlike the British and Dutch, the opinions of the two French age groups drew closer together during the tense atmosphere of 1981, in the aftermath of the Iran hostage crisis and the Soviet invasion of Afghanistan. In fact, during 1981 the clear age differences that had existed earlier in France were reduced to a barely noticeable level. This appears to be a classic case of social differences being reduced by a rise in international tensions, and it closely follows the evolution of French political and intellectual currents after the Soviet invasion of Afghanistan and the suppression of Solidarity in Poland. None the less, by 1983 the generational consensus had dissipated. As overall French opinions grew less supportive of defense, the age differences that had existed earlier re-emerged by a slightly larger margin.

West German opinion provides a final variant. The Federal Republic is the one country in which only marginal age differences existed in both 1979 and 1981. Despite a rise in tensions, neither overall attitudes nor age differences changed between 1979 and 1981. It is only in 1983 that the two generations diverged in support for a strong defense. These opinions obviously do not match the "crisis-consensus" image, but, like French opinions, they do follow the course of policy debates during the period. Between 1979 and 1981 West German politics were characterized by a cautious concern for Soviet actions in Afghanistan and elsewhere. Chancellor Schmidt's government supported the Moscow Olympics boycott in 1980, and it was Schmidt who stimulated NATO's decision for INF deployment. Yet by 1981 debate over INF and East–West relations in general began a period of polarization in West German politics that culminated in Schmidt's resignation and the famed "missile election" of 1983. The surveys track this evolution almost perfectly: by 1983 generational differences replaced the consensus among age groups that had characterized West German opinions since 1979.

In summary, one of the most interesting features of these surveys about "strengthening defense" is the variation in the age patterns over time. Although we generally suppose that international tension fosters consensus, the generational breakdowns indicate that such a reaction is hardly universal. In Britain and the Netherlands, age differences change little if at all during wide swings in international tension. West German generations changed little during the height of East–West tensions in 1981, but they did diverge as controversy broke out over how to respond to those crises. Only in France did the tensions of 1981 reduce previously existing generational differences, but the French generational consensus was shortlived.

The volatility in age differences suggest a qualification to the successor generation thesis. A key argument of theorists of generational change is that the experience and values of the young have produced both a lower priority for security and a lesser tendency to react to threat. Yet the French and West German surveys show that age differences are volatile. In France, they vary drastically from strong generational differences to consensus and back again. In West Germany, age differences emerge only two years after near identical opinions had characterized the generations. And although age differences in Britain and the Netherlands are clear and stable, even this stability might throw the generational theory into question: if values and priorities are fundamentally different, should not the reaction to events also be different? Put another way, if theories of generational change suggest that basic values and policy views are different, should the young not react differently to change in the environment than do their elders?[15]

None the less, perhaps judgment on the generational thesis should be suspended, for these questions did not directly broach the issue of *spending* to strengthen defense. In March and October 1980 USIA surveys asked respondents directly if defense *spending* (or spending "in support of NATO") should be increased, kept the same, or decreased. The results were strikingly different, both in overall response and in generational distribution (Table 6.5). Despite the tension surrounding events in Iran and Afghanistan, only in the British responses was there substantial support for increasing the defense budget. Overall, the distribution of support for defense

Table 6.5 Opinions of Defense Spending: Younger and Older Generations

	March 1980			October 1980		
	Age under 35 (%)	Age over 35 (%)	Difference (%)	Age under 35 (%)	Age over 35 (%)	Difference (%)
FRANCE						
Decrease	36	18	−18	53	37	−16
Keep same	49	63	+14	42	59	+17
Increase	15	18	+ 3	6	4	− 2
n=	341	524		225	287	
BRITAIN						
Decrease	11	9	− 2	18	17	− 1
Keep same	37	35	− 2	52	50	− 2
Increase	52	55	+ 3	30	33	+ 3
n=	340	562		354	515	
WEST GERMANY						
Decrease	14	15	+ 1	20	20	0
Keep same	64	60	− 4	54	58	+ 4
Increase	23	26	+ 3	26	22	− 4
n=	307	537		314	548	
NETHERLANDS						
Decrease	not available			40	27	−13
Keep same				52	58	+ 6
Increase				8	15	+ 7
n=				442	523	

NOTES: In March the question asked "Do you think that the level of [country's] expenditures for military purposes should be increased, decreased, or kept at about their present level?" In October the question asked "Should our defense spending in support of NATO be increased, decreased, or kept at its present level?" The difference column subtracts the views of those under 35 from those over 35.

SOURCES: Computed from: Machine-Readable Branch, US National Archives and Record Service, *USIA Multi-Regional Security Survey, March 1980* (Washington, D.C.: Study nos I8007, I8010 and I8005); and J.-R. Rabier *et al.*, *Eurobarometer 14, October 1980* (Ann Arbor, Mich.: Inter-university Consortium for Political and Social Research, Study no. 7958).

spending is not unlike that found in surveys presented previously: the French and Dutch are least supportive of the defense budget, with somewhat greater support found in West Germany and Britain. In any event, a comparison of this survey on defense spending to the more symbolic question on "strengthening defense" confirms that defense *spending* is viewed far less positively than is the more general goal of strengthening defense.

Given the dominance of social spending priorities, perhaps it is not surprising that generational differences are both less dramatic and less general in these surveys than in the more symbolic surveys. There are no age differences of consequences among British and West German respondents. In France and the Netherlands, age differences are quite marked. A further complication is that age differences on this spending question do not always match the pattern of age differences on the "strengthen defense" question. Once again, diversity marks the national profiles. In France and the Netherlands there are large age differences on both types of question. In West Germany age differences are not noticeable in either question. And in Britain there are age differences on the "strengthen defense" question but not on the spending question. In summary, only in France and the Netherlands are age differences clear and consistent across different surveys. When present, age differences generally support the successor generation thesis, although no age group in any country shows much enthusiasm for increasing defense spending.

YOUNG AND OLD, GUNS AND BUTTER

My interpretation of the "successful" generation of the post-war welfare state is predicated upon the trade-off between defense and social spending, a choice that will surely remain salient in an era of uncertain economic growth. In the March 1980 survey this additional question was put to European publics directly. The first question, just discussed, asked simply if defense spending should be increased, kept the same, or decreased. A second question focused on the "guns--butter" choice by further asking those who favored an increase in defense spending if they would change their view if "social spending were to be cut or taxes had to be increased". As noted earlier, overall support for defense declines when this choice is forced. An additional question is whether the change in views is more pronounced among

Table 6.6   Reaction to the "Guns–Butter" Trade-off: Younger and Older Generations

"Do you think [we] should spend more for military purposes even though taxes might go up or social services might decline as a result? Or do you think we should not increase military spending under those conditions?"

	Age under 35 (%)	Age over 35 (%)	Difference (%)	n
FRANCE				
Should still increase	40	59	+19	46
Should not increase	59	41	−18	95
BRITAIN				
Should still increase	66	77	+11	161
Should not increase	34	23	−11	293
WEST GERMANY				
Should still increase	62	70	+ 8	58
Should not increase	38	30	− 8	130

NOTE: The difference column subtracts the views of those under 35 from those over 35.

SOURCE: See Table 6.5.

particular age groups. As shown in Table 6.6, there is an age difference on the "trade-off" question in France – now a familiar pattern. But age differences are also present in Britain and (to a lesser extent) in West Germany. Although there was little age difference in the original percentage favoring increases in defense, when the "guns––butter" trade-off is pushed, support turns slightly "softer" among the young. It runs against the grain of budgetary self-interest, but these age differences also show that the older, successful generation in these countries are moderately *more* tolerant of a potential guns––butter trade-off than are the younger, successor generation. Nor does this result from combining age groups – in Britain and France the retired population (65 and older) is even more willing to absorb a trade-off in favor of defense.[16]

Taken together, the surveys presented to this point suggest caution in attempting to generalize about generational differences in public opinions of the defense budget. True, in France and the Netherlands the generations differ significantly in the direction suggested by theorists of generational change. However, the British responses are quite diverse, ranging from large age differences on the symbolic "strength" and trade-off questions to no age differences on defense spending in general. In West Germany, noticeable age differences are present in only one of five surveys from 1979 to 1983. Finally, in the "strengthen defense" question posed from 1979 to 1983, age differences appear volatile rather than firmly engrained.

But neither do the polls support the argument that the older members of the successful, welfare generation are less supportive of defense. Indeed, although there is nowhere strong support for increasing defense, among the minorities who do favor increases, support is moderately greater among older respondents. This is a significant finding, although it is part of a general pattern that is not favorable to increases in the defense budget. Overall, the percentage who would accept a sacrifice in favor of defense was nowhere greater than 17 per cent (in Great Britain). Reading across the surveys cited here and above, it is clear that the option of "keeping defense the same" is far and away the dominant view in all countries and all age groups. Recent surveys indicate that this pattern has changed little.

THE YOUNG, THE OLD, AND THE EDUCATED

Before examining the implications of these trends, it is important to examine a specific segment of the successor generation – those young people who took part in the tremendous expansion of European universities in the post-war period. As noted in previous chapters, theorists have emphasized the importance of the educated, successor generation for two reasons. First, they experienced the "cognitive" effects of higher education, which could produce a more cosmopolitan, "less threatened" set of attitudes. Secondly, the "socialization" effects of the 1960s are important to national security attitudes. The Vietnam War, the emergence of strategic parity, and the détente of the 1970s exposed this generation to considerable debate about the utility of military force. For both sets of reasons, would it not be on the question of defense spending that the successor generation reveals its doubts about the marginal utility of force?

Table 6.7 presents some evidence on the matter. The table shows the percentage of each age and educational group who preferred that the defense budget be decreased in 1980 and 1985. The "difference"

| | "Defense spending should be decreased" | | | | | |
| | Under 35 Education | | | Over 35 Education | | |
	Lower (%)	Higher (%)	Difference (%)	Lower (%)	Higher (%)	Difference (%)
FRANCE						
1980	28	51	+23	18	18	0
1985	15	27	+12	16	10	−66
BRITAIN						
1980	9	20	+11	9	14	+ 5
1985	26	33	+ 7	15	40	+25
WEST GERMANY						
1980	13	18	+ 5	15	19	+ 4
1985	43	64	+21	31	49	+18
NETHERLANDS						
1980	38	43	+ 5	30	20	−10
1984	33	58	+25	24	17	− 7

NOTE: In this and following tables, higher education is defined as nineteen years or older on completion of full-time education. The difference column subtracts the views of the lower educated from those of the higher educated.

SOURCE: US National Archives and Records Service, *USIA March 1980 Multiregional Security Survey*, and USIA, *November 1985 Post-Geneva Survey [Contractor's Reports]*.

column subtracts the views of those with lesser education from those with higher education.

The breakdown by both age and education generally indicates that the young educated are indeed more hostile to the defense budget. Once again, the difference is most consistent in France where in 1980 the young with higher education were almost twice as likely to favor cuts in defense than their cohorts. The gap is smaller in 1985 but visible none the less. The same is true in the Netherlands, but the successor generation is most distinct in 1984. In contrast, French and Dutch educated respondents over 35 are *less* in favor of cutting defense. In these two countries, clearly the group most hostile to defense spending are the young with higher educational attainments.

The successor generation is similarly distinct in Britain, although the differences are not as large as in France and Holland. In West Germany, there was only a minor generation gap in 1980, but by 1985 the young educated had become very critical of defense spending – much more so than their cohorts with lesser education. Reading down the table, then, by the mid 1980s a distinctively negative successor generation was visible in all four countries.

However, there is an additional finding of interest in Britain and West Germany. Especially in 1985 there is also evidence of greater sentiment to cut defense spending among *older* respondents with higher education. Recall that there was a similar pattern in some opinions of the military balance (the data were presented in Tables 3.7 and 3.8); in France and West Germany some of the older educated (like their successor generation counterparts) were more likely to see parity in the military balance. The pattern also characterizes French, German, and British opinions on the "defense spending in support of NATO" question presented above. In France and to a lesser extent in West Germany, both the younger *and* older respondents with higher education are more negative toward defense spending than are their contemporaries with lesser education. In Britain young graduates are not significantly different from their contemporaries, but the higher educated over age 35 are more critical of defense spending than those without similar education.[17]

Finally, the surveys inquiring of Europeans' desire to make a "stronger defense effort" confirm the consistency in the skepticism of both educated generations. Table 6.8 tracks age and educational differences in this question between 1979 and 1983. In both Britain and West Germany the older educated generation came to match the skepticism of the younger educated generation over time – in 1983 they were much less likely than their cohorts to agree on the strong defense question. In France and the Netherlands, the younger successor generation stands out as the most negative about "strengthening defense".

An additional finding of interest in Table 6.8 is the combination of generational effects and "period effects". Notice that the educated successor generation in Britain and West Germany reacted exactly the opposite from their cohorts to the increasing tensions of the 1980s. The former moved away from "strong defense", while the latter came to favor it more. Were period effects the only influence, we would expect the generations to move in unison. The fact that they react differently suggests that their generational experience had indeed left a predisposition to react differently to threat. In France

Table 6.8 Support for a "Stronger Defense" by Age and Education

| | Per cent "Agree" | | | | | |
| | Under 35 Education | | | Over 35 Education | | |
	Lower (%)	Higher (%)	Difference (%)	Lower (%)	Higher (%)	Difference (%)
FRANCE						
1979	47	31	−16	54	52	− 2
1981	70	59	−11	68	71	+ 3
1983	51	44	− 7	66	67	+ 1
BRITAIN						
1979	73	57	−16	85	77	− 8
1981	69	43	−26	81	56	−25
1983	68	54	−14	79	59	−20
WEST GERMANY						
1979	61	63	− 2	66	62	− 4
1981	66	54	−12	65	68	+ 3
1983	55	27	−32	56	42	−14
NETHERLANDS						
1979	55	42	−13	63	65	− 2
1981	49	29	−20	57	68	+11
1983	34	30	− 4	42	50	+ 8

SOURCE: See Table 6.4

and the Netherlands the successor generation actually moved closer to its cohorts.

Particularly in the latter countries, it is difficult to explain this movement, for on every other question described in this and previous chapters, the French and Dutch successor generations remained the most proportionately skeptical of security policies. It may be that the mention of "Western Europe" in the survey question colors responses. Or perhaps respondents felt that the controversy of 1983 – the INF deployment – had passed them by, for the decision did not affect France, and a Cabinet decision on deployment had been postponed in the Netherlands.

In any case, the examination of the combined effect of age and education provides strong support for the generational theorists. In questions on defense spending as well as "strong defense", the young educated are indeed the most hostile to the defense budget in every country. However, there is also evidence that the *older* educated are more hostile to defense spending than their cohorts, especially in Britain and West Germany, but also in France in some surveys. This could be taken as evidence that, for whatever reason, it is the experience of higher education in general rather than of generation that influences security opinions. Although the young educated are the more critical of defense spending than are the older educated, both groups are more critical than those without higher education. Could it be that the education of these groups taught them that investment in the defense budget was of little marginal utility?

THE LEFT AND THE RIGHT

One clue is Inglehart's finding, described above, that attitudes toward defense spending remain strongly correlated with ideology and party affiliation. This correlation is consistent with the argument that traditional party positions on both public spending and security issues provide an orientation in an area where public attention or information is generally low. This interpretation is reinforced by the fact that on issues of budgetary politics, European parties have a well-developed set of positions that have been underscored recently by the growing conflict between defense and social priorities and by the general polarization of the parties on economic and budgetary issues.

That polarization is clearly evident in the variety of polls on defense spending brought together in Table 6.9. The table summarizes *opposition* to defense spending. Two types of survey are set out in the table. The portion on the left displays the percentage who favored decreases in defense spending in USIA polls. The portion on the right shows the percentage who *disagreed* in the Eurobarometer questions on "strengthening defense".

Table 6.9 reveals a uniquely uniform pattern: in every country there is a clear alignment of views along the Left–Right spectrum. Generally, the polarization is greatest in France and the Netherlands, where the gap among parties reaches as much as 30 to 35 percentage points, but the distance between parties of the Left and the Right is also evident in Britain and to a lesser but noticeable extent in West Germany. Not surprisingly, the French and West German surveys also show the near-total rejection of defense spending among supporters of the Ecologist and Green Parties.

The USIA surveys in Table 6.9 do not allow conclusions about

Table 6.9   *Opposition to Defense Spending by Political Party Affiliation*

	USIA surveys					Eurobarometers		
	May 1979 (%)	March 1980 (%)	Oct. 1980 (%)	July 1982 (%)	Nov. 1985 (%)	April 1979 (%)	Oct. 1981 (%)	April 1983 (%)
FRANCE								
Total population	30	25	43	24	16	53	33	43
Ecologist	–	44	63	42	29	67	50	66
PCF	44	45	72	36	26	75	63	56
Socialist	35	29	48	25	19	57	36	51
UDF (Giscard)	16	9	20	17	16	42	17	29
Gaullist (RPR)	17	7	16	11	14	28	13	27
BRITAIN								
Total population	–	10	18	16	28	22	28	29
Labour	–	14	25	23	40	35	31	43
Social Democrats	–	–	–	19	36	–	27	32
Liberal	–	11	18	14	–	25	32	22
Conservative	–	4	8	6	15	14	17	19
WEST GERMANY								
Total population	11	40	21	34	36	35	36	50
Greens	–	64	69	70	71	69	92	94
Social Democrats	14	42	19	39	37	40	41	60
Free Democrats	14	49	25	35	36	35	41	46
CDU/CSU	7	31	15	21	30	30	25	34
NETHERLANDS								
Total population	10	–	33	–	29	43	48	62
PvdA (Labour)	11	–	47	–	43	57	63	79
D'66	14	–	36	–	32	51	67	72
CDA	4	–	13	–	17	24	33	44
Liberals (VVD)	1	–	11	–	5	30	21	41

NOTE: Figures displayed for USIA surveys are the "decrease" response to defense spending queries; for *Eurobarometer* surveys, they are the percentage responding "disagree" to the query on "strong defense", as listed in Table 6.4. For all countries, total population percentages include responses of parties not shown separately.

Surveys are not always available for the years listed. The following are taken from adjacent years: Netherlands 1979 (1978), 1985 (1984); West Germany 1982 (1983).

SOURCES: For *Eurobarometer* surveys, Table 6.4; for the 1980 USIA surveys, Table 6.5. Additional figures are computed from Machine-Readable Division, US National Archives and Record Service, *USIA Per-*

change in the degree of party polarization *within* each country, for the surveys employed different question wordings in each year. The Eurobarometers, in contrast, were posed identically in 1979, 1981, and 1983, and the changing distance among party views can therefore be traced in light of the rapid changes in the international climate that spanned these surveys.

The evolution of *French* opinion once again reveals deep divisions, and it also provides evidence of the greater significance of party affiliation as compared to generational or educational factors. The three French parties of the Center-Left to Center-Right (Socialists, UDF, RPR) show a consistent difference of at least twenty percentage points in *all three surveys*. And whereas age and educational differences in these same French surveys fluctuate (recall Figure 6.1 and Table 6.8), this breakdown by political party shows that partisan polarization did not. For example, the consensus *between* age groups in 1981 masked considerable partisan differences *within* both the younger and older samples.

West German opinions are similar. Age differences in 1979 and 1981 were minor, but Table 6.9 shows that the views of SPD and CDU/CSU supporters differed by 10 to 15 percentage points in those same years. By 1983, when age and educational differences had begun to reflect the polarization of the West German security debate, party differences had also deepened considerably. In fact, the West German surveys show the most dramatic increase in the depth of partisan polarization over the 1979 to 1983 period.

Finally, the British and Dutch responses provide slightly different variants. In both countries, the distance between the labour parties (Labour, PvdA) and the more conservative parties (CDA, VVD) is deep and stable from 1979 to 1983. Unlike the French and West German figures, which show some variation in the degree of partisan conflict, the British and Dutch figures suggest a less changing landscape of political difference among major parties, but it is certainly a divided one.

Table 6.9 – cont.

ceptions of the Soviet Military Threat, West Germany [France] (Washington, D.C.: Study nos I7904.RS260 and I7904.RS220); *1978 NATO Summit Rider: Netherlands* (Washington, D.C.: Study no. 7801); and *USIA July 1982 NATO Summit Follow-Up* (Washington, D.C.: Study nos I8230 and I8235). The remaining years are drawn from Office of Research, USIA, *November 1985 Post-Geneva Survey [Contractor's Reports]*, and *1984 Security Issues Survey [Contractor's Reports]*.

In summary, a variety of surveys using different question wording over a number of years reveals a clear patterning of opinions along party lines, a pattern that is consistent across all the four countries under study. The diverse selection of surveys in Table 6.9 therefore suggest that partisan affiliations are more consistently related to opinions of the defense budget than are the "new" cleavages resulting from generational change or the expansion of university education in the 1960s and 1970s.[18]

There is one potential qualification to this conclusion. If the pattern of partisan alignments on defense issues results from a disproportionate degree of partisan polarization within particular groups – such as the young or the educated – it would be misleading to so characterize the entire population. For example, since there is evidence that the young educated identify disproportionately with parties of the Left, the patterns observed in Table 6.9 are conceivably due to concentration of the young and educated in the ranks of parties on the Left of the political spectrum.

Further examination of the defense spending surveys suggests that no such simple explanation will do. The breakdown of responses by party affiliation, education, and age produces a complicated table, but close study of these figures reveals an interesting picture. Table 6.10 shows this three-way breakdown for the "decrease" response from the March 1980 USIA survey. In France the alignment of views according to party holds for *all* age and educational groups. In fact, the addition of party views differentiates some groups that otherwise appear homogeneous. In this 1980 survey, those older than 35 show no difference by level of education – 18 per cent of both groups favor a decrease in defense spending. But we can also see that *within* the over-35 groups, there is a substantial degree of division by party affiliation, a pattern that holds for both younger groups as well.

But the French data also confirm generational effects, for the young in general are more hostile to defense spending, and the young with higher education are both most hostile to defense spending *and* the most severely polarized by party. Not only is this group the most negative about defense spending, it is also the most divided within itself. For example, among the higher educated under 35, the gap between supporters of the Socialist Party and supporters of the UDF is 34 percentage points. Supporters of these two parties who are over 35 are divided by only 13 percentage points.

The breakdown for Great Britain produces a slightly different story. Once again, a division along party lines characterizes most age

*Table 6.10   Opposition to Defense Spending by Age, Education, and
Political Party Affiliation (March 1980)*

| | "Decrease defense spending" | | | | | |
| | Under 35 Education | | | Over 35 Education | | |
	Lower (%)	Higher (%)	Difference (%)	Lower (%)	Higher (%)	Difference (%)
FRANCE						
Total population	**28**	**51**	**+23**	**18**	**18**	**0**
PCF	37	75	+38	48	50	+ 2
Socialist	31	53	+22	20	18	− 2
UDF (Giscard)	6	19	+13	9	5	− 4
Gaullist (RPR)	13	0	−13	7	0	− 7
n=	225	116		441	79	
BRITAIN						
Total population	**9**	**20**	**+11**	**9**	**14**	**+ 5**
Labour	8	35	+27	14	33	+19
Liberal	8	22	+14	10	29	+19
Conservative	6	9	+ 3	3	3	0
n=	257	80		507	51	
WEST GERMANY						
Total population	**44**	**48**	**+ 4**	**39**	**40**	**+ 1**
Social Democrats	51	60	+ 9	37	64	+27
Free Democrats	55	57	+ 2	41	*	*
CDU/CSU	23	25	+ 2	36	25	− 9
n=	192	41		443	31	

SOURCE: See Table 6.5.

and educational groups. We have previously seen that there are no simple age differences in this British survey and that hostility to defense spending was highest among the better educated of *both* age groups. Here we can see that both age groups with higher education are also the most polarized by party affiliation. In fact, it is apparently the greater hostility of Labour and Liberal party members to defense spending that underlies the more negative opinion of the older educated that we saw earlier. Among older Conservatives, the higher educated do not differ from their cohorts. In Britain, then, hostility to defense spending is greatest in both the younger and older educated Left.

Table 6.10 shows that West German opinions are more similar to the British than to the French, although particular caution is war-ranted with the German survey due to the extremely small size of the university-educated sample. Generally, the alignment of defense spending views follows the Left–Right spectrum of German parties. Like the British, however, the university-educated of both age groups are more negative about defense spending than are their cohorts, but this skepticism of the university-educated is confined to the parties of the Center and the Left (FDP and SPD). Older, educated Social Democrats in particular are much more hostile to defense spending than are their age cohorts with lesser education.

Finally, it is worth noting that this pattern of more critical opinions among both younger and older members of the educated Left is not confined to the 1980 survey. It also appears in West Germany in two of the three *Eurobarometer* surveys on "strong defense", and it is clearest in the 1983 survey – when defense debates had polarized the German parties. In Britain the pattern is evident in one of the three surveys. As in Table 6.10, the French and the Dutch do not show the same pattern.

A SYNTHESIS

Opinion surveys since 1979 show a strong pattern of partisan align-ment on defense spending. This finding is uniquely uniform cross-nationally. The strength of this alignment probably results from several factors, including the role of parties as "cue givers" in an area where the policy views of many citizens are normally inchoate or nonexistent. Where there is an existing tradition of party conflict on defense or budgetary issues, party loyalty provides an organizing device for the general public. Furthermore, party orientations on the appropriate distribution of budgetary resources have been high-lighted in the recent past by increasing debate over whether and where to cut government budgets.[19]

None the less, this finding is overlayed by a second: the successor generation of the young and educated are indeed the most hostile to defense spending. But the data also reveal some familiar faces. In Britain and West Germany, the older "élite" of the educated Left is also disproportionately hostile to defense spending. In any case, the strength and consistency of the correspondence between party affilia-tion and views on defense spending means that, in general, know-ledge of a person's party membership would provide the single best clue to opinions of defense spending. Although there has been much discussion of the effects of social changes that have produced "new" political cleavages, these analyses suggest that the primary line of division within European publics is the familiar one of Left and Right.

SUMMARY, CAVEATS, AND IMPLICATIONS

I began this chapter in a search for general lines of division in European opinions of defense spending. Whether the focus is generational change, the increasing constraints of welfare politics and the "successful" generation, or the presumably rebellious group of 1960s university students, I have pursued hypotheses regarding social and political factors that should affect citizen views of the monetary resources allocated to defense.

The surveys examined in this chapter cast doubt on general explanations based on generation, education, budgetary self-interest or any other factor taken in isolation. There *is* consistent evidence of a "successor" generation phenomenon, but it is overlayed and complicated by strong partisan divisions that encompass all subgroups of the population – but especially the older educated. Put simply, defense spending is an issue that divides the entire population along partisan lines, but the successor generation is both more critical and more divided than others.

However, despite the strength of the *correlation* between party affiliation and views of defense spending, several caveats are in order about the political significance of partisan versus generational or educational factors. In the first place, it is fairly obvious that the structure of citizen opinions in a nationwide survey do not automatically translate into influence on government policy. Normally, it is in fact useful to know the correlation between social and political characteristics and the policy views of all members of the population, for citizens will indeed express their preferences in a regular political decision – the vote in elections. However, between elections most citizens do not actively express their views. Rather, the expression of political views is usually dominated by the most organized, motivated, and informed members of the electorate. Most analysts agree that the young and educated are more likely to take such an active interest in politics.[20]

As we have seen, it is indeed young and educated citizens who are most hostile to defense spending and most divided among themselves on the issue. A focus on the partisan alignment of the entire population should not distract attention from these numerically small but potentially more influential sectors of the electorate. Moreover, the significance of the younger generation is quite clear in one very important respect: their support for the "new" parties that are clearly more hostile than any group to traditional defense policies. A singular feature of the young, university-educated is their support for the new "anti-party" parties; the Greens in West Germany and the Ecologists in France.[21] Not surprisingly, these parties are the most hostile to defense spending in any country. Moreover, despite their small numbers, they may exert an impact in two very important ways. First, if they gain in electoral strength, their numbers and policy views will be crucial to the stability and platforms of fragile coalition governments. Secondly, by unsettling the electoral landscape, they may trigger a shift in the positions of other parties who must compete with them at the all-important electoral margin. In short, despite their minority status, these parties – and their young adherents – may take on a significance that outweighs their numbers.

None the less, if these smaller groups and parties represent the politically crucial result of social and political change in Western societies, the evidence also shows the continuing importance of traditional lines of political conflict. Even if one accepts that younger (or older) educated activists are likely to have an impact in policy debates on most issues, they may not dominate the politics of the defense budget. Although the older, more established members of society may not take to the streets or the halls of parliaments when the issue is nuclear weapons or the utility of military alliance, on budget issues there is a strong network of interest and party groupings that can assert influence. Moreover, among all older citizens there are still strong partisan divisions that will surely complicate debates about the appropriate level of defense spending. In Britain and West Germany, the "élite" of older university graduates who identify with parties of the Center and Left are every bit as skeptical of defense spending as their younger cohorts. Thus, although the young may be the most vocal, considerable potential for partisan conflict exists beyond the problem of the young so often cited by policy makers.

The image of a "glacier" process is once again appropriate: to the extent that the young and the educated have developed distinct views on defense, generational change will complicate politics by revealing a more vocal, informed *and* polarized voice in policy-making. Yet a considerable residue of traditional partisan conflict on defense issues remains below the "tip" of the generational glacier, and these divisions are equally significant on budgetary issues. In summary, opinions of defense spending demonstrate the need for synthesis in explaining security attitudes. Traditional ideological conflicts over the utility of force and the precedence of social spending remain clear in the polls, despite much discussion of a "new" politics of national security. The views of the successor generation magnify this division, but the fact that it is confined to the young, educated *Left* suggests that in substance the conflict is similar.

Finally, we should also note that public opinions on defense spending present something of a unique case among the issues studied in this book: there is a little of every social cleavage in opinions. This by itself should indicate caution in generalizing about the public's stand on defense issues. But it may also say something about the peculiar nature of defense spending as a political issue. In this chapter I have speculated along with other theorists about which groups should favor defense spending and which should oppose it, but, by and large, the overall population percentages are very telling: very few people favor increases in defense spending. The most that is conceded is that the defense budget should stay the same. In times of budgetary retrenchment, perhaps the message of the polls is that every social and political grouping has become part of the post-war "successful" generation.

This presents a dismal picture for European governments under pressure to reform or modernize their defense establishments. At a time of rising defense costs and budget austerity, they face a public ambivalence about defense spending that is complicated by broad partisan differences and vocal hostility from the young and the educated of all ages. Does public opinion thus confirm what is now widely assumed: that European governments have no room for maneuver as they attempt to modernize their forces and respond to calls for lowering the nuclear threshold?

The answer is ambiguous. True, public opinion in all European countries is hardly favorable, but that has been the case virtually since the beginning of the post-war period. European defense budgets did not stagnate as a result. In the historical surveys cited at the beginning of this chapter, support for increasing defense never exceeded 20 per cent of the population of any country but Britain, and the "guns–butter" choice in surveys almost always yielded a preference for social spending. Yet defense budgets in these four countries increased in real terms by a yearly average of 1.88 per cent during the 1960s and by 2.75 per cent during the 1970s. Indeed, defense increases have been *highest* in the countries with the least supportive public opinion (France, West Germany, Netherlands) and *lowest* in Great Britain, where opinion has been more tolerant – if volatile. Excluding the British, the average defense increases of the other three countries was 2.6 per cent in the 1960s and 2.82 per cent in the 1970s. In short, the historical impact of public opinion on actual defense spending does not support the popular picture of European defense budgets held hostage to a recalcitrant public opinion.

Of course, current conditions are unique in the post-war period. Although opinion surveys indicate that hostility to defense spending does not arise from a fundamental "anti-defense" mood, they also reveal a desire to avoid cuts in social and other domestic programs. And for the first time, European governments now feel constrained in their ability to avoid such trade-offs through deficit spending or higher taxes. Concern about "Eurosclerosis" and international competitiveness has brought with it a distinctly cautious mood about deficits and taxes.

Even so, the difficulties should not be exaggerated, for there are several reasons why public opinion might again tolerate modest increases in defense. First, while growth in the European economies remains halting, it has averaged 2 to 3 per cent since recovery began in 1982.[22] Although hardly spectacular, we should recall that the defense budget increases of the 1970s were financed on the basis of a 3 to 4 per cent annual rate of real economic growth.

Secondly, there are signs that Europeans have begun to accept marginal cuts (if not drastic reductions) in civilian programs. There is even evidence that tax increases would be accepted if necessary to avoid budgetary trade-offs. Tellingly, this sentiment is most noticeable in Britain and the United States – the two countries that have most increased defense and most slowed the growth in social spending. The response of the British public has been particularly noteworthy during Thatcher's government. Between 1979 and 1985 the percentage of the British who preferred higher taxes to cuts in social programs grew from 37 per cent to 63 per cent. Other European countries also show a preference for taxes over cuts in services.[23]

Thirdly, the general economic malaise of the 1980s has distracted attention from the fact that European governments have already

considerably consolidated their budget deficits. In addition, with the
reduction of American interest rates and the decline of the dollar,
there has been some relief for European concerns about the effect of
deficits on domestic investment. There may even be some room for
modest increases in deficit spending. In fact, we are now witnessing
calls for Europeans to reflate their economies to support global
demand. In the same vein, although observers often suppose that
there is a political ceiling on defense budgets, it is also true that
economic considerations provide a floor. Jobs in the steel, aircraft,
and shipbuilding industries are precious at times of stagnation in
employment, and these sectors are often sensitive for reasons of
regional politics. Surveys reveal this sensitivity. According to USIA
polls, among those who oppose increasing defense, half in France
and one-third in other countries would change their minds if defense
increases would protect jobs.[24]

Finally, we saw in Chapter 4 that there is overwhelming sentiment
against first or even early use of nuclear weapons. The "double-zero"
arms control agreement may increase this sentiment by focusing
debates on the use of tactical nuclear weapons. Together, these
forces might provide the basis for consensus on the need to modernize or reorganize conventional forces. It is true that, when asked
directly, Europeans generally feel that conventional forces are
"adequate". However, fragmented polls suggest that this sentiment
is not absolute. In the Netherlands, for example, support for increasing defense spending "if that would reduce NATO's need to use
nuclear weapons" was 41 per cent in 1984 – higher than in any other
poll on defense spending. More significantly, the normally critical
successor generation in the Netherlands does not dissent on this
question: their support is identical to the general populations. Also in
1984, 40 per cent of the British population and 54 per cent of the
successor generation felt that NATO should strengthen its conventional forces rather than its nuclear weapons.[25]

Taken together, the factors discussed above suggest that there is a
potential coalition in favor of modest increases in defense to improve
conventional defense and contribute to economic growth. The incremental growth of 2–3 per cent that characterized the defense budgets
of the 1970s are not out of the question. To be sure, there are many
"ifs" in this scenario that mirror the more general economic uncertainties of the immediate future. Clearly, one would not expect
defense increases beyond the levels of the past. And whether modest
defense increases are sufficient to the Alliance's needs is a question

that will surely be debated.[26] None the less, past patterns would suggest that *some* increases are politically possible. That in itself is a considerable challenge to the assumptions that underlie current discussions of NATO's strategic choices.

7 Two Track: Continuity, Change, and Consensus in the Politics of European Security

In many ways, the turbulent years of the 1980s were not really unique in the history of the NATO Alliance. As early as the 1950s, popular opposition to nuclear weapons had brought demonstrators to the streets of European cities. Even among governments, the dilemma of how to implement NATO's policy of flexible response has been a persistent and seemingly insoluble source of anxiety and disagreement. The so-called "out-of-area" question and disputes over East--West trade are also longstanding. From an historical perspective, the quarrels of the recent past seem less than novel.

What made the 1980s unique was the increasing importance of public opinion and the concern that was expressed by governments about the breakdown of the domestic security consensus. Unlike the 1950s, this time public concern seemed more deeply rooted, unlikely to pass as it had before. Although the causes of change were as yet unclear, it seemed to many that neutralism and pacifism had somehow taken hold among broad sectors of the populace. Public opinion surveys provided ample cause for concern. In newspapers, magazines, and even scholarly works, public opinion surveys seemed to document a rise in neutralism, an emerging refusal to spend money for defense, and a rejection of the deterrence strategy that had guided the Alliance for many years. For many observers, this collapse in the security consensus would bring profound change, if not in the Alliance itself, then certainly in the policies that NATO could pursue with assurance of domestic support. Defence Minister Pym solemnly warned in 1982 that the job for NATO governments was no less than to recapture the "hearts and minds" of their citizens.

CHANGE, CONTINUITY, AND CONSENSUS

As I argued in the opening chapter of this book, much of the concern for the state of public opinion was based on a superficial reading of the evidence. Single polls were used to infer historical trends, and flawed or hypothetical question wording formed the basis for sweeping judgments about citizen views. Admittedly, much of this analysis was limited by gaps in available sources, for the eruption of public concern had found scholars with no comparative, historical analysis of public opinions. Moreover, even comparative surveys lacked the depth and detail that was needed to test the sensitivity of public opinion to the trade-offs inherent in security policy. Until this information could be collated and analyzed, researchers could not go forward with the "natural experiment" of comparing responses to a large number and variety of survey questions.

The historical trends examined in this book provide evidence that continuity in public opinion was far more prevalent than change. This is particularly clear on three issues. First, attachment to the NATO Alliance has remained very strong. Indeed, the evidence suggests that the attachment to NATO is even stronger than it was in the 1950s, when the options available to Europeans seemed more open than they are today. Even when confronted with a number of alternatives that appeal to other sensitivities (such as nervousness with American policies), Europeans continue to choose NATO as the preferred framework of their national security policies.

A similar continuity characterizes opinions of defense spending, which have been surprisingly stable during the 1970s and 1980s. It is true that there is little enthusiasm for increasing defense spending, but this has been the case since at least the 1960s. If a consensus on the defense budget has been lost, the erosion did not begin with the defense debates of the 1980s. This characterization is also true of opinions on the nuclear issue, although here the historical evidence is not as extensive as it is in other policy areas. Certainly, it is clear that the public's objection to the possible *use* of nuclear weapons is longstanding, but as I argued in Chapter 4, this is neither surprising nor particularly unique to public opinion. The use of nuclear weapons is a distasteful possibility that will hardly find endorsement in hypothetical questions. As for deterrence, there are recent surveys which suggest that – despite the outcry over INF – public opinion accepts the argument made so persistently by European governments (especially after the announcement of SDI): given the constraints, nuclear weapons are necessary for deterrence in Europe. To be sure, the public strongly supports arms control initiatives, and citizens were opposed to any INF deployment that was not accompanied by negotiation. Yet it is hard to identify any radical change in such a view, and in any case it accorded with the INF decision that NATO had formulated in 1979. It was a "dual track" approach based on deployment and negotiation.

None the less, these continuities were also accompanied by change. The most dramatic change is the deterioration in European images of America and in their confidence in the wisdom of the dominant Alliance partner. To judge from the polls, these negative images are profound. Recent years have brought little improvement in these readings, and perhaps understandably so. Beginning with President Reagan's announcement of the SDI initiative, and continuing with the Reykjavik summit and the Iran/Contra scandal, the substance and process of American foreign policy have taken a heavy beating, from press and European governments alike. Of course, a major question is whether this decline in Europeans' confidence will be arrested or reversed. As noted in Chapter 4, the American image has declined before (especially at the time of the Watergate scandal), but it eventually recovered. The answer to this question depends on what one sees as the cause of the decline, a question I address below.

The second issue on which there has been change is in estimates of the military balance, although the change is not really of recent origin. Beginning in the early 1970s, Europeans saw a decline in American (and NATO) military power, a perception that was accompanied by estimates of growing Soviet power and especially by the growing perception of parity in the military balance. This change will surprise few military analysts. None the less, it *is* surprising that, contrary to what many strategists expected, these trends in estimates of the military balance did not drastically alter perceptions of security. There is hardly optimism concerning NATO's ability to deter the Soviet Union, but to judge from historical polls, this is not new (and perhaps not even surprising). Yet the change in perceptions of power has had a significant political consequence. Although the evidence is limited by the paucity of historical surveys available for reanalysis, more recent polls suggest that the emergence of parity has polarized opinions of national security. Not only is the perception of parity an increasing point of view; those who see parity also feel most secure and are less receptive to the view that additional increments of military force are necessary. As I concluded in Chapter 3, the most significant impact of the changing military balance was not, as many feared, to make Europeans feel less secure. The effect was to make security more ambiguous and thus more debatable.

EXPLAINING TRENDS IN PUBLIC OPINION

These historical trends raise an important question: why has there been continuity in some public opinions and change in others? Three answers seem pertinent.

The first is the role of structural factors, especially those that are rooted in the balance of power and the national interests of the Western states. These considerations are often neglected in studies of public opinion, both by the pollsters who administer surveys and by those would interpret them. Surveys often offer respondents a number of hypothetical options, but in reality both citizens and governments are more constrained in their choices. This is particularly clear in surveys that inquire of the utility of the NATO Alliance. As argued earlier, a dominant explanation for the longevity of NATO is structural: given the East–West (and European) power structure and the unpopularity of alternative security arrangements, NATO has been the option most favored by governments. The Alliance may be *faute de mieux*, but from an analytical perspective that is precisely the point. Thus, despite a number of polls which show the popularity of hypothetical options, such as neutrality, a "Gaullist" membership in NATO, or a stronger European "pillar", surveys which reflect the choices available to Europeans usually find a preference for NATO. Moreover, it is likely that opinions will continue to reflect the options available to Europeans. As I noted in Chapter 5, there is indeed some movement among European governments to strengthen the European pillar, but barring drastic changes in Soviet policy – or the French policy of deterrence – it is unlikely that these changes will go far enough to produce a drastic shift in public opinion. Unless there is a fundamental change in the power relations that underlie European choices, public opinion is unlikely to shift away from its preference for alliance in NATO. Ironically, then, although recent concerns about public opinion suggested that the Alliance was eroding from *within*, the evidence suggests that public opinion is conditioned more by *external* factors, an observation that will please scholars whose theories are based on the structure of the international system.[1]

A second explanation for the coexistence of change and continuity is that some public opinions are conditioned by factors unrelated to national security. The best example is opinions of defense spending, which remained relatively stable during the 1970s and 1980s despite changes in other opinions and despite the fact that the 1970s were at least partially characterized by détente and arms control. This stability was unexpected. During the détente period, some observers feared that successful arms control would erode public support for the defense budget, and during the INF outcry, it was feared that support for defense spending would fall victim to a more general trend toward antimilitarism. None of this happened, it seems, because the public judged defense spending on budgetary rather than security grounds. During the 1970s, defense increases were tolerated because both guns and butter were increasing. During the tight budgetary situation of the early 1980s, governments restrained defense spending, and certainly in Europe they did not engage in an all-out attack on social spending. Thus, the public's long-held preference for civilian spending – evident since the 1960s – was not challenged.[2] The prediction would therefore be that public opinion will tolerate the defense budget so long as governments do not engage in a "trade-off" that favors defense. For governments, this may very well allow little room for maneuver. On the other hand, it would also suggest that support for defense spending will be immune from wider controversies surrounding security policy.

A final reason for the coexistence of change and continuity is found in the obvious distinction between opinions that are rooted in long-term forces and those that react to short-term forces. Long-term forces are anchored in processes of political and social change. Examples would be the evolution of the military balance or the expansion of educational levels among the population. Short-term forces, in contrast, are events and forces that *may* pass quickly. Examples would include a temporary downturn in economic fortunes or a global event that catches the notice of the public before passing from attention.

On past experience, the rapid decline in Europeans' confidence in the United States should be seen as a reaction to short-term events. As I noted in Chapter 4, the American image has declined before, as at the time of the Watergate episode, but it eventually recovered. This suggested that Europeans' views of the United States had not changed fundamentally, a conclusion supported by parallel polls which showed that Europeans continued to perceive a harmony of interests and values with the United States. This sentiment continued through the mid 1980s even as broader assessments of the United States had deteriorated. If this hypothesis is correct, one should ascribe the recent deterioration of European views to the extraordinary confluence of (short-term) events that characterized the early 1980s. In the first place, it was a time of intense crisis, with events in Iran, Afghanistan, and Poland following in quick succession. As we have seen, fear was at an extremely high level, and there is little doubt that Europeans reacted negatively to what they saw as an unnecessarily bellicose American response to these events. These feelings were reinforced by bitter transatlantic exchanges on economic issues.

If these opinions were indeed a reaction to the events and policies of the moment and not the culmination of a long-term trend toward distrust in the United States, there is clearly the possibility that they will improve. Recent events have made the testing of this hypothesis difficult, for the Iran/Contra controversy, with its much-publicized failures in American decision-making, could hardly have improved perceptions of confidence. Yet this scandal too will pass, and in any case the United States now has a new administration. On past experience, what conditions could lead to a short-term *improvement* in European confidence?

To judge from the events of the 1980s, European public opinion seems to mirror the persistent urgings of its leaders for a consistent American approach to East–West relations that reflects the Harmel formula of strength *and* negotiation (it would help were there no further scandals). This interpretation would suggest that a consistent, balanced approach to East–West relations would lead to an improvement in Europeans' confidence. Indeed, the paradox of the domestic "crisis" of the 1980s is that the elements of consensus were there all along. Attitudes towards nuclear weapons had already improved by 1982, and as we have seen repeatedly, other basic attitudes on security issues had never really changed. In many ways, then, there is an optimistic outlook for the Alliance and its leaders. On the fundamentals of security policy, the basis of domestic consensus is still in place. What remains is to find a transatlantic meeting of the minds on the proper mix of policies for dealing with the Soviets. There is nothing in past opinion surveys to suggest that this consensus will require successful arms control, cuts in defense spending, reform of NATO, or change in nuclear strategy. Given the alarm about pacifism in recent years, this is an ironic conclusion, but it is supported by the available evidence.

Yet there is one sense in which consensus formation has been rendered more difficult. One long-term trend – the emergence and perception of parity – has polarized opinions. It is inevitable that short-term events will interact with this trend to challenge governments. Crises are not completely preventable, and in any case the dynamics of the East–West arms competition will continue to present both governments and publics with challenges to existing policies. In an age of ambiguous parity, the relevance of military solutions to these challenges is by no means clear. The pursuit of a common approach will also be complicated by growing polarization *within* European publics about the proper balance of strength and negotiation in East–West relations.

FAMILIAR FACES: ARE THE OLD POLITICS THE NEW POLITICS OF NATIONAL SECURITY?

In the midst of NATO's domestic controversies of the early 1980s, the theory of generational change was the dominant explanation for the apparent erosion of the security consensus. Citizens who had grown to political maturity in the secure and prosperous environment of the 1960s and 1970s were less attuned to the priority of national security and less attached to Western institutions, such as NATO, that had been formed during the Cold War period. Along with broader value changes that had brought a "new politics" to Western systems, both scholars and politicians predicted fundamental changes in the politics of national security.

However, the initial rush of scholarship that examined the generational hypothesis brought more confusion than confirmation. There were numerous surveys in which the views of the young were more critical of security policies, but there were also a number of surveys showing a similarity of views among the young and the old. Age differences in surveys also varied by country and by the time of the survey, and they were not uniform across security issues. When a variety of individual surveys were collected and compared, it turned out that age differences in survey responses were far less prominent than the polarization of opinions along the traditional "old politics" continuum defined by partisan affiliation.[3]

As noted in Chapter 2, the problem with this early body of research was its univariate focus and secondary methodology. Because researchers were limited to the published percentages of secondary sources, they were of necessity constrained by the usual "one way" breakdown of opinions by age, education, party affiliation, or other factors. Although one could compare differences among age groups or adherents of different parties, it was impossible to combine these breakdowns in a detailed analysis of opinions *within* particular groups. Was the concentration of critical opinions in the parties of the Left confined to the views of younger members of those parties? Was it not possible, as generational theorists such as Inglehart and Szabo had in fact argued, that the real source of generational change was in the combined impact of age and education? If so, would it not be more revealing to examine opinions *within* generations according to their level of education?

The analyses in this book have shown that these sorts of question are crucial, and – as is usual as research progresses – they suggest that the answers are more complex than any single-factor theory would have it. Certainly, the strength and generality of the partisan factor has been repeatedly confirmed. Across countries, generations, and educational levels, the correlation of partisan affiliation with opinions of security issues is far and away the most consistent finding.

None the less, the data also show that the generational thesis, somewhat discounted in recent scholarship, should be resurrected. Especially in France and the Netherlands, the successor generation of the young educated shows consistently more critical views in almost all policy areas. In West Germany, there is also a successor generation effect, although it is not as strong or consistent as in France and the Netherlands. Only in Britain is there lesser evidence of a more critical younger generation, but even there it appears occasionally. As suggested at several points in this book, then, a detailed analysis of opinions *between* and *within* different groups in the population suggest the applicability of a "glacier" metaphor. Within all age and educational groups, public opinions are aligned along the "old" politics continuum of Left and Right. Yet in terms of both the singularity of their opinions and the degree of partisan polarization, the young educated – the generation of the "new" politics – also show a distinct profile.

These correlations are now well-established, but it remains to *explain* them. Later in this chapter I will argue the importance of party leaders as "cue givers" who contributed to the polarization of their followers' opinions, but here it is important to acknowledge the substantial historical basis of these ideological differences. Ideological conflict on issues of national security is nothing new in Western democracies. Especially since the Enlightenment, conflicting evaluations of military force have been part of the more general ideological division of Left and Right. Whether or not one chooses to accept the "Idealist/Realist" dichotomy, it seems clear that disagreement about the utility of military force is a central component of this ideological conflict. For the Left, military force is not the solution – it is the problem. The accumulation of arms and the balancing of power are themselves the causes of war. Real security can only be achieved through negotiation or through the integration of societies through law and trade.

This ideological conflict was not confined to the late nineteenth century, when Socialists and Communists added the critique of capitalism and imperialism to the classic idealist argument. In France, it was an influence in the Socialist Party well into the post-war period. In West Germany, proposals for collective security arrangements were part of the Social Democratic attack on rearmament, and of course the SPD became the party of détente *par excellence*. In the Netherlands, the Labour Party has long argued for a policy of détente to supplement deterrence. Given the dominance of economic issues in Britain, perhaps it is not surprising that ideological conflict has found its greatest expression in defense budget debates, but the competing nuclear policies of Labour and Tory are also longstanding.

Of course, a challenge to this interpretation is found in the observation that these conflicts were overcome in the security "consensus" of the 1960s. Beginning with the Bad Godesberg program of the German Social Democrats in 1959, the parties of the European Left came to embrace both NATO and its policies. Even old quarrels, some of them transatlantic, were muted, as in the "end of ideology" that accompanied the liberal welfare economies and open trading system of Bretton Woods.

There is little question that the 1960s were a period of muted conflict on security issues, but one must ask if this "consensus" resulted from a *convergence* of party approaches or from a *compromise* of those approaches. The latter characterization is more convincing. In fact, one might argue that the NATO consensus of the 1960s was a classic compromise, for it combined by addition the competing preferences of Left and Right. Certainly, the maintenance of NATO commitments and the adoption of flexible response signalled an acceptance of the central components of a policy of strength. Yet the 1960s were also a time of "mini-détente" and arms control. Indeed, the US–Soviet negotiations of the 1960s brought a series of agreements that have not been matched since (seven agreements were signed and ratified between 1961 and 1968). Finally, NATO institutionalized the hybrid policy of strength and negotiation in its 1967 Harmel Doctrine. Henceforth, the official policy on which the consensus rested was the "dual track" compromise of Harmel:

> The Atlantic Alliance has two main functions. Its first is to maintain adequate military strength and political solidarity to deter aggression . . . its second function [is] to pursue the search for progress towards a more stable relationship in which the underlying political issues can be solved. Military security and a policy of détente are not contradictory but complementary.[4]

If this consensus has now broken, it seems less because of "new" views on the part of Left and Right than because of the reassertion of their respective emphases on strength or negotiation as the crucial component of security policy. Faced with the security challenges of the late 1970s and early 1980s, Left and Right reverted to traditional views, and as several surveys reviewed above have shown, the polarization grew more severe as the 1980s wore on. Initially sensitized by the INF decision that had carried forward the "dual track" approach, the parties were increasingly polarized as the Left urged negotiation and the Right emphasized the need to maintain strength and deterrence.

West German politics illustrated this process dramatically. While journalists had discovered the successor generation as the source of pacifism in the wake of the INF controversy, a quick survey of the political scene in Bonn revealed many familiar faces from the debates of the 1950s and the détente battles of the early 1970s. Although public attention was focused on such "new" figures as Petra Kelly of the Green Party, the initial criticisms of INF (and earlier, the neutron bomb) came from such old hands as Wehner, Brandt, and Bahr. Later proposals from the SPD, such as that for "nuclear free zones", were almost identical to similar proposals made by the SPD in the 1950s. One such proposal was offered in the Bundestag by Helmut Schmidt in 1959.[5]

Indeed, in retrospect, Schmidt's position does not seem paradoxical. Although often cast as the victim of his support for the INF deployment, Schmidt never wavered from his insistence that negotiation was equally crucial. There is even some evidence that he intended all along that the INF issue be addressed through negotiation rather than weapons deployments.[6] After leaving office in 1982, he was bitter at the failure of both the Americans and the Soviets to proceed with negotiations. In 1978, he argued, he had made it clear to President Carter that the INF issue should be included in the forthcoming SALT III talks. Later, Schmidt was disturbed to discover that the issue had never been raised by Carter at the final round of the SALT II negotiations. Thereafter, the INF negotiations were shelved by the Soviet invasion of Afghanistan and the hesitation of the Reagan administration. Serious negotiation did not begin until 1982. True, as late as 1983, Schmidt continued to assert the correctness of NATO's 1979 decision, but he also maintained the importance of negotiation: "Above all I want to hold to the dual philosophy that the North Atlantic Alliance adopted in the Harmel Plan fifteen years ago: on the one hand, security from the Soviet threat and on the other, cooperation and 'détente' with the Soviet Union."[7]

Thus, what made Schmidt unique was not that he favored strength *or* negotiation. Rather, as he had for many years, Schmidt favored both in equal measure, a position he could not uphold as positions polarized during the INF debate. Helmut Schmidt fell from power because he was nearly alone in favoring the position that NATO had endorsed for many years.

In summary, the strong correlation of party affiliation and security opinions suggests that traditional approaches to security had not been erased during the so-called decade of consensus during the 1960s. In fact, even the views of the "successor generation", the putative representatives of a "new politics", might be interpreted as part of this same process of re-polarization. After all, the security questions that dominated the socialization period of this "détente generation" had an important similarity to traditional arguments about the utility of military force. Strategic parity had raised the choice between additional competition and arms control. Had the codification of parity not symbolized the futility of this competition? As for improving conventional forces, was it really necessary given the protection of the strategic stalemate, and in any case, had Vietnam not revealed the limits of conventional military power? Finally, in an age of social solidarity and welfare consensus, should the pursuit of social justice and security be sacrificed to military investments of questionable marginal utility?

The argument could thus be made that the views of the successor generation were really nothing new. This generation was socialized and educated in an environment of rapid international change and debate about the utility of military force. Their views certainly reinforced, indeed they magnified, the ideological polarization of the security debate, but in substance the debate was familiar.

A crucial question is therefore whether the polarization will recede – re-establishing the "consensus" that prevailed in earlier years. Based on the interpretation offered above, this is not an unlikely prospect. During the period of the Harmel compromise, the gap in party approaches was much less than it is today. Should NATO succeed in reestablishing a consistent "dual" approach that appeals both to the public's appreciation of deterrence and its desire for political management of relations, past patterns would suggest that polarization in public opinions would decline. Indeed, it seems apparent that this process has already begun. With the thaw in East–West relations that began with the INF negotiations in 1982 and continued with the signing of the INF Treaty in 1987, public unrest in Europe has declined noticeably. The public calm has been somewhat hidden by US–European disagreements on such matters as the US raid on Libya and the question of how to maintain the flow of oil through the Persian Gulf. None the less, in terms of basic security opinions, there is much less concern than was the case five years ago. Certainly, these issues do not constitute the "crisis" in NATO that was widely feared in the early 1980s.

The future of generational conflict is less certain, in part because it is difficult to tell if it is truly new. Historical breakdowns of the opinions of the successor generation are simply not available in sufficient wealth to ascertain whether the peculiar socialization environment of this "détente generation" is the causal factor in their more critical views. A plausible alternative explanation would be that, like their elders who are polarized on the basis of partisanship, the successor generation is simply reacting to the (short-term) breakdown of the security policy compromise that governed during the 1970s. It is true that they are far more critical of NATO policies than are their elders, but perhaps this simply means that, due to the emphasis on détente and arms control of the 1970s, they are far more committed to the Harmel formula of peace and strength – a supposition that was supported by the "détente sensitivity" revealed in surveys of the Dutch and West German successor generations. If so, a return to balanced policies would also reduce their concern.

Thus, it may be that the critical views of the successor generation represent what generational theorists call a "period effect" – a short-term reaction to contemporary conditions rather than a long-term outgrowth of true generational change. We have seen some evidence of this phenomenon, particularly in surveys on defense spending. In France and the Netherlands, an existing generation gap was narrowed by the rising tensions of the 1980s.

Yet these data do not totally rule out the generational thesis, for even after the gap between generations narrowed, there remained some distance between the younger French and Dutch and their age cohorts. Moreover, generational theory does not exclude the possibility of period effects (public opinion should, after all, respond to events). Rather, the theory predicts that particular generations, such as the "détente generation", should react differently or in different measure to the same events. There is, in fact, some evidence for this combination of period and generational effects. Again, the best data come in surveys on defense spending. In Britain and West Germany there were indeed period effects that moved the opinions of all sectors of the population, but in the successor generations, the movement is much more in a critical direction, widening the gap between young and old. Once again there is a combination of long-term and short-term processes: the long-term process of generational change produces a sector of the population with different predispositions, and these are revealed when short-term events put these attitudes to the test.

As I have argued, the substantive basis of successor generation views can be interpreted as an extension and magnification of the traditional critique of military force that has been prevalent on the Left (the successor generation is, after all, concentrated in parties of the Left). Thus, it seems likely that European political systems will continue to be faced with the challenge of maintaining consensus in the "glacier" politics of national security. Older citizens are also polarized ideologically, and party positions are historically derived and unlikely to be transformed. Generational change, on the existing evidence, is real rather than apparent – it is not the result of a life-cycle effect arising from the temporary "idealism" of the young.[8] And in any case, the latter point may be irrelevant for policy purposes. The successor generation may eventually outgrow its critical views, but the Alliance faces its challenge now.

A TRANSATLANTIC GAP IN OPINION?

If the foregoing interpretation is correct, clearly the prospect for the reestablishment of domestic consensus in the politics of European security will depend on American politics and policies. As the most powerful Alliance partner, the United States sets the tone in East–West relations, and as we have seen, its actions have an important impact on European opinions in such areas as arms control and support for the transatlantic Alliance. It is therefore unsurprising that much of the concern of Europeans during the 1980s was due to a perceived imbalance in American policies. Especially in the crisis atmosphere of the early 1980s, Europeans were demanding greater moderation in policies, but the United States seemed to hesitate on arms control, and in any case the dominant mood in America was for rearmament and reassertion – not for negotiation.

In the early 1980s, public opinion in the United States hardly suggested optimism for a transatlantic meeting of the minds. Quite the opposite, the American public had been growing increasingly distrustful of the Soviet Union since the mid 1970s, and support for defense spending and "standing up to the Russians" was revealed in a myriad of surveys. The election of Ronald Reagan in 1980 symbolized these sentiments, for after the frustration brought on by the Iran hostage crisis and the Soviet invasion of Afghanistan, the new President promised above all to reestablish the strength of the United States. Opinion analysts captured the American mood: in the words of Daniel Yankelovich, public opinion definitely revealed an "Assertive America".[9]

Yet American public opinion changed rapidly. By 1982, support for defense spending had collapsed to the levels of the Vietnam era, and demonstrations in support of the Nuclear Freeze confirmed a consistent finding of opinion surveys: Americans favored arms control. Moreover, despite the Reagan administration's repeated warnings about Soviet advances in Central America and elsewhere, the American public remained stubbornly cautious about the overseas commitment of American aid or troops. At the same time, the public continued to support the notion of deterrence, and the commitment to alliance with traditional partners (including NATO) actually increased over this period. Writing in 1985, William Schneider drew a conclusion that is remarkably similar to my analysis of European public opinion: "the American public does not favor strength over peace or peace over strength. They favor a 'two-track' policy that engages both values".[10] In an interesting analysis of American attitudes towards the Soviets, Miroslav Ninic went a step further. He found that opinions systematically react to extremes of hawkishness *or* dovishness in Presidents' policies: "this places limits on policies that deviate too far, either in a conciliatory or a confrontational direction, from what expectations have defined as a 'moderate' foreign policy: one combining peace and strength".[11]

Paradoxically, then, far from revealing a transatlantic chasm in attitudes toward national security, the trend of American public opinion during the 1980s revealed much in common with European attitudes. Table 7.1 summarizes this evolution. In 1981, American public opinion differed from European public opinion primarily in the huge level of support for increased defense spending. By the mid 1980s, however, European and American opinion became much more similar.

The polarization of European and American opinions is also similar, although this similarity is less than apparent at first glance, for both in conception and methodology, the study of American public opinion has been quite different from studies of European opinion. As we have seen, the study of cleavage in European public opinion has been strong on hypotheses and weak on data to test those hypotheses. That is, there are a number of theoretical expectations from the fields of international and comparative politics that would suggest why security attitudes should be associated with such characteristics as age or level of education, but with few exceptions, evaluation of these ideas has been restricted to the task of collating and comparing secondary survey results. Lacking comparative opinion surveys on a variety of security issues that could be subjected to primary analysis, researchers have contented themselves with a comparison of breakdowns to single questions.

The research tradition in the United States has been quite different. American researchers are fortunate to have available a number of exhaustive surveys that were designed specifically to allow the study of both public and élite opinions on a very large number of issues. Chief among these are the surveys of the Chicago Council on Foreign Relations, but there are other valuable surveys as well.[12] These studies are available from archives, allowing for re-analysis, replication, and far more cumulation than has been possible in the study of European opinion.

Perhaps because the data are so rich, students of American opinion have generally not started with hypotheses relating independent variables to security opinions. Rather, the primary focus has been the exploration of the underlying structure of opinions – the dependent variables. Using a variety of statistical techniques, scholars have sought to discover the extent to which a number of individual opinions are interrelated in broader attitude clusters. Although there has been

Table 7.1　A Comparison of American and European Public Opinion

	1980 (%)	1982 (%)	1985 (%)
Defense spending should be increased			
France	15	16	12
Britain	29	40	9
West Germany	17	10	7
Netherlands	11	11	8
United States	56	29	14
NATO is essential			
France	44	34	48
Britain	79	65	76
West Germany	88	66	75
Netherlands	76	76	76
United States	67	67	70
US and Soviet power are equal			
France	38	37	40
Britain	24	28	36
West Germany	30	30	47
United States	39	40	48

NOTES: Wording of the defense spending and military balance questions are as in the tables noted below. In the United States the figures for commitment to NATO are from a question which asks "Some people feel that NATO . . . has outlived its usefulness and that the US should withdraw. Others say that NATO has discouraged the Russians from trying a military takeover of Western Europe. Do you feel that we should increase our commitment to NATO, keep our commitment what it is now, decrease our commitment, or withdraw from NATO entirely?" The "increase" and "keep commitment" figures are shown in the table.

SOURCES: For European figures, Tables 3.1, 5.1 and 6.1. For the United States: William Schneider, "Peace and Strength: American Public Opinion on National Security", in Gregory Flynn and Hans Rattinger (eds), *The Public and Atlantic Defense* (Totowa, N.J.: Rowman and Allanheld, 1985) p. 328; and John E. Rielly (ed.), *American Public Opinion and US Foreign Policy, 1987* (Chicago, Ill.: Chicago Council on Foreign Relations, 1987) pp. 21, 86.

a good deal of theoretical and methodological debate concerning the number of clusters that characterize American attitudes and the labels that should be assigned to them, these studies have produced a great deal of substantive convergence.

For example, in virtually every study of the Chicago Council surveys, researchers have concluded that a major restructuring has taken place in American public opinion. According to William Schneider, a prominent analyst of these surveys, American opinions have experienced three distinct phases. The first, lasting until the post-Second World War period, encompassed the familiar isolationist/internationalist cleavage: the primary distinction among Americans was their willingness to accept a global role for the United States that included commitments or collaboration with other states. The second phase, evoked by the Cold War, produced a consensus in favor of containment and internationalism: Americans accepted both the need to contain the Soviet Union and the need to commit the United States to alliances in pursuit of the containment strategy.[13]

The third phase was brought on by the Vietnam War. Although some had thought that the effect of Vietnam was to reawaken the isolationist/internationalist split in the United States, research shows that the actual effect was more complex. Isolationists *per se* were a minority. Certainly, there remained a rather unilateralist sector (labelled "non-internationalist" by Schneider) that believed in the need for global involvement to contain the Soviets but preferred a "go it alone" approach. But the major cleavage that developed in the post-Vietnam era was a split among internationalists themselves. In the words of Mandelbaum and Schneider, the American public became increasingly split between "liberal internationalists" who emphasized economic interdependence, arms control and the use of international organizations, and "conservative internationalists" who emphasized the Soviet threat, military containment and the global defense of liberal economic values.[14] This division of the American public (and leadership) into non-internationalist, liberal internationalist, and conservative internationalist has been variously labelled by other scholars. None the less, the political substance of the cleavage is very similar in all studies, and its presence has been documented well into the 1980s.[15]

According to Schneider, the dynamics of American security politics are governed by this cleavage. Since there are far fewer non-internationalists among leaders and activists, they tend to divide in a competition for allies, which must be sought not only among sympathetic members of the public but among the non-internationalist public as well. Yet the latter have somewhat ambivalent sentiments. To be sure, they are sensitive to Soviet power and to the need to defend American interests (a sentiment they share with conservative internationalists), but in the wake of Vietnam they have also become very wary of overseas commitments (a sentiment they share with liberal internationalists). To this must be added the consistent finding that, despite its distrust of the Soviet Union, a large majority of Americans support the notion of at least attempting to control weapons. For Schneider, then, not only is it unsurprising that American security policy undergoes swings from militancy to conciliation (for a potential coalition exists for both), it is also unsurprising that the public seems to exhibit a contradictory profile: concerned about Soviet power yet overwhelmingly in favor of a nuclear freeze; concerned about potential Soviet influence in Central America yet unwilling to commit American aid or forces there. Depending on short-term conditions, either the liberal or conservative internationalists might prove capable of tapping one or the other sentiments of the non-internationalists.[16]

Despite the fact that these divisions in American public opinion have evolved in reaction to quite specific circumstances, the correlates of American opinion are actually quite similar to patterns in Europe. Although American party affiliation does not have the link to ideology that it has in Europe, ideology itself is by far the strongest correlate of liberal and conservative internationalism in public and élite opinion. As in Europe, education and (to a lesser extent) age are strong but secondary influences. In fact, one of the most surprising and consistent findings of this body of research is that the presumed generational effects of the Vietnam War have not materialized in either élite or public opinion.[17]

To summarize, as in Europe, the primary correlates of American opinion are found in the ideology, educational level, and age of the citizen. Those toward the left of the political spectrum are generally less threatened, less disposed to defense spending and less inclined to adopt a militant attitude in security matters. Those on the right are more concerned with Soviet power and more favorable to hardline policies. On both sides of the Atlantic, younger citizens and especially those with higher educational attainments are more inclined to be critical of military policies.

As noted earlier, American and European opinion also exhibit similarities in the movement of overall population sentiments. Despite acrimonious debates on a number of issues, the populations of the United States and Western Europe remained committed to deterrence and to the Atlantic Alliance, and both show a decided preference for a "dual" policy of deterrence and negotiation.

Although defense spending is nowhere popular, this is not a new development. Thus, despite a number of transatlantic differences over the past several years, the weight of the evidence suggests that the pattern of political conflict is much the same on both sides of the Atlantic.

Why should this be the case? Despite obvious differences in interest and circumstance, the basic issue facing the Western democracies is really quite similar: the appropriate role of military force in national security policy. Of course, in the United States this issue was highlighted above all by the Vietnam War, but the emergence of strategic parity and the pull of domestic problems has played a role as well. In any case, as the studies cited above suggest, the American public is divided less by the traditional question of whether to seek security through international involvement than by the question of *how* to do so. The crucial distinction between liberal and conservative internationalists is the degree to which they accept the use of military force in the pursuit of national security. This question, in turn, resurrects ideological divisions that were revealed by the war in Vietnam.

European opinion is similar, although it has evolved in reaction to different traditions and national interests. Certainly Vietnam and strategic parity highlighted the debatability of force, but for Europeans this debate was not new. As noted in the opening sections of this chapter, ideological conflict on the question of military force has a long tradition in Europe. Indeed, the new "liberal/conservative" cleavage that has arisen in the United States is quite familiar to Europeans. Perhaps it is a simplification to tag this distinction with the well-worn labels of "idealism" versus "realism", but that distinction seems useful and appropriate. After all, what has always separated these two schools of thought is their contrasting views of the utility of military force. For idealists, security is to be sought above all in negotiation and reconciliation of conflicting interests. Indeed, idealism is rooted in an explicit critique of policies of power balance. For realists, of course, a balance of military power has always been primary, and the reconciliation of conflicting interests has been seen as a distant goal, if not a Utopia. In recent decades, while all sides of the political spectrum in Europe have come to agree that a dual policy of strength and negotiation is the appropriate approach to security, in emphasis the Left and the Right remain noticeably different.

In fact, the issue is so fundamental that one wonders whether the "liberal/conservative" division in American opinion is really of recent origin. The strong clustering of opinions around issues of military force, clusters that are correlated with ideology, does indeed suggest that Vietnam touched deep fissures in American politics. Yet the fissure may be older than that. In fact, the distinction between idealists and realists is as old as the United States itself. It found its first expression (imported from Europe) in colonial America, where the enlightenment critique of the balance of power found a strong echo. In the words of Felix Gilbert, "American foreign policy was idealistic and internationalist no less than isolationist."[18] This idealistic internationalism has emerged periodically ever since, most notably in the ideas of Presidents Wilson and Carter. And as Huntington observed thirty years ago, American thinking about the military was affected by ideological debates even during the Cold war period.[19] Although recent studies of both American and European public opinion often conclude with the observation that the politics of national security have entered a "new phase", the basic line of division may be as old as the Enlightenment.

THE CORRESPONDENCE OF ELITE OPINION AND PUBLIC OPINION

The paradoxical conclusion of most studies of public opinion of the early 1980s was that governments enjoyed great leeway in policy making. Despite fears of a youth revolt and a broader popular drift toward pacifism, the survey data revealed a considerable basis of support for NATO and its policies. As the authors of one comprehensive study concluded:

> Restrictions on the range of national security options open to decision makers are far more strongly imposed by the positions taken and articulated by political and social élites and counterélites than by public opinion at large. In terms of popular acceptance, the decision latitude of policy makers still appears to be rather wide.[20]

One author of this study also argued that the increasing polarization of public opinion is itself a reflection of élite debates. These debates have political consequence only in so far as they reflect party conflict at the élite level: "Most of this disagreement [in public opinion] would not take its current partisan shape, much of it would not even be there without the stimulation by debates among élites for whom these matters are of utmost importance."[21]

My research suggests that this view, while correct in some respects, also requires modification. The depth and consistency of partisan polarization in public opinion has been confirmed, but to interpret this pattern as a mechanical reaction to contemporary debate among party leaders is to ignore the considerable historical tradition of ideological conflict on these issues. The association of individuals with political parties is deeply rooted in family, class *and* issue philosophies. The polarization in the views of both party leaders and individual citizens therefore suggests both a substantive component (different emphases on the priority of strength and negotiation in national security policy) and a cognitive component (reaction and alignment of views as the conflict is articulated by party and other élites).

The difficult task for the political scientist is to sort out the exact nature of this process of élite and public polarization. Theoretically, three "models" can be described. A first model might be called "shared predispositions": because of common beliefs and interests, leaders and party members share a predisposition to react to changing circumstances and issues. In the case of the recent turmoil in the field of security policy, this model would suggest that leaders and members of political parties, long tied by common beliefs about the usefulness of military force, reacted similarly to the challenge that external events presented to the Harmel philosophy.

The second model, "élite leadership", is well stated in Rattinger's argument. On both theoretical and empirical grounds, we should expect public opinion to *react* – to follow – the positions and arguments of political élites. One reason is the low level of information that most citizens bring to issues of security policy. At the level of facts, most citizens know little about the details of security issues. As these issues reach the political agenda, they look to party leaders or party tradition in formulating an opinion. Secondly, security issues have a low salience for the average citizen. Unlike economic or other domestic issues, defense and security remain low on the list of public concerns, a pattern that prevailed even during the vociferous debates of the 1980s. In addition to these reasons for the dominance of the élite leadership interpretation, we can add a third argument recently offered by Joffe: it is the job of political parties and political leaders to mobilize opinion. Political parties are opportunistic institutions.

They gravitate to issues that will increase their support in the polls and their showing in elections. According to Joffe, security issues became an attractive mobilization device during the 1970s precisely because other issues offered fewer opportunities, especially for parties of the Left. On economic issues, the Left's position had been eroded by a decade of halting growth that pushed budget deficits high at precisely the time that a philosophy of retrenchment had become the dominant political mood. With economic and welfare policy foreclosed as vehicles for political advancement, the parties turned to the peace issue. Moreover, parties of the Left had learned an important political lesson during the height of the Cold War: conservatives usually benefit from external threat and tension, while the Left profits from détente and arms control. Admittedly, issues of security policy were not uncontested even *within* parties. In fact, in Joffe's view, it was the internal struggle between the moderate and "détente" wings of the Left that foreshadowed later public debates. What is important in Joffe's interpretation is that this debate flowed in a "top down" direction: faced with threats to their domestic base, party leaders adopted the peace issue as a mechanism for mobilizing support within the party and the electorate. These debates were later reflected in the polarization of public opinion.[22]

Ironically, despite the theoretical coherence of the "leadership" model and the evidence that has supported it, a third model, more "populist" in flavor, has in fact dominated interpretations of NATO's crisis of consensus. As Joffe notes, much of the commentary on the recent period has suggested that changing public views of security policy were "mobilized from below" in an attempt to influence recalcitrant governments.[23] Government officials seem to accept this interpretation. As noted earlier, élites in Europe reacted to the polls and protests of the 1980s with the observation that citizens (especially young citizens) had developed "alien" conceptions of security, and in any event they stressed the need for intensified public relations to combat the pressure from below.

LEADERS AND CITIZENS: A SURVEY OF THE EVIDENCE

One would like to confront these competing models in a direct test of the direction of élite–public interaction on security issues. However, despite the centrality of this issue to the study of democratic politics, this linkage is among the most difficult to study. One reason is clear.

It is not enough to determine the *correspondence* between élite and public opinion, for this alone cannot establish who is leading whom. At a minimum, it is also necessary to establish the temporal sequence of influence. Does public opinion change *after* a change in élite opinion or in government policies, or does it *precede* such changes – suggesting a "populist" influence?

Since a thorough evaluation of this question requires historical data covering both public opinion and the opinions and actions of leaders, perhaps it is not surprising that studies of this linkage are very rare. Among the few studies that do exist, the predominant conclusion favors the "élite leadership" model. For example, Abravanel and Hughes analyzed the interaction of foreign policy and public opinion in France, Britain, West Germany, and Italy, and their analysis showed that public opinion tended to follow the articulation of foreign policy by leaders. Similarly, Dalton and Duval studied the British public's enthusiasm for membership of the EC and found that, in the short term, the public's attitudes were sensitive to public events. Since leaders can manipulate such events, the possibility of "élite leadership" of opinion seems clear. Finally, Shapiro and Page conducted a wide-ranging study of the reactiveness of American opinion and found that it reacts to international events "as these matters have been reported and interpreted by the mass media and by policy makers and other elites".[24]

Historical data such as those used in these studies are simply not available for the types of issues under study here, but there are recent studies of leadership opinion that allow examination of a more restricted set of questions. At least for recent years, we can examine the extent of overall correspondence between élite and public opinions on the issues studied in this book. Once again, the presence or absence of shared attitudes will not by itself reveal the direction of opinion influence, but the analysis of opinion correspondence is useful for an additonal reason: whatever the direction of opinion influence, such data will reveal the extent to which élites face a consensus problem with the public. Do leaders favor increases in the defense budget against the wishes of a recalcitrant public? Is the public's affinity for negotiations resisted by political élites?

A second type of data addresses the "leader–follower" issue indirectly. By comparing the pattern of polarization among élites with the polarization of public opinion, we can further describe the extent to which the "shared predispositions" model holds. In addition, surveys of élite polarization can address other issues of interest. For example, one criticism of theories of generational change is that the attitudes of a rebellious youth may very well moderate as younger leaders move into positions of responsibility that require compromise. To the extent that such a maturation effect is visible among élites, generational differences in public opinion would be cast in a different light, for presumably they would moderate as the "successor generation" move into positions of leadership.

Finally, to ascertain the direction of influence of élite opinions and public opinion, we need to study the evolution of both over time. As noted above, that is not possible using systematic surveys of opinion. However, we can address the issue by reviewing the historical context, especially as concerns the "opportunism" of the parties described by Joffe. Here the major question is whether the polarization of the 1980s was simply a reaction to immediate events or whether, in contrast, they had their origins in earlier partisan struggles that had already been communicated to party followers.

LEADERS AND PUBLIC COMPARED

Some initial evidence comes from a 1974 survey that compared public opinions of the military balance to those of "opinion leaders" in four European countries.[25] The survey asked respondents in both groups whether they preferred US superiority in the military balance or parity. The results were clear cut: large majorities or pluralities of both public and élite opinion preferred parity. In addition, in every country but France, élites were *more* favorable to parity than was public opinion. In France, the overwhelming preference of both public and élites (62 per cent) for parity seems unsurprising in light of French policy.

None the less, there is a double irony in the affinity for parity revealed in other countries. First, this survey in 1974 came at a time of great concern on the part of strategists about the perceptions of Europeans in the age of strategic parity. As reviewed in Chapter 3, American strategic policy was shifting toward "flexible nuclear options", in part to reassure Europeans that strategic parity and mutually assured destruction had not undermined the basis of extended deterrence in Europe. Yet this survey shows that, among both leaders and public, there was in fact great satisfaction with parity. The second irony is that the détente and arms control of the early 1970s had concerned many observers because they feared that negotiations would seduce the public with the belief that parity had rendered military strength less relevant. Yet these figures show that leaders were far more satisfied with the parity established through arms control than were the public at large. In Britain, for example, 61 per cent of élites favored parity versus 47 per cent of the public.[26]

In any case, additional studies during the 1970s confirmed the preference of élites for strategic parity. Mahoney and Mundy describe the results of an ambitious study conducted on behalf of the US Arms Control and Disarmament Agency. The study included a systematic evaluation of all statements on security issues by European political leaders from 1946 to 1978, supplemented by detailed studies of party programs and specialized publications in the security field. The results of the study revealed a preference for parity during the 1970s. Moreover, throughout the 1970s, there was a trend indicating that leaders perceived an improvement in national security. Thus, leaders' opinions match the profile of public opinion discussed in Chapter 3: although the shift to parity in the military balance was noticed, there was not an erosion in perceptions of security. Put another way, there is no evidence from this European leadership study that the détente period had left a perceptual gap between governments and citizens. Neither leaders nor citizens felt less secure in the face of a changing military balance.

This congruence between the overall pattern of public and élite opinion was strikingly revealed in a 1983 survey of European élites conducted by the Science Center in West Berlin. Administered to over 800 respondents from government, civil service, parliament, labor, business, and interest groups (including military and peace associations), this study is the only comparative, quantitative sounding of élite opinion from the period of the INF debate and the eruption of the peace movements.[27] Table 7.2 displays the percentage responses of these élites to a series of questions on the INF issue. With the exception of the French responses, the overall pattern of these élite opinions is strikingly similar to the pattern of public opinion on the INF issue.[28] Neither unconditional support nor unconditional opposition to the deployment is favored by more than a minority. However, when the deployment is related to Soviet deployments or to efforts to negotiate arms control, support is much higher.

To judge from these results, the public's insistence on a "dual track" policy is hardly novel – it is precisely the pattern that governs élite opinions. The clear exception is France, where élites unconditionally

Table 7.2   Elite Opinions of the INF Deployment (Spring 1983)

	Germany	Per cent "agree" Britain	Holland	France
NATO should deploy INF under any circumstances	11	16	12	65
NATO should not deploy INF under any circumstances	33	31	29	3
NATO should deploy if the Soviets reduce to a mutually agreeable number of SS-20's	61	55	58	67
NATO should accept a moratorium on INF so long as negotiations continue	50	45	40	11

NOTE: The figures are responses to a mail survey of élites. The questions were presented separately.

SOURCE: Wolf-Dieter Eberwein and Heinrich Siegmann, *Bedrohung oder Selbsgefährdung? Die Einstellungen Sicherheitspolitischer Führungsschichten aus fünf Ländern zur Sicherheitspolitik* (West Berlin: International Institute for Comparative Social Research, 1985) p. 182.

favored the INF deployment and showed no enthusiasm for delaying the deployment while awaiting the results of negotiation. The French leaders are distinct in another way: their opinions are not shared by public opinion. We saw in Chapter 4 that French public opinion is really not much different from opinion in other European countries. French citizens shared a conditional, "two-track" view of the INF deployment, and they opposed first use of nuclear weapons.

This gap between French élites and citizens is not confined to the INF issue. Table 7.3 displays élite and public opinions on four security issues. The most striking thing about this comparison is the consistent gap between the French élites and public. While 45 per cent of French élites favored increasing defense, the figure is only 16 per cent among the public. There is also a huge gap in support for "no-first-use", and the public's opposition to the INF deployment is not shared by élites. Clearly, these data suggest a potential consensus problem in France. None the less, whether a French consensus problem will in fact emerge is probably dependent on other factors, which I discuss in the final section of this chapter.

In the remaining three countries, there appears to be a substantial amount of agreement between élites and the public. Concerning the

Table 7.3   A Comparison of European Public Opinion and Elite Opinion in 1983

	Elites (%)	Public (%)	Opinion gap (%)
NATO is essential			
France	80	34	46
Great Britain	69	76	−7
West Germany	75	86	−11
Netherlands	81	76	5
Defense spending should be increased			
France	45	16	29
Great Britain	23	12	11
West Germany	11	12	−1
Netherlands	23	8	15
Oppose INF deployment unconditionally			
France	3	33	−30
Great Britain	31	28	3
West Germany	33	29	4
Netherlands	29	52	−23
Favor "no-first-use"			
France	19	79	−60
Great Britain	67	88	−21
West Germany	64	92	−28
Netherlands	50	75	−25

NOTES: The wording to public opinion questions is as in the Tables noted below. The élite questions were worded as follows. *NATO*: "Only the Alliance with the United States can guarantee security [agree/disagree]"; *Defense spending*: "What do you think of the current level of defense spending in your country [decrease, about right, increase]; *No-first-use*: "East and West should agree to no first use of nuclear weapons [agree/disagree]; *INF*: "NATO should not deploy INF under any circumstances [agree/disagree]".

SOURCES: Public opinion figures are taken from Tables 4.3, 4.5, 5.1, and 6.1. The opinions of élites are from Eberwein and Siegmann, *Bedrohung oder Selbstgefährdung?* pp. 177, 182, 186, 189.

NATO Alliance, support is overwhelming in both samples, making the small gaps that do appear of minor political relevance. In the case of defense spending, the opposite is true: support is so low among both élites and public that the minor differences that do appear are unlikely to be politically relevant. Yet on the nuclear issue, as indicated by support for "no first use", there appears to be a substantial gap. To be sure, there is a surprising amount of support among élites for "no-first-use" – surprising because European governments have been so vehement in asserting the continuing relevance of nuclear deterrence in the face of the peace movements and the Star Wars movement. We should recall, however, that this élite sample contains both government officials and "leaders" in business, unions, and parliament. The latter are presumably less attuned to the orthodoxy of nuclear deterrence, so the gap between the views of officials and citizens is probably larger than it appears here. In any case, this comparison suggests that it is above all on the nuclear issue that élites and the public diverge.

This comparison of élite and public opinions confirms the characterization of NATO's consensus problem that has been developed throughout this book. Certainly the popular picture of a broad erosion of consensus on security policy is not confirmed. On most issues, public opinion has changed only little. The élite surveys summarized here indicate that there is not a large gap between public and élite opinions. Further, élites seem to share the public's dual sensitivity to Soviet capabilities and arms control negotiations. Except in France, only on the "no first use" question do élites and public diverge. This reinforces a conclusion first suggested in Chapter 4: élites, although fully in tune with the public's desire for negotiation as well as strength, differ from the public in their willingness to live with the uncertainties of flexible response. Indeed, for élites, *some* nuclear deterrence is a positive value, for it has worked far better than earlier systems of deterrence.

This gap in opinions of nuclear weapons may soon be tested once again. The United States and the Soviets have agreed on the "double-zero" elimination of medium-and short-range missiles from Europe, and attention has already shifted back to one of NATO's oldest and most divisive questions: when and how to use nuclear weapons of battlefield (tactical) range. In addition, the Alliance is once again debating the issue of whether and how to modernize nuclear weapons of shorter range. Paradoxically, then, the arms control agreement that was widely seen as the required condition of domestic consensus may bring renewed debate on exactly those issues that most divide European citizens from their leaders.

THE DIVIDED ELITE

A second type of correspondence between citizen and élite views is the degree to which polarization within the public matches polarization among élites. Whether such a correspondence would indicate a *communication* of polarization or its *representation* is a question left for later. Here we must ask if the partisan and generational polarization of public opinion is matched by similar divisions at the élite level. Is there a unified élite facing a worried and divided public, or have élites themselves also become divided?

The 1983 Berlin survey of élites provides some limited evidence on the matter, and it suggests that partisan polarization is also a prominent line of division in élite opinion. For example, in West Germany 57 per cent of SPD respondents believed that defense sending should be cut; among CDU/CSU supporters, the figure was 3 per cent. In Britain, Labour élites chose defense spending when asked to name which government spending programs should be cut first; among Conservatives, defense spending was the most protected priority. In both Britain and Germany, élites were also polarized along partisan lines on a number of other issues.[29]

Do these figures reflect longstanding differences among party élites, or do they simply mirror – perhaps they were caused – by the public polarization that erupted in the wake of the INF controversy? There are few comparative studies that can answer these questions for earlier years, but there are some earlier studies of élites in West Germany. In 1975, for example, Reif and Schmitt studied the opinions of delegates to each of the major party's annual convention, and the results presaged later debates: 78 per cent of CDU delegates believed that the European Community should engage in "more policy coordination with the United States than hitherto", while 80 per cent of SPD delegates believed that the EC should "strive toward more independence from both superpowers".[30] Similar differences were found in a detailed survey of West German élites conducted by Schössler and Weede in 1976. The study documented clear lines of élite polarization in 1976: élites who identified with the SPD were far more favorable (by 30 percentage points) than CDU/CSU affiliates to the idea of securing peace through trade, and they displayed a consistent distance from the conservatives on such questions as the effectiveness of deterrence, the need to raise defense spending, and the effect of détente on the prospects for peace. In fact, in a statistical analysis of opinion clusters similar to those employed in studies of American opinion, Schössler and Weede characterized the alignment of West German élite views in terms of the "idealist/realist" ideological clusters discussed above. For those on the Left, arms races are seen as the cause of conflict, and peace can best be pursued through policies of negotiation, trade, and conciliation.[31] In short, not only did the alignment of West German élite views match what we have found for public opinion. It is also clear that the division among élites predates the controversies of the early 1980s.

There are only two broadly comparative studies of the correspondence of élite and public opinion in all of Western Europe, both carried out by Russell Dalton. In the first, Dalton studied the policy views of candidates for the European Parliament in 1979, using many of the same public opinion questions that have been used in the *Eurobarometer* surveys. Among a host of interesting findings concerning the correspondence of élite and public opinion, Dalton found that correspondence in opinions of defense spending was among the highest of any political issue. Morever, using an innovative technique to ascertain which factors most influence the correspondence of opinion, Dalton found that a clear ideological image on the part of political parties increased élite–public correspondence on the defense issue. Correspondence is also highly related to such party characteristics as centralized control of the party organization and national-level selection of candidates for office. Dalton concludes:

> The political awareness and interest of most voters is limited; characteristics that clarify party positions make it easier for voters to select a party consistent with their issue beliefs. A centralized party is more likely to project clear party cues, and a distinct ideological or social group image helps voters and élites agree on a party's general political orientation. . . . Diversity in party choice clarifies party options and makes it more likely that voters can find a party that supports their mix of policy preferences.[32]

Dalton's study could be interpreted to mean that, however visible the generational cleavage revealed in public protests and opinion polls, the primary line of division in both public and élite opinion remains the traditional one of Left and Right.

That would be only partially correct, as a second study by Dalton has shown. Focusing once again on the 1979 survey of EC Parliament candidates, he confirms that élites are polarized along partisan lines, but there are some additional findings of interest. As was the case in public opinion surveys, there are notable generational differences in the policy views of élites. For example, younger élites are significantly less supportive of defense spending – indeed, generational differences on this issue are among the highest in a list of thirteen policy issues.[33] Yet, as was also true in public opinion surveys, the élite surveys reveal the continuing significance of partisan polarization among both young and older élites. In fact, partisan polarization *within* the younger generation of élites is extremely high. With one exception, it is the issue of defense spending that most divides the younger élites: the Left–Right gap in support for defense spending among younger leaders is two to three times larger than the gap among older élites.[34] In summary, Dalton's study confirms the "glacier" image that I have discussed with respect to public opinion. Certainly younger élites are more skeptical of defense policy than older élites, but there is an even larger degree of cleavage *within* the younger generation along the Left–Right ideological spectrum. Like public opinion, élite opinion is doubly polarized on issues of national security.

WHO IS LEADING WHOM?

Previous sections have established that, with the exception of the nuclear issue, there is generally correspondence between public and élites on issues of national security. At a minimum, this suggests the plausibility of the "shared predispositions" model of élite–public interaction on security issues. In terms of the nature of the interaction, we can say that élite and public opinion responded in similar ways to the events of the 1980s, both in overall profile and in the nature of polarization. In terms of substance, the presence of both partisan and generational cleavage suggest that these differences arise from conflicting assessments of the utility of force, a difference that is longstanding for Left and Right and magnified by the "détente" socialization environment of the successor generation.

This evidence also establishes the necessary condition for an "élite leadership" model of opinion influence, for one could hardly conclude that élites are leading were the overall pattern and polarization of the public's views different from those communicated by élites. Yet the presence of opinion correspondence is not sufficient to establish élite leadership. As noted above, élite leadership requires evidence that change or polarization in leadership views preceded similar change in the public's views.

In a broad sense, it is not difficult to document a conflict in the ideological views of party élites. As argued earlier, the ideological critique of military force has been an integral part of the overall "system critique" of working-class parties since the nineteenth century. Of course, the problem with this argument is the equally obvious observation that these differences appeared to have subsided during the "decade of consensus" that found its symbolic expression in the Bad Godesberger program of the West German Social Democrats in 1959. With the apparent acquiescence of British Labour to nuclear deterrence in 1964, the oulines of the NATO consensus appeared complete. The historical pacifism of the working-class parties had been overridden in their acceptance of deterrence, and their acceptance of mixed capitalist policies removed an ideological barrier to the Western Alliance. It is this consensus that observers now believe has "broken", for major segments of the Left, at least in Britain, Germany, and the Netherlands, have either rejected deterrence entirely or put conditions on its operation that threaten the cohesion of NATO.[35]

The dominant interpretation of this "breakdown" in consensus is the "populist pressure" model referred to above. The break with the past was not initiated by leaders, to be followed by loyal partisans among the citizenry. Rather, pushed from below – if only by minorities – leaders of the parties of the Left gradually responded by deserting the consensus. The conflict that erupted within and between parties of Left and Right were only later reflected in public opinion.

There are two problems with this interpretation, the first with the definition of the NATO consensus, the second with the assumption that the consensus first "broke" in 1979.

What was the NATO consensus of the 1960s? The observation that it rested on the acceptance of nuclear deterrence is broadly accurate (NATO did deploy nuclear weapons and adopt flexible response), yet it is also misleading, for on the specific issue of when and how NATO would implement its strategy, NATO's consensus has been fragile, to say the least. In fact, in light of the interminable quarrels that have accompanied NATO's nuclear planning, Sigal argues flatly that "No consensus has ever existed on the place of nuclear weapons in NATO strategy."[36] Moreover, the acquiescence of the Left to NATO's strategy appears in hindsight to have been conditional. Especially after the Cuban Missile crisis, the 1960s were largely a period of relaxation in East–West relations and progress in arms control. Nor was the drift to détente confined to the US–Soviet relationship: the *Ostpolitik* of West Germany and others had their roots in the mid 1960s, especially in the UN "Group of Nine" that was established in 1965 to further contacts between East and West.[37]

Thus, to characterize the 1960s as a decade of consensus on strength and deterrence is to overlook the emerging transition to negotiation and détente that was a traditional theme for the parties of the Left.

In fact, by at least the late 1960s, détente had become more than an ideological priority for the Left – it was an explicit demand that was soon tied to heated debate on other defense issues. In the Netherlands, Foreign Minister Luns came under pressure to cultivate more active relations with the East, and under pressure from Parliament, he joined the Group of Nine in 1967. During the mid to late 1960s, the Dutch defense budget was under near-constant attack, from the Labour party, the media, and others. In 1969, the Prime Minister was forced to make a national television broadcast to overcome opposition to his plan to increase defense spending after the Soviet invasion of Czechoslovakia. Especially on the Left wing of the Labour Party, NATO membership itself also came under attack. The controversy peaked in 1975 when the Labour Party Congress adopted a resolution calling on the Netherlands to leave NATO unless "an essential contribution to détente" was made within three years.[38] Also in 1975, Labour passed resolutions favoring "no-first-use", the establishment of a European nuclear free zone, and the elimination of nuclear tasks from the Dutch armed forces.[39]

The détente issue was also actively contested in Belgium, where the transfer of NATO headquarters became the object of Socialist demands for negotiation and disarmament. The Belgian government had, in fact, initiated a number of contacts with the East beginning in 1965, but the proposed transfer of NATO headquarters brought a "détente challenge" from the Socialist Party. That debate led to the dramatic repudiation of Paul-Henri Spaak, the senior statesmen of the Socialists and a "father" of NATO. In the vote in the Lower Chamber of Parliament, his fellow Socialists deserted him.[40] As one Belgian diplomat later observed:

I was somewhat surprised to hear that it was INF which broke down the consensus over foreign policy. If I may refer to Belgium, in 1968 . . . it was the entire Belgian Socialist party, except for Paul-Henri Spaak and Antoine Spinoy, who voted against NATO coming here. Our breakdown had already occurred by then. . . . I wonder what other European countries would have said then. We might have had no NATO whatsoever in Europe had it not been for the other political parties. So I cannot really see this break-up having happened only recently.[41]

Yet, despite the bitterness of the NATO debate in Brussels, détente had hardly been the special preserve of the Socialists. Foreign Minister Harmel, whose name is attached to the institutionalization of détente within NATO, said during the NATO debate that "as long as the level of armament doesn't change, the Belgian Government will not give up the security provided by NATO. But we are convinced that the efforts with respect to détente and peace are more important than the defense efforts . . . at least for the sake of peace, at least as many diplomatic as military risks should be taken."[42]

As noted earlier, Josef Joffe also disputes that the NATO consensus, such as it was, first collapsed in the wake of the INF imbroglio. According to Joffe, the roots go back further, especially to intra-party struggles in the British Labour Party and German Social Democratic Party: "the established parties of the democratic Left began to push nuclear weapons toward front-stage while the activists were still demonstrating against nuclear power plants". [43] The public battle began only after the Left wings of Labour and SPD rose to challenge the moderate (pro-nuclear) policies of James Callaghan and Helmut Schmidt. Reinforced by a younger generation of party activists long determined to wrest power from the older moderates, the anti-nuclear issue became the banner in a struggle for party control. The neutron bomb episode was a catalyst, but hardly a cause, of this conflict.[44]

Joffe's analysis is convincing, but perhaps it does not go far enough, for especially in the case of West Germany, the conflict between the Left and the Right, as *within* the SPD, has much older roots. The SPD defense consensus, much-heralded in the wake of Bad Godesberg, was hardly unconditional. Far from rejecting the party's traditional affinity for negotiation, the Bad Godesberg program *integrated* them as part of SPD policy. While the Bad Godesberg document certainly conceded that German security would be predicated on membership in NATO, it did not depart from the SPD's traditional affinity for negotiation, collective security and disarmament. In fact, the chapter on "National Defense" contains the following sentence: "The Social Democratic Party seeks the inclusion of a unified Germany in a European zone of détente and controlled limitation of armament. . . ."[45] Nor does this appear to have been a last hurrah to soothe the party faithful. During the 1960s, American proposals for arms limitation (as opposed to complete disarmament) found a receptive audience in the SPD. In 1960 Fritz Erler, a prominent leader of the SPD, declared that "national defense and arms control are not contradictory . . . they belong together". The SPD's election platform for the 1961 election stated that "defense policy and arms control are the two sides of our indivisible security policy". Helmut Schmidt, the SPD's most prominent security expert, declared in 1960 that military strategy and arms control were "Siamese twins". In his comprehensive history of the SPD's security policy, Lothar Wilker concluded that these were not simply the adjustments of dependent allies to the growing popularity of arms control in American doctrine. Rather, they represented fundamental notions that animated SPD thinking on security policy before and after Bad Godesberg.[46]

The "two-track" thinking of the SPD was thus longstanding, and the prominence of such older, familiar faces as Brandt, Wehner, and Bahr in the INF debate is hardly surprising. According to Jonathan Dean, it had been the urging of (then) Foreign Minister Brandt (and his planning chief, Egon Bahr) that pushed the Harmel Report forward.[47] And of course, it was Brandt's *Ostpolitik* that thrust West Germany into the role of leader of European détente. Opposed by the conservative opposition, Brandt survived a no-confidence vote and a subsequent election, but the battle over the merits of détente and defense had been deeply bitter.

The one country not covered by this historical review is France, where, unlike the other countries of Europe, the traditional ideological quarrel about defense and détente was of limited relevance during the 1960s and 1970s and was barely visible during the 1980s. As we have seen throughout this book, this certainly was not due to a lack of skepticism on the part of the Left, for the French Left continues to hold opinions that are similar to their colleagues elsewhere in Europe. Rather, the reason must be sought in the special dynamics of French defense policy – meaning the orthodoxy created by President Charles de Gaulle. How could the pursuit of détente be championed by the Left when de Gaulle had predicated his policies and actions on the very concept? Nor could the Left criticize nuclear deterrence, for this was the most Gaullist concept of them all, which ultimately forced the Left to embrace the French deterrent. Finally, as many observers have noted, the Socialists' traditional critique of the military was inhibited by the presence of the Communist party to its Left and the need to maintain distance from its Moscow orientation.

In summary, with the unusual exception of France, we can assert two conclusions. One is straightfoward. To characterize the 1960s as the "decade of NATO consensus" is misleading. To be sure, all parties embraced NATO and tolerated nuclear deterrence – although the latter to widely varying degrees. None the less, the consensus was contingent. No party of the European Left had foresworn the traditional affinity for détente. Indeed, the movement toward détente was well underway from the mid 1960s, and parties of the Left battled toward the end of the decade to institutionalize détente in national defense polices and in NATO's Harmel Report. Nato's consensus was very much a "two-track" affair.

The second conclusion follows from the first. The leaders of the democratic Left had pushed the détente track from the beginning, sometimes asserting it in very explicit ways, as in Dutch Labour's conditions for NATO membership and Brandt's role in the initiation of Harmel. Later, it was these same leaders who questioned INF because of what they saw as the failure to uphold the negotiating track of NATO's decision in the crisis atmosphere of the 1980s. Moreover, the American ally was conducting a frontal assault on détente. The link with the past was clear. In 1979 – long before the first peace demonstration had taken place – the security policy commission of the SPD's executive board suggested the possibility of a moratorium on INF deployment by stating that "Without the longing for peace, antimilitarism and an active peace and disarmament policy, the SPD would lose its identity as a social democratic party."[48]

In summary, party leaders had been arguing for over a decade that détente was an essential element of the security equation. Well before 1979, they asserted this priority in domestic battles over NATO policy. Citizens therefore had ample "cues" that the parties placed unequal emphasis on the pillars of strength and détente. The parties' historical programs reinforced these emphases. When we recall that the level of public interest and information in the security field remained low even during the time of most intense public debate after the INF decision and the crises of the early 1980s, it would suggest that the alignment of public opinion reflects the "élite leadership" rather than the "populist" model of élite–public interaction.

POPULIST MUSCLE

Yet it also seems obvious that élite leadership has not totally dominated the politics of national security. As we have seen, the public has resisted the leaders' insistence that nuclear deterrence is essential to NATO strategy, and it would take an extreme myopia not to see that there are vocal minorities of citizens who reject the deterrence argument and even the legitimacy of NATO itself. In 1981 and 1982, evidence for this rejection was quite literally walking in the streets in what Josef Joffe characterized as "the most impressive display of populist muscle in the postwar era".[49]

It is true that leaders, public, and peace movements often talked past each other – sometimes in a fragmented stream of contradictory voices. True, the clash between the movements and governments of the Center-Right was clear cut, for the latter placed a clear priority on the need for deployment as a basis for the INF negotiations – a strategy clearly rejected by the movements. The relationship between popular sentiment and governments of the Center-Left, however, was less clear. The only example is West Germany, and I have already discussed Schmidt's paradoxical position. He grew increasingly isolated as his argument for deployment with negotiation found little support in a polarized domestic environment. While his critics wanted one or the other, Schmidt wanted both. And although Schmidt, as well as every Center-Right government, increasingly exhorted Washington to negotiate and to cease uncontrolled rhetoric about the use of nuclear weapons, both public opinion and the peace movements seem unconvinced. Although negotiation calmed the atmosphere by 1983, clearly there had been a failure of "élite leadership" on the nuclear issue.

Populist muscle is also evident when one considers the *impact* of polls and protests. Admittedly, there was one clear failure: the INF deployments were not prevented. Yet the broader impact of the anti-nuclear sentiment seems self-evident.[50] One result was the dramatic increase in the amount and quality of technical information that found its way into public debates for the first time. Through the publications of research institutes, parliamentary hearings, press discussions, and party conferences, the sophistication of public strategic debates reached a level never before seen in Western Europe. Moreover, although NATO's strategy had been debated among experts for over thirty years, now governments and critics were engaged in sophisticated – if emotional – seminars on such topics as the limits and dangers of extended deterrence, no first use, and strategic nuclear doctrine.

For the moment at least, this discussion has changed the agenda of official and scholarly discourse on security matters. As I argued in Chapter 4, governments have not always correctly interpreted the drift of public opinion of these issues, but it is significant that they act on such judgments at all. Their expectations about public pressure to accept the "double zero" accord is a good example. In addition, subjects that previously enjoyed the status of Bohemian curiosities – alternative defense strategies are an example – are now a regular topic of scholarly and governmental study. Although the strengthening of conventional defense is a timeworn theme in NATO circles, the anti-nuclear neuralgia has reinvigorated the topic and even given it acronymic status, as in NATO's conventional defense initiative (CDI). And all of this has brought serious discussion of ways to create a stronger "European pillar" within the alliance. None of these topics, it could be argued, would have received this amount of serious attention without the concern that was revealed in opinion polls and in public protests.

Finally, perhaps the most important impact of the anti-nuclear sentiment has been its contribution to change in European party systems. The effect has been twofold. First, it has reinforced the strength of the small environmental and peace parties that already existed. For example, although anti-nuclear sentiment hardly created the German Greens, their emergence as a party with parliamentary strength might not have occurred without the emotional impact of the nuclear issue. Furthermore, in Britain, Holland, and West Germany, Labour and Social Democrats moved rapidly to the Left in an attempt to respond to what they interpreted as a groundswell of anti-nuclear sentiment. By 1983 all of these parties had taken positions that, while not questioning NATO itself, did raise the prospect of serious controversy in NATO should they return to governmental authority. This was no small result for "populist muscle".

There seems no question, then, of the populist dynamic of security politics in recent years, but several final caveats should be noted. One is the warning to avoid "either–or" characterizations. As we have seen, there is also ample evidence that, on the crucial choice of "strength versus negotiation", party élites had long ago begun the process of polarization, a process that may have contributed to the polarization of the public. In this regard, it is useful to note that the recent shift of the democratic Left has been in the direction of traditional positions: unilateral disarmament in Britain; anti-nuclear pacifism in the Netherlands; and unconditional détente in West Germany. The populists have pushed the parties back to familiar positions.

A second concerns the limits of populist influence. That influence has been clear on the nuclear issue, where public sentiments and organized protest converged to create the image of a groundswell of nuclear neuralgia. Yet the push had its limits. As for the peace movements, their calls for abolition of the blocs and for unilateral disarmament found only minority support. The parties of the Left have therefore been careful to avoid any renunciation of NATO or of sudden, unilateral moves that could throw the Alliance into turmoil.

The third caveat follows from the second: Labour and Social Democrats have learned that absolute anti-nuclear sentiments remain a distinct minority with little political appeal. The preference for NATO remains the overwhelming choice of voters. As a result, the nuclear issue did nothing to help the Left back to power. The least that can be said is that the nuclear issue did not influence election outcomes at all (as in West Germany). More likely, the shift to an anti-nuclear posture actually hurt the electoral fortunes of the Left (as in Britain in 1983 and 1987). There is therefore a paradox in the recent drift of Social Democratic defense policy: if these parties return to government, it will be *in spite of rather than because of* their positions on defense issues. More likely, they will learn the lesson discussed earlier: in security politics as in other areas, a winning policy is found in the center.[51]

SOME FINAL COMPARISONS

The opinion patterns presented in this book point to two contradictions – both involving the French. First, despite the common interpretation of scholars that France enjoys a widely shared "defense consensus", the opinion data examined in this book show that it is above all the French who are polarized on issues of national security. In terms of both ideological and generational conflict, there is no question that France shows the deepest and most consistent polarization. This leads to the second contradiction: it is the French government – whose public is most polarized – that appears to operate with least consideration for public concerns. Despite wide cleavages on such issues as defense spending, the Alliance, and even nuclear weapons, the drift of French policy in the 1980s has been in the direction of greater Atlanticism and heavier dependence on nuclear weapons.[52]

The first contradiction raises the issue of the origins of domestic polarization. Why is it that some countries are more divided than others, independent of the drift of their country's policies? The factors emphasized in this book do not totally explain the difference. The French, for example, are hardly more sensitive to the détente theme that appears to be the major ideological divide in recent debates – yet they are even more polarized than the West Germans, who *are* sensitive to this issue. Nor can ideological tradition explain it. True, the French Left has a history of anti-militarism, but that is equally true of the Left in other countries.

The answer must be sought in a basic hypothesis from the field of comparative politics: given that citizens look for "cues" on complicated issues of public policy, the polarization of views is likely to reflect the choices available in the party system and the incentives to party competition defined by the electoral system. In multi-party systems, there is a greater variety of party "cues". In systems of proportional representation, minority views are more "competitive" in an electoral sense. Indeed, given the importance of even minor swings in voter percentages in systems of proportional representation, there is an incentive to develop a clear profile on the issues in the hopes of making marginal gains in votes. Larger parties, in turn, must be attentive to minority sentiment or risk losing votes on their flanks. In plurality based systems (such as Britain's "first past the post"), parties can ignore minority sentiment as they seek the center – the location of majorities.

Students of comparative politics have found that these variations in party systems are indeed related to the dynamics of public opinion on political issues. Ronald Inglehart, for example, shows that fundamental values are more likely to be expressed in the votes of citizens in multi-party systems. It is in France, Italy, and the Netherlands – all multi-party systems – that citizens are most likely to express their issue positions in the vote.[53] Similar evidence is available in other studies. In Dalton's research on the correspondence of élite and

Table 7.4 The Relationship between Party System and Polarization on Security Issues

	Number of parties	Electoral system	Average party polarization 1980	
			1980	1982
France	9	TTC	24	21
Netherlands	11	P	26	24
West Germany	5	LP	7	10
Great Britain	4	FPP	10	13

NOTES: The number of parties is taken from the electoral list offered to survey respondents in J.-R. Rabier, *et al.*, *Eurobarometer 14: Trust in the European Community* (Ann Arbor, Mich.: Inter-University Consortium for Political and Social Research, Study no. 7958, 1983). The "average partisan polarization" is calculated by averaging the absolute percentage distance between parties of the Left and Right for three questions presented in previous chapters: NATO Essential (Table 5.4); the military balance (Table 3.6) and defense spending (Table 6.9). Left and Right are defined as follows: France (Communist/Gaullist); Netherlands (PvdA/VVD); Germany (SPD/CDU–CSU); and Britain (Labour/Conservative).

The symbol "P" refers to proportional representation; "LP" to limited proportional representation; "FPP" to Britain's system of "first past the post" constituencies; and "TTC" to France's two-tiered elections with single constituencies.

public opinions, there is a clear effect of party and electoral systems: the correspondence between citizen and élite views is highest in multi-party systems and systems of proportional representation.[54]

The summary in Table 7.4 shows that this pattern also holds for the degree of polarization in public opinions of security issues. The table provides a summary of the number of parties that compete in elections and the electoral system that governs in each country: pure proportional representation in the Netherlands; limited proportional representation in West Germany (where parties must exceed 5 per cent of the vote to gain representation in parliament); and plurality-based constituencies in Britain and France. The table also summarizes the distance between major parties on three issues described earlier in this book: NATO, defense spending, and the military balance. As we have seen repeatedly in previous chapters, opinion is most polarized in France and the Netherlands, with the West Germans and British less divided.

The data support what might be called an "institutional" effect on public opinion: in the multi-party systems (France and the Netherlands) the diversity of viewpoints is reflected in the greater polarization of public opinion. Where the party system offers fewer choices (Britain and West Germany), opinions are less divided, perhaps reflecting the pressure to seek votes in the moderate center.

At first glance, the effect of electoral systems seems less uniform, for the two countries with plurality-based systems (Britain and France) differ greatly in the degree of polarization on security issues. Yet the French electoral system is not a simple plurality system, as is the case in Britain's one round, "first past the post" elections. Rather, French elections proceed in two rounds, with all parties competing in the first round to place among the two finalists for a second round to decide constituency representatives. The initial round in French elections have been decidedly multi-party affairs, with up to seven parties competing effectively. In this sense, the French systems bears some political resemblance to systems of proportional representation, for the first round of legislative elections provides incentives for parties to stake out a clear profile, either to qualify for the second round or to place pressure on the parties that do. This contrasts sharply with Britain's "first past the post" elections, where there are incentives to seek the center in the single, deciding vote. In sum, although the French system is not governed by proportional representation, its singular type of election offers many of the same incentives as do systems of proportional representation.

Obviously, this same hypothesis might explain the variations in generational cleavage seen in previous chapters, for like these partisan gaps, generational differences are also highest and most consistent in France and the Netherlands. Since the young educated do identify with parties of the Left, these generational differences might be nothing more than an institutional effect, since the Left in these systems may be capturing the support of the successor generation. It is difficult to evaluate this hypothesis, for as Table 7.5 shows, France and the Netherlands also provide support for the competing hypothesis of the generational theorists: it is in these countries that access to higher education has been historically highest, and during the crucial socialization period of the "détente generation" during the 1960s, it was in these countries that access to higher education expanded most rapidly. Generational division on security issues is also highest in these countries. If the cognitive and socialization effects of higher education are as hypothesized by generational theorists, this comparison of access to higher education would support the theory.

It is impossible to sort out the relative impact of the institutional

Table 7.5   The Expansion of University Education and Generational
Conflict on Security Issues

	University attendance as Per cent of 20–24 age group			
	1965	1970	% Change	Generation gap in security opinions
France	9	18	100	11
Netherlands	8	13	63	11
West Germany	6	12	100	7
Britain	4	6	50	5

NOTES: The first three columns show the percentage of eligible young people who attended university in 1965 and 1970 and the percentage growth rate in these figures between 1965 and 1970. The generation gap in security opinions is the average absolute difference of "successor generation" opinions and the opinions of the overall population on three questions in 1980: NATO essential, defense spending and the NATO–Warsaw Pact military balance.

SOURCES: Educational statistics are taken from Peter Flora, *et al., State, Economy and Society: a Data Handbook for Western Europe* (Chicago, Ill. and Frankfurt: St James's Books, 1983) Ch. 10. The generation gap in opinions was computed from Tables 3.8, 5.4, and 6.5

effects of the party system and the generational impact of access to higher education, for in statistical terms these variables are perfectly "colinear": access to education is highest in the multi-party, proportional systems. Yet the consistent finding that domestic polarization is highest in France and the Netherlands leads to the second contradiction raised above: why has the *impact* of these cleavages varied so widely?

France is the obvious paradox. French public opinion is really not much different from opinion in other countries. French support for increasing the defense budget has always been low. On many questions that touch on the "nuclear neuralgia"·, French opinion matches the "no first use" sentiments visible elewhere. Moreover, on all of these issues the French public is deeply divided.

Yet the impact of these popular sentiments has been very low. Despite an "anti-nuclear" public in the 1960s, de Gaulle moved rapidly forward with the *force de frappe*. In the 1980s the peace movements that erupted in Holland, Britain, and West Germany had no counterparts in France. And in any case, public skepticism about nuclear weapons and defense spending have little impact on the

French government. Like other countries, France increased defense spending throughout the 1970s, and the government has been moving toward greater rather than lesser reliance on nuclear weapons. What explains this French immunity?

The answer must be sought in institutional factors. What distinguishes France, of course, is the unique superimposition of the Presidency on an otherwise parliamentary system of government. Elected for a seven-year term, the President, like his American counterpart, is insulated from the popular pressures and divisions that affect Prime Ministers in pure parliamentary systems. Moreover (and unlike his American counterpart), the President's powers are far more independent of legislative interference than is the power of other heads of government. Although no French President could claim the equation of state and President in the manner of de Gaulle, all French Presidents profit from a governmental system that provides them with considerably more independence than is the case elsewhere. To these factors we must add the intangible but no less important variable of national tradition. In France, defense begins with *l'Indépendance*, a tradition that enjoys universal support and that stigmatizes even modest proposals for reform.[55] In addition, the presence of the Communist Party on the Left delegitimizes dissent, for to agree with its views would be to identify with its Moscow orientation at a time of decidedly negative evaluations of the Soviet Union.

In fact, one could argue that these institutional and traditional factors also explain the ability of British governments to resist popular pressures and to withstand domestic polarization on security issues. Part of the independence of the Prime Minister arises from the electoral system, for minority viewpoints have little chance of upsetting a government or clouding the electoral horizon – witness the elections of 1983 and 1987, which found the Tories with large legislative majorities based on less than 50 per cent of the vote. But there are intangible factors similar to those that operate in France. In both countries, foreign and defense policy are considered the preserve of a very small group of executive officers – not always elected – who operate in what Heclo and Wildavsky have called a "private village" or culture of policy-making.[56] In France, of course, the culture of the Presidency is, in fact, anti-populist: the President is leader of all France, with the emphasis on leading.

In summary, both institutional provisions and the culture of executive power help explain why the governments of France and Britain have managed, despite deep domestic divisions, to proceed largely independent of popular pressures. In West Germany and the Netherlands, in contrast, there is neither a tradition of strong executive power (least of all in West Germany) nor an electoral system that can provide a buffer from popular pressures. Therefore, despite similar levels and divisions in public opinion across all four countries on controversial issues of national security, the *impact* of public opinion probably has less to do with the particular level of support for defense spending, nuclear weapons, arms control, or American policy. The significant factors in the impact of public opinion are found in the mediating effect of institutions and traditions quite unrelated to national security.

The final paradox is therefore that, as concerns the impact of public opinion on security issues, the most dramatic future development would come not in a fluctuation of the percentage of the public who support defense spending or arms control. It would come in the reform of electoral systems. In Britain, for example, there has been persistent discussion of electoral reform that would introduce proportional representation. If my analysis is correct, such a change would do more to bring pressure on British governments than would any change in global events or NATO policy. Despite the uproar of concern about pacifism, denuclearization, and the "democratization" of security policies, this analysis suggests that the crucial variables are to be found in such basics of governance as constitutions, electoral laws, and party systems.

Appendix 1: Statistical Significance between Sub-samples

Estimated Sampling Error for Differences between Two Percentages for Stratified Probability Samples Conducted by Survey Research Center

Part A For percentages from 35 to 65

Number of interviews	2000	1000	700	500	400	300	200	100
2000	3.2–4.0	3.9–4.9	4.4–5.5	5.0–6.2	5.5–6.9	6.2–7.8	7.4–9.2	10–12
1000		4.5–5.6	4.9–6.1	5.5–6.9	5.9–7.4	6.6–8.3	7.7–9.6	10–13
700			5.3–6.6	5.9–7.4	6.3–7.9	6.9–8.6	8.0–10	11–13
500				6.3–7.9	6.7–8.4	7.3–9.1	8.4–10	11–13
400					7.1–8.9	7.6–9.5	8.7–11	11–14
300						8.2–10	9.1–11	12–14
200							10–12	12–15
100								14–17

Part B For percentages around 20 and 80*

Number of interviews	2000	1000	700	500	400	300	200	100
2000	2.5–3.1	3.1–3.9	3.5–4.4	4.0–5.0	4.4–5.5	5.0–6.2	5.9–7.4	8.2–9.8
1000		3.6–4.5	3.9–4.9	4.4–5.5	4.7–5.9	5.3–6.6	6.2–7.8	8.4–10
700			4.3–5.4	4.7–5.9	5.0–6.2	5.5–6.9	6.4–8.0	8.6–10
500				5.1–6.4	5.4–6.8	5.8–7.2	6.7–8.4	8.8–11
400					5.7–7.1	6.1–7.6	6.9–8.6	9.0–11
300						6.5–8.1	7.3–9.1	9.2–11
200							8.0–10	9.8–12
100								11–14

NOTE: The values are the differences between two subgroups in a sample (or subgroups in two different samples) necessary for considering the difference between the two subgroups to be significant. Significance is defined here as results that are two standard errors apart.

*For differences around 10% or around 90% the percentage difference for a "significant" difference between two subgroups is smaller. For percentages near 5% or 95%, the percentage difference needed for a "significant" difference is smaller still.

SOURCE: Ronald Freedman, Pascal K. Whelpton, and Arthur A. Campbell, *Family Planning and Sterility* (New York: McGraw-Hill, 1959); reprinted with permission of the publishers.

Appendix 2: A Note on Sources of Public Opinion Data

Two types of public opinion data are available to researchers. First, there are a large number of data summarized in percentage form in government reports, scholarly works, periodicals, and news sources. Secondly, some original surveys are deposited in archives and are available for re-analysis. This Appendix provides a brief guide to both types of source. I have limited the discussion to sources that provide data for a substantial period or that are especially rich in data on a particular issue or a particular point in time. Other sources are listed in the Bibliography. In addition, some of the sources listed in the Bibliography contain additional bibliographies of numerous surveys conducted by news organizations or scholarly organizations in single countries. The books by Capitanchik and Eichenberg and by Flynn and Rattinger (listed in Part A.4 of the bibliography) are useful for this type of data.

1. COMPARATIVE SOURCES

Office of Research, United States Information Agency (301 4th St SW, Suite 352, Washington, D.C. 20547). This is the richest source of comparative, historical data. The USIA has conducted surveys in Europe since the 1950s, and until recently, their reports were deposited in government repository libraries in the United States. However, the sensitivity of the INF missile issue led to some restrictions in access to USIA reports. As of this writing (early 1988), the policy of the Agency seems to be that the survey data themselves are available to scholars one year after the survey date. The reports, however, remain restricted, and USIA prefers that researchers request data from the National Archives, where all USIA Surveys are deposited.

Machine-Readable Branch, US National Archives and Records Service (Washington, D.C. 20408). The original USIA surveys are now available from the US National Archives, although several limitations should be noted. First, there is a delay between the administration of the surveys in Europe and delivery to the Archives by USIA. Secondly, the Archives are understaffed, and "accessioning" of surveys (the cleaning and documenting of the data) is a halting process, although it is usually expedited by scholarly interest. It was only in Spring 1987 that the Archives received USIA surveys conducted between 1982 and 1984, but these had not been "accessioned" at that time.

ICPSR: Inter-University Consortium for Political and Social Research (PO Box 1248, Ann Arbor, Mich. 48106). For American scholars the ICPSR is a valuable source of opinion data. Not only does ICPSR archive American data (see below). Through its affiliation with European archives, it also acquires election and other surveys. Most useful among these is the *Eurobarometer* series, listed separately in the Bibliography below. The *Eurobarometers* have included numerous questions on security issues in recent years, and they remain a valuable source of data on European Community and domestic policy issues. The ICPSR also archives important European election studies on a routine basis, and it can request others from European archives. The ICPSR *Guide to Resources* (yearly) provides a detailed listing of these surveys.

Other Comparative Sources. Several periodicals occasionally publish comparative articles and data on European public opinion on security issues. Most useful in this regard are *Public Opinion* magazine, *The Public Opinion Quarterly,* and *World Opinion Update.* In addition, the Stockholm International Peace Research Institute (SIPRI) now publishes a summary of public opinion in its *Yearbook* (Oxford University Press) and maintains a file of public opinion data for researchers who visit the Institute.

2. NATIONAL SOURCES

West Germany

Zentralarchiv für Empirische Sozialforschung (Bachemerstrasse 40, 5000 Köln 41). The Zentralarhiv is the headquarter archive for West German scholarly studies. It archives German election studies, which have recently increased their coverage of security isssues, as well as other surveys of interest to students of security. The holdings of the Zentralarchiv, listed in its *Catalog*, are available to Americans through the ICPSR.

Press and Information Office, Federal Ministry of Defense (Postfach 1328, 5300 Bonn). The Ministry sponsors numerous surveys devoted entirely to security issues. These are listed below in Part B.1 of the Bibliography. These surveys are also occasionally summarized in the Ministry's newsletter *Material für die Presse*.

Commercial Survey Organizations. West Germany has more commercial polling than any European country. The best-known agencies are the Allensbacher Institut für Demoskopie (7753 Allensbach Am Bodensee) and the EMNID Institute (Bodelschinghstr. 23–5a, Postfach 2540, 48 Bielefeld). Allensbach and EMNID publish newsletters (*Allensbacher Berichte; EMNID Informationen*). In addition, Allensbach's director, Elisabeth Noelle-Neumann, edits a series of volumes summarizing Allensbach surveys. A list of these volumes is in Part B.1 of the Bibliography.

Netherlands

Steinmetz Archives (Herengracht 410–412, 1017 BX Amsterdam). The Steinmetz Archive is the headquarter archive for scholarly (and other) studies of Dutch public opinion. It holds copies of the *Dutch Continuous Surveys* and of Dutch election studies, both of which have increasingly touched on security issues. The holdings of the Steinmetz Archive are available to Americans through the ICPSR.

POLLS Archive (Baschwitz Institute, Weteringschans 100–102, 1017 XS Amsterdam). The POLLS Archive is unique and invaluable, but it is not a machine-readable archive. That is, it does not archive the original survey responses. However, it does index and file summaries of the responses to surveys from throughout the world. Users of the archive can therefore search the files for responses to particular types of questions administered anywhere in the world.

Press Office [Voorlicting], Ministry of Defense (Postbus 20701, 2500 ES, The Hague). The Ministry conducts yearly surveys on security issues. Occasional reports of the Ministry are listed in Part B.4 of the Bibliography.

Commercial Survey Organizations. Very good coverage of security issues is provided by NIPO (Netherlands Instituut voor de publieke opinie, Westerdokhuis, Barentzplein 7, 1013 NJ Amsterdam). Occasional NIPO reports are listed in Part B.4 of the Bibliography. NIPO also issues frequent press releases under the title *NIPO Berichten*. There are a number of other commercial surveys in the Netherlands, frequently sponsored by newspapers and television stations. These are well covered in the works of Professor Philip Everts, listed in Part B.4 of the Bibliography.

Britain

Economic and Social Research Archive (University of Essex, Colchester, Essex, England C04 3SQ). The British equivalent to the ICPSR, the ESR Archive maintains copies of British election studies and some commercial surveys.

Commercial Survey Organizations. I know of no publicly available government surveys in Britain, but this gap is redressed by the wealth of commercial survey material. The best source is the British Gallup poll (Social Surveys, Ltd, 202 Finchley Road, London NW3 6BL). British Gallup repeats a number of interesting survey questions and publishes them regularly in *Gallup Political Index*. Other commercial organizations, such as MORI (Market and Opinion Research International), conduct frequent polls for British newspapers and magazines. This material is brought together in an excellent doctoral dissertation by Oksana Dackiw, listed in Part B.2 of the Bibliography.

France

Commercial Survey Organizations. Opinion data is most scarce for France. In early years, commercial surveys were published in *Sondages*, a periodical that ceased publication in 1978. A new publication, *L'Opinion Publique*, has been published yearly since 1985 (Paris: Gallimard). In addition, the periodical *L'Armée d'aujourd'hui* publishes a yearly report on its survey of public opinion on security issues. Finally, some machine-readable surveys are available from the Banque de Données Sociopolitiques (University of Grenoble, Grenoble, France).

United States

Inter-University Consortium for Political and Social Research (address above). The ICPSR has rich holdings of American opinion data. These include the entire series of American election studies, the surveys of the Chicago Council on Foreign Relations, and occasional surveys conducted by individual scholars and commercial organizations (such as the CBS/*New York Times* election surveys).

Scholarly Works. American opinion is much better documented through scholarly works than is the case with European opinion. Historical trends in opinions are described in the works of Graham, Holsti, Hughes, Mueller, Page, and Shapiro (all listed in Part B.5 of the Bibliography). Detailed analyses of more recent surveys are contained in the works of Holsti and Rosenau, Rielly, Russett and Hansen, Schneider, and Wittkopf.

Commercial Survey Organizations. Virtually every American survey firm (Gallup, Harris, CBS/*New York Times*) conducts surveys on security issues. These are usually reported in newspapers and in the periodicals listed above under "Other Comparative Sources". In addition, the Bureau of Public Affairs of the US Department of State maintains a clipping file of American public opinion on foreign policy issues.

Notes

Notes to Chapter 2: Crisis or Consensus?

1. On the theme of continuity, see Stanley Hoffmann, "NATO at Thirty: Variations on Old Themes", *International Security*, 4/2 (Summer 1979) pp. 88–107; and Anton W. DePorte, *Europe Between the Superpowers: The Enduring Balance* (New Haven, Conn: Yale University Press, 1979).
2. Eliot A. Cohen, "The Long-Term Crisis of the Alliance", *Foreign Affairs*, 61/2 (Winter 1982/3) pp. 325–43; Irving Kristol, "Does NATO Exist?", in Kenneth Myers (ed.), *NATO: The Next Thirty Years* (Boulder, Col.: Westview Press, 1981) pp. 361–72.
3. Lawrence Freedman, "NATO Myths", *Foreign Policy*, 45 (Winter 1982) p. 48.
4. Francis Pym, "Defense in Democracies: the Public Dimension", *International Security*, 7/1 (Summer 1982) pp. 40, 44; emphasis as in the original.
5. In the voluminous literature on public opinion in the 1980s, I found only three studies that provide this type of detailed "three-way" breakdown. All deal with West Germany: Stephen Szabo, "West Germany: Generations and Changing Security Perspectives", in Stephen Szabo (ed.), *The Successor Generation: International Perspectives of Postwar Europeans* (London: Butterworth, 1983); Gregory F. T. Winn, "Westpolitik: Germany and the Atlantic Alliance", *Atlantic Community Quarterly*, 21/2 (Summer 1983) pp. 140–50; and Harald Mueller and Thomas Risse-Kappen, "Origins of Estrangement: the Peace Movement and the Changed Image of America in West Germany", *International Security*, 12/1 (Summer 1987) pp. 52–88.
6. Michael Howard, *The Causes of Wars* (Cambridge, Mass.: Harvard University Press, 1983) pp. 4–5.
7. Gregory Flynn and Hans Rattinger (eds), *The Public and Atlantic Defense* (Totowa, N.J.: Rowman and Allanheld, 1985) p. 381.
8. As cited in Lawrence Freedman, *The Evolution of Nuclear Strategy* (London: Macmillan, 1981) p. 364.
9. Robert Keohane and Joseph Nye, *Power and Interdependence* (Boston, Mass: Little, Brown, 1977) esp. pp. 27–9.
10. Cited in ibid., p. 26.
11. Pym, "Defense in Democracies", p. 40.
12. The most comprehensive statement of Ronald Inglehart's theory is *The Silent Revolution: Changing Values and Political Styles Among Western Publics* (Princeton, N.J.: Princeton University Press, 1977); see also his later study, "Postmaterialism in an Environment of Insecurity", *American Political Science Review*, 75/4 (December 1981) pp. 880–900.
13. Peter Flora, *et al.*, *State, Economy and Society in Western Europe, 1815–1975* (Chicago, Ill.: St James Press, 1983) ch. 10.
14. Inglehart, *Silent Revolution*, p. 76.

15. Seyom Brown, *New Forces in World Politics* (Washington, D.C.: Brookings Institution, 1974); see also Mueller and Risse-Kappen, "Origins of Estrangement".

16. Two excellent reviews of the problems involved in the study of generational change are Paul Beck, "Young versus Old in 1984: Generations and Life Stages in Presidential Nominating Politics", *PS*, 17/3 (Summer 1984) pp. 515–25; and Kent Jennings and Richard G. Niemi, *Generations and Politics* (Princeton, N.J.: Princeton University Press, 1981).

17. Beck, "Young vs. Old in 1984", p. 521.

18. Inglehart, "Post-Materialism in an Environment of Insecurity"; and Russell Dalton, "Was There a Revolution? a Note on Generational versus Life-Cycle Explanations of Value Differences", *Comparative Political Studies*, 9/4 (January 1977) pp. 459–75. For an informative exchange of views between Inglehart and his critics, see the entire issue of *Comparative Political Studies*, 17/4 (January 1985).

19. Kent Jennings, "Residues of a Movement: the Aging of the American Protest Generation", *American Political Science Review*, 81/2 (June 1987) pp. 367–82.

20. A number of these studies is reviewed in Richard C. Eichenberg, "Strategy and Consensus: Public Support for Military Policy in Industrial Democracies", in Edward Kolodziej and Patrick Morgan (eds), *National Security and Arms Control: A Reference Guide to Theory and Practice* (Westport, Conn.: Greenwood Press, 1989).

21. Flynn and Rattinger, *The Public and Atlantic Defense*, pp. 377–9.

22. Ronald Inglehart, "The Changing Structure of Political Cleavages in Western Society", in Russell Dalton, Scott Flanagan and Paul Beck (eds), *Electoral Change in Advanced Industrial Democracies* (Princeton, N.J.: Princeton University Press, 1984) pp. 34, 22.

23. Michael Howard, *War and the Liberal Conscience* (New Brunswick, N.J.: Rutgers University Press, 1978); on the similarity of idealist thinking and the demands of the peace movements, see Stanley Hoffmann, "Realism and its Discontents", *The Atlantic* (November 1985) pp. 131–6.

24. This review follows Howard, *War and the Liberal Conscience*, as well as Felix Gilbert's history of the influence of European idealism on American thought: *To the Farewell Address: Early Ideas of American Foreign Policy* (Princeton, N.J.: Princeton University Press, 1961) esp. ch. 3.

25. The peace movements of the 1950s were not the only examples. See Alfred Grosser, *The Western Alliance* (New York: Vintage Books, 1982).

26. A good introduction to survey analysis is found in Paul Abramson, *Political Attitudes in America* (San Francisco, Calif.: Freeman, 1983) chs 2 and 3.

27. Kenneth Adler, "The Successor Generation: Why, Who, and How?", in Szabo, *The Successor Generation*, p. 9.

28. Views of INF are described in Chapter 4 and views of defense spending in Chapter 6.

29. Michael Harrison, "The Successor Generation, Social Change and New Domestic Sources of Foreign Policy in France", in Szabo, *The Successor Generation*, p. 35; Kenneth Adler and Douglas Wertman, "West Euro-

pean Concerns for the 1980s: Is NATO in Trouble?", paper presented to the 1981 Annual Meeting of the American Association of Public Opinion Research, Buck Hills Falls, Pa, p. 11; Werner J. Feld and John K. Wildgen, *NATO and the Atlantic Defense* (New York: Praeger, 1982) pp. 103–4.

30. The full responses to this question are presented in Chapter 4; they are drawn from Office of Research, USIA, *West European Public Opinion on Key Security Issues, 1981–82*, Report R–10–82 (Washington, D.C., June 1982).

31. Surveys presented in Chapter 5 show that West German support for NATO rarely falls below 60 per cent.

32. *Washington Post*, 17 April 1980, p. A–1. Surveys on alternatives to NATO are presented in Chapter 5 below.

33. I am grateful to Jan Siccama of the Dutch Institute of International Affairs for this characterization.

34. *Allensbach Report*, E–4 (1980) p. 4.

35. Ibid., p. 4 and Table 5.

36. Feld and Wildgen, *NATO and the Atlantic Defense*, p. 97.

37. Office of Research, USIA, *Multi-Regional Security Survey: Questions and Responses* (Washington, D.C.: April 1980) p. 3.

38. Werner Kaltefleiter, "Public Support for NATO in Europe", in Meyers, *NATO: The Next Thirty Years*, p. 399.

39. These relationships are explored at length in Chapter 3.

40. Hans Rattinger, "National Security and the Missile Controversy in West Germany", paper delivered to the Annual Meeting of the American Political Science Association, Washington, D.C., September 1982.

41. John Mueller, *War, Presidents and Public Opinion* (New York: Wiley, 1973); Richard Merritt, "Public Opinion and Foreign Policy in the Federal Republic of Germany", in Patrick McGowan (ed.), *Sage Yearbook of Foreign Policy Studies* (Beverly Hills, Calif: Sage Publications, 1973); Martin Abravanel and Barry Huges, "Public Opinion and Foreign Policy Behavior: a Cross-National Study of Linkages", in Patrick McGowan (ed.), *Sage Yearbook of Foreign Policy Studies* (Beverly Hills, Calif.: Sage Publications, 1974).

42. Stephen Szabo, "The West German Security Debate: the Search for Alternative Strategies", paper presented to the Annual Meeting of the International Studies Association, Atlanta, Ga, March 1984.

43. Gregory Flynn, "Public Opinion and Atlantic Defense", *NATO Review*, 31/5 (December 1983) p. 5.

44. The German poll on flexible response is reproduced in Richard C. Eichenberg, "Public Opinion and National Security in Europe and the United States", in Linda Brady and Joyce Kaufmann (eds), *NATO in the 1980s* (New York: Praeger, 1985) p. 240. On the relative salience of security issues, see Flynn and Rattinger, *The Public and Atlantic Defense*, pp. 366–9.

45. For a review of this literature, see Adler, "The Successor Generation: Why, Who, How?".

46. Since the surveys analyzed here are available from archives (listed in Appendix 2 and the Bibliography) other scholars can retrieve them to

test their own definitions of generations for particular countries, issues, or years.

47. Karl Mannheim, "The Sociological Problem of Generations", in Paul Kecskemeti (ed.), *Essays on the Sociology of Knowledge* (London: Routledge and Kegan Paul, 1952) p. 291.
48. The literature on generational differences in American security opinions is reviewed in Robert Wells, "The Vietnam War and Generational Difference in Foreign Policy Attitudes", in Margaret Karns (ed.) *Persistent Patterns and Emerging Structures* (New York: Praeger, 1986) pp. 99–125.
49. See Jennings and Niemi, *Generations and Politics* p. 20–2.
50. Inglehart, *Silent Revolution*, p. 11.
51. Most theories of generational change emphasize young adulthood – age 18–25 – as the crucial period in the crystallization of political attitudes. For a review, see Adler, "The Successor Generation: Why, Who, How?".

Notes to Chapter 3: The Ambiguous Politics of Parity: Power and Deterrence in European Public Opinion

1. Anton W. DePorte, *Europe Between the Superpowers: The Enduring Balance* (New Haven, Conn.: Yale University Press, 1979) pp. ix–xii, 243–4; the quote is from p. ix.
2. For a forceful analysis along these lines, see Edward Kolodziej, "Europe: the Partial Partner", *International Security*, 5/3 (Winter 1981) pp. 104–31.
3. Arnold Wolfers, "National Security as an Ambiguous Symbol", in Arnold Wolfers, *Discord and Collaboration* (Baltimore, Md: Johns Hopkins University Press, 1962) pp. 147–66.
4. The following summary is taken from two works: Robert Keohane and Joseph Nye, *Power and Interdependence* (Boston, Mass.: Little, Brown, 1977) pp. 27–9; and Robert Keohane, Joseph Nye and C. Fred Bergsten, "International Economics and International Politics: a Framework for Analysis", in C. Fred Bergsten and Lawrence B. Krause (eds), *World Politics and International Economics* (Washington, D.C.: Brookings Institution, 1975) pp. 6–9.
5. On the "dominance" of military power and its relative utility, see Keohane and Nye, *Power and Interdependence*, p. 17. Other theorists also wrote of the paradox of military power in an age of nuclear parity. Edward Kolodziej, for example, wrote in 1982 that "If military power has never been so pervasive, its utility has never been more questionable"; see "Living with the Long Cycle", in Edward Harkavy and Edward Kolodziej, (eds) *American Security Policy and Policy-Making* (Lexington, Mass.: Lexington Books, 1980) p. 35.
6. Werner Kaltefleiter, "Public Support for NATO in Europe", in Kenneth Myers (ed.), *NATO: The Next Thirty Years* (Boulder, Col.: Westview Press, 1981) p. 399.

7. Josef Joffe, "Peace and Populism: Why the European Anti-Nuclear Movement Failed", *International Security*, 11/4 (Spring 1987) p. 35. Samuel Huntington made a similar argument in "Broadening the Strategic Focus: Comments on Michael Howard's Paper", in International Institute for Strategic Studies, *Defence and Consensus: The Domestic Aspects of Western Security* (London: Adelphi Paper no. 184, 1983) p. 27.

8. Edward Morse, *Foreign Policy and Interdependence in Gaullist France* (Princeton, N.J.: Princeton University Press, 1974) p. 202.

9. Compare the arguments in Robert Art, "To What Ends Military Power?", *International Security* 4/4 (Spring 1980) pp. 3–35; and David Baldwin, "Power Analysis and World Politics", *World Politics*, 31/2 (January 1979) pp. 161–94, esp. p. 181.

10. Edward Lutwak, "The Missing Dimension of US Defense Policy: Force, Perceptions and Power", as cited in Lawrence Freedman, *The Evolution of Nuclear Strategy* (London: Macmillan, 1981) p. 368.

11. Richard Betts, "Elusive Equivalence: the Political and Military Meaning of the Nuclear Balance", in Samuel P. Huntington (ed.), *The Strategic Imperative* (Cambridge, Mass.: Ballinger, 1982) p. 120.

12. John Mearsheimer notes that concern for European confidence has infused American strategic policy throughout the postwar period: "Nuclear Weapons and Deterrence in Europe", *International Security*, 9/3 (Winter 1984–5), esp. pp. 23–4.

13. Richard M. Nixon, *US Foreign Policy for the 1970s: The Emerging Structure of Peace* (Washington, D.C.: Government Printing Office, 1972) p. 158.

14. The statement is from the Secretary's *Annual Report 1976*, as cited in Freedman, *Evolution of Nuclear Strategy*, p. 369. As Freedman notes (p. 383), Schlesinger explicitly related the flexible options policy to the need to reassure the Europeans of the credibility of extended deterrence.

15. Ibid., p. 370.

16. Ibid.

17. Warner Schilling, "US Strategic Nuclear Concepts in the 1970s: the Search for Sufficiently Equivalent Countervailing Parity", *International Security*, 6/2 (Fall 1981) p. 63. Schilling concedes that the phrase is carefully chosen. For a similar conclusion based in part on opinion surveys, see George Quester, "The Superpowers and the Atlantic Alliance", *Daedalus*, 110/1 (Winter 1981) pp. 23–40.

18. Art, "To What Ends Military Power?", p. 29. In fairness to Keohane and Nye, it should be pointed out that they also made this observation: *Power and Interdependence*, p. 28.

19. Catherine M. Kelleher, "The Conflict Without: Europeans and the Use of Force", in Sam Sarkesian (ed.), *Non-Nuclear Conflicts in the Nuclear Age* (New York: Praeger, 1979). Many of the topics in the previous paragraphs are covered by Kelleher in an incisive essay, "The Nation-State and National Security in Western Europe", in Catherine M. Kelleher and Gale Mattox (eds), *Evolving European Defense Policies* (Lexington, Mass.: Lexington Books, 1986) pp. 3–14.

20. See the discussion by Freedman, *Evolution of Nuclear Strategy*, pp.

362–3 and the strong statement of this position in Jane Sharp, "Arms Control, Alliance Cohesion and Extended Deterrence", paper presented to a conference on Prospects for Peacemaking, Minneapolis, Minn., November 1984. For research on political versus military determinants of deterrence, see Bruce Russett and Paul Huth, "What Makes Deterrence Work?", *World Politics*, 36/4 (July 1984) pp. 496–526.

21. In a 1979 speech in Brussels, Henry Kissinger said: "to be tactless – the secret dream of every Europeans was, of course, to avoid a nuclear war but, secondly, if there had to be a nuclear war, to have it conducted over their heads by the strategic forces of the United States and the Soviet Union". The speech is reprinted in Myers, *NATO: The Next Thirty Years*, pp. 3–14, with the quote at p. 8.

22. The surveys on US and Soviet strength "in Europe" are found in Office of Research, USIA, *West European Public Opinion on Key Security Issues, 1981–1982*, Report R–10–82 (Washington, D.C.: June 1982) Tables 8 and 9.

23. Ibid., Table 8.

24. The 1982/3 edition of the *Military Balance* concluded that "even with the inclusion of the Poseidon/Trident [submarine systems] on the Western side, the balance is distinctly unfavorable to NATO and is becoming more so" (International Institute for Strategic Studies, *The Military Balance, 1982/1983* (London: 1982) p. 135).

25. Pieter Dankert, "US–European Relations: Defense Policy and the Euromissiles", in Richard C. Eichenberg (ed.), *Drifting Together or Apart?* (Lanham, Md: University Press of America, for the Harvard Center for International Affairs, 1986) p. 68. Earl Ravenal offers a slightly different characterization: "even the whiff of American nuclear retaliation is probably enough to keep the Soviet Union from invading Western Europe"; cited in Mearsheimer, "Nuclear Weapons and Deterrence in Europe", p. 22.

26. The figures in the preceding paragraph are from the following reports of the Office of Research, USIA: *West European Perceptions of NATO*, Report M–7–78 (Washington, D.C.: 8 May 1978) p. 7; *West European Perceptions of NATO and Mutual Defense Issues*, Report R–27–79 (Washington, D.C.: 20 December 1979) pp. 24–5; *Multi-Regional Security Survey: Questions and Responses* (Washington, D.C.: April 1980) p. 6; and *March 1986 Multi-Issue Survey [Contractor's Reports]* (Washington, D.C.: 1986).

27. The literature on the European conventional force balance is voluminous. For recent contributions, see Steven Miller (ed.), *Conventional Forces and American Defense Policy* (Princeton, N.J.: Princeton University Press, 1986); and Andrew Pierre (ed.), *The Conventional Defense of Europe: New Technologies and New Strategies* (New York: Council on Foreign Relations, 1986).

28. Office of Research, USIA, *West European Public Opinion on Key Security Issues, 1981–82*, Report no. R–10–82 (Washington, D.C.: 1982) Table 18; and Office of Research, USIA, *NATO and Burden-Sharing*, Report M–9–11–84 (Washington, D.C.: July 1984) Tables 5 and 6.

29. Office of the [West German] Federal Chancellor, Press and Information

Staff, "Dreissig Jahre NATO", report of surveys conducted on the occasion of NATO's thirtieth anniversary (Bonn: 29 October 1979); surveys by Allensbach.

30. Ronald Inglehart, *The Silent Revolution: Changing Values and Political Styles among Western Publics* (Princeton, N.J.: Princeton University Press, 1977) p. 11.

31. Ibid., p. 76.

32. Francis Pym, "Defense in Democracies: the Public Dimension", *International Security*, 7/1 (Summer 1982) p. 40.

33. Given the difference in wording, the levels of responses should not be compared across the two questions. Rather, the focus of comparison is the degree of polarization *within* each question.

34. SINUS [Sozialwissenschaftliches Institut Nowak und Sorgel], *Rückwirkungen weltpolitischer und weltwirtschaftlicher Ereignisse auf die politische Lage unseres Landes* (Munich: October 1982) p. 25. The survey was conducted for the Office of the Federal Chancellor.

35. Age differences were examined in five surveys, including the 1979 survey shown in Table 3.6 and the USIA's *Multi-Regional Security Survey* for 1980. Educational differences were examined in eleven surveys conducted between 1979 and 1981. Only in West Germany (in 1979) and the Netherlands (in 1978) were age or educational differences of any significance. These are discussed below.

36. The term moderate is used because differences of this magnitude are not statistically significant given the extremely small size of the educated sub-samples. None the less, we shall see this "successor generation" pattern repeatedly in later chapters.

37. The three-way breakdowns were also computed for the 1980 survey (available in Britain and France only). In France, there is a patterning of views along the Left–Right axis only for those under 35 years of age, with young, educated Socialists being the most optimistic about the power balance. In Britain, the Left–Right pattern prevails throughout the population, but *older*, educated Labourites are the most optimistic.

38. Another hint that this may be the case is that the correlation of power perceptions with age, education, and party affiliations in this chapter is much lower than with opinions on other security issues presented in later chapters.

39. Public opinion is not the only example of outwardly "inconsistent" reasoning. Governments also base their defense policy decisions on economic and political grounds. Citizens are no different. They may discount or ignore their view of the military situation because of competing concerns.

40. All of these associations approach or exceed the .01 level of significance.

41. Exactly the same pattern was found in two German studies of opposition to INF deployment. The deployment was opposed most by those who perceived East–West military parity. See Karlheinz Reuband, "Issueorientierung und Nachrüstungsprotest", in Jürgen Falter, *et al.* (eds), *Politische Willensbildung und Interessenvermittlung* (Opladen: Westdeutscher Verlag, 1984) p. 596; and Harald Mueller and Thomas Risse-Kappen, "Origins of Estrangemement: the Peace Movement and the

Changed Image of America in West Germany", *International Security* 12/1 (Summer 1987) p. 67.

42. Etienne Davignon, "Europe and the United States: Relations on a Threshold?", in Eichenberg, *Drifting Together or Apart*, p. 52; emphasis in the original.

43. The West German threat index is from Press and Information Office, Federal Ministry of Defense, *Meinungsbild zur Wehrpolitschen Lage: Herbst 1983* (Bonn: August 1983) p. 16; British surveys are from Social Surveys Ltd, *Gallup Political Index*, February 1968 through January 1980.

44. Surveys on arms control negotiations and détente in general will be presented in Chapter 4, but one example will illustrate the point made here. In West Germany, the percentage of poll respondents who thought that *Ostpolitik* had reduced "the extent to which we must fear an attack from the East" was never higher than 36 per cent from 1974 to 1980, while the percentage who thought that "in this context *Ospolitik* has changed nothing" was never less than 52 per cent. See Press and Information Office, Federal Ministry of Defense, *Meinungsbild in der Bundesrepublik Deutschland zur Sicherheitspolitik* (Bonn: 1 October 1984) p. 2.

45. Surveys on defense spending are presented in Chapter 6. The Dutch poll is reported in Netherlands Institute for Public Opinion [NIPO], *Bericht* Nr 1650. During the 1970s, the West German Defense Ministry conducted a survey asking if the Bundeswehr was "sufficiently armed" or "underarmed"; the percentage answering "sufficiently armed" rose from 41 per cent in 1972 to 63 per cent in 1978; see Press and Information Office, *Hinweise für Öffentlichkeitsarbeit*, Nr 7/79 (Bonn: 14 September 1979) p. 78.

46. Lloyd Free, *How Others See Us: Report of the Commission on Critical Choices for Americans* (Lexington, Mass.: D. C. Heath, 1976) p. 69.

47. Kenneth Adler and Douglas Wertman, "West European Security Concerns for the 1980s: Is NATO in Trouble?", paper delivered to the 1981 Annual Meeting of the American Association for Public Opinion Research, Buck Hill Falls, Pa, Table 2; and Office of Research, USIA, *West European Opinion on Key Security Issues*, Table 10.

48. Figures for 1981 are in Office of Research, USIA, *West European Opinion on Key Security Issues*, Table 11. For later figures, see Kenneth Adler, "West European Attitudes Toward Peace, Defense and Disarmament", paper delivered to the 1985 Annual Meeting of the World Association for Public Opinion Research, Wiesbaden, Table 4.

49. Schilling, "US Strategic Nuclear Concepts in the 1970s", p. 65.

Notes to Chapter 4: Collision and Collusion

1. Helmut Schmidt, "Europa muss jetz handeln", *Die Zeit* (Overseas Edition), 11 January 1985, p. 1.
2. Helmut Schmidt, "The 1977 Alastair Buchan Memorial Lecture", reprinted in *Survival*, 20 (January/February 1978) p. 2–10.

3. The 1979 decision and its aftermath are reviewed in David Schwartz, *NATO's Nuclear Dilemma* (Washington, D.C.: Brookings Institution, 1983); and Leon V. Sigal, *Nuclear Forces in Europe: Enduring Dilemmas, Present Prospects* (Washington, D.C.: Brookings Institution, 1984).

4. The best history is Schwartz, *NATO's Nuclear Dilemma*. For an interesting statement of the dilemmas involved, see Jane Sharp, "Arms Control, Alliance Cohesion and Extended Deterrence", paper delivered to a Conference on Prospects for Peace, Minneapolis, Minnesota, 29 November 1984.

5. "A Europe of Two Minds", *New York Times*, 3 March 1987, p. 1; "Commander of NATO is Opposed to Ridding Europe of All Missiles", *New York Times*, 21 April 1987, p. 6; and "Analysts: Soviet Forces in Europe Exaggerated", *Boston Globe*, 26 April 1987, p. 2. For a summary of the impact of the zero option, see Jane Sharp, "After Reykjavik: Arms Control and the Allies", *International Affairs*, 63/2 (Spring 1987) pp. 239–57.

6. This point is nicely illustrated by Sharp, "Arms Control, Alliance Cohesion and Extended Deterrence"; for a theoretical statement of the "abandonment/entrapment" dilemma, see Glenn Snyder, "The Security Dilemma in Alliance Politics", *World Politics*, 26/4 (July 1984) pp. 461–94.

7. Michael Howard, *The Causes of Wars* (Cambridge, Mass.: Harvard University Press, 1983) p. 4.

8. "Bonn Now Seeking New US Missiles", *New York Times*, 8 April 1987, p. 18.

9. Strobe Talbott, *Deadly Gambits: The Reagan Administration and the Stalemate in Nuclear Arms Control* (New York: Alfred A. Knopf, 1984) p. 163; emphasis as in the original.

10. Nitze was referring to polls commissioned in Europe by the United States Information Agency (USIA). In most European countries, at least two government agencies are involved in public opinion polling: the Prime Minister's office and the Ministry of Defense.

11. Walter Laqueur, "Hollanditis: a New Stage of European Neutralism", *Commentary*, 19 August 1981, pp. 19–26.

12. Joseph Joffe, "The Eclipse of the Peace Movement", *New Republic*, 11 June 1984, pp. 21–3.

13. Seyom Brown, *New Forces in World Politics* (Washington, D.C.: Brookings Institution, 1974); and Robert Keohane and Joseph Nye, *Power and Interdependence* (Boston, Mass.: Little, Brown, 1977).

14. The British public's endorsement of the Falklands operation is reported in *The Economist*, 26 June 1982, p. 64.

15. Richard C. Eichenberg, "The Myth of Hollanditis", *International Security*, 8/2 (November 1983) pp. 152–4.

16. Laqueur, 'Hollanditis: a New Stage of European Neutralism".

17. Figures in the preceding paragraph are from Eichenberg, "The Myth of Hollanditis", pp. 146–7, 151–2; and Philip Everts, "The Impact of the Peace Movement on Public Opinion and Policy-Making: the Case of the Netherlands", paper prepared for the 21st European Conference of the Peace Science Society (International), Amsterdam, September 1986, Figures 1 and 2.

18. On these issues, see Reinhard Mutz, *Sicherheitspolitik und demokratische Öffentlichkeit in der Bundesrepublik Deutschland* (Munich: Oldenburg Verlag, 1978), and Ralph Zoll (ed.), *Wie Integriert ist die Bundeswehr?* (Munich: Piper Verlag, 1979).
19. Opinions of détente are presented later in this chapter. Surveys summarized in the preceding paragraph are drawn from Ralph Zoll, "Militär und Gesellschaft in der Bundesrepublik – Zum Problem der Legimität von Streitkräften", in Zoll, *Wie Integriert ist die Bundeswehr?*, p. 48; Hans Rattinger, "The Federal Republic of Germany: Much Ado About (Almost) Nothing", in Gregory Flynn and Hans Rattinger (eds), *The Public and Atlantic Defense* (Totowa, N.J.: Rowman and Allanheld, 1985) p. 129; Press and Information Office, [West German] Federal Ministry of Defense, *Meinungsbild in der Bundesrepublik zur Sicherheitspolitik* (Bonn: 1 October 1984) p. 6.
20. The general deterrence item is reported in Rattinger, "The Federal Republic of Germany", p. 133; the nuclear deterrence item is from Press and Information Office, *Meinungsbild in der Bundesrepublik zur Sicherheitspolitik*, p. 6.
21. *World Opinion Update*, 1/4 (July/August 1982) p. 91, and Connie de Boer, "The European Peace Movements and Deployment of Nuclear Missiles", *Public Opinion Quarterly*, 49 (Spring 1985) p. 122.
22. The latest survey in 1987 did show a decline, but it is difficult to tell whether this presages a downward trend. Note that the two questions in 1986 and 1987 which mentioned the Soviets elicited responses that are consistent with the high support of the past.
23. Renate Fritsch-Bournazel, "France: Attachment to a Nonbinding Relationship", in Flynn and Rattinger, *The Public and Atlantic Defense*, pp. 84–5, 87–8.
24. "L'opinion sur l'armée et la défense en 1983", *Armées d'aujourd'hui*, no. 88 (March 1984) p. 9.
25. "Opinions et défense en 1985", *Armées d'aujourd'hui*, no. 104 (October 1985) p. 15.
26. For French polls (now somewhat dated), see Edward Morse, *Foreign Policy and Interdependence in Gaullist France* (Princeton, N.J.: Princeton University Press, 1974) p. 175. British polls deal largely with the costs of acquiring the Trident nuclear submarine. See *Gallup Political Index*, no. 286 (June 1984); and Oksana Dackiw, "Defense Policy and Public Opinion: The Campaign for Nuclear Disarmament, 1945–1985", doctoral dissertation, Columbia University, 1986, ch. 4.
27. Josef Joffe, "Europe and America: the Politics of Resentment (Cont'd)", *Foreign Affairs*, 61/3 ("America and the World", 1982) pp. 569–90; and Stanley Hoffmann, "Cries and Whimpers: Thoughts on West European Relations in the 1980s", *Daedalus*, 113/3 (Summer 1984) pp. 221–52.
28. Commission of the European Communities, *Eurobarometre: Public Opinion in the European Communities*, no. 22 (Brussels: December 1984) Table 3.
29. *Washington Post*, 17 April 1980, p. A–1, and Office of Research, USIA,

West European Public Opinion on Key Security Issues, 1981–1982, Report R–10–82, (Washington, D.C.: June 1982) Table 14.

30. The favorability rating calculated by the USIA subtracts the percentage with unfavorable opinions of the United States from the percentage with favorable ratings to yield the "net favorable" figures mentioned in the text. Although the US ratings have declined considerably, it should also be noted that they remain "net favorable". Similar ratings for the Soviet Union have always shown very negative scores and also declined in the early 1980s. See Office of Research, USIA, *Long-Term Trends in Some General Orientations Toward the United States and USSR in West European Public Opinion*, Report R–12–83, (Washington,D.C.: July 1983) Tables 1 and 4.

31. Ivor Crewe reviews these data in two articles: "Britain Evaluates Ronald Reagan", *Public Opinion*, 6 (October/November 1984) pp. 46–9; and "Why the British Don't Like Us Anymore", *Public Opinion*, 9 (March/April 1987) pp. 51–6.

32. Based on four reports of the Office of Research, USIA: *Trends in US Standing in Western European Public Opinion*, Report R–4–82, (Washington, D.C.: February 1982) Tables 6 and 6a; *West European Public Opinion on Key Security Issues, 1981–1982*, Table 2; *Differences in Some Foreign Policy Views between Supporters of the Major West German Parties*, Report N–11/7/83 (Washington, D.C.: November 1983) Table 9; and *Multi-Issue Survey: March 1986 [Contractor's Reports]* (Washington, D.C.: mimeographed).

33. Office of Research, USIA, *Long-Term Trends in Some General Orientations Toward the US and USSR*, Tables 3, 6, 8, 10 and 11; and Ben J. Wattenberg, "Bad Marx: How the World Sees the Soviets", *Public Opinion* 9/6 (March/April 1987) p. 10.

34. Pieter Dankert, "US–European Relations: Defense Policy and the Euromissiles", in Richard C. Eichenberg (ed.), *Drifting Together or Apart? US–European Relations in the Paul-Henri Spaak Lectures* (Lanham, Md: University Press of America, 1986) p. 69.

35. Jan Stapel, *De Nederlander en het Kruisvluchtwapen* (The Hague: Netherlands Institute of International Relations [Clingendael], 1986) p. 4.

36. "The Cruise Missile Debate", *British Public Opinion*, 5/10 (October 1983) pp. 3–4.

37. Office of Research, USIA, *West European Public Opinion on Key Security Issues, 1981–1982*, Table 44, and *West Europeans Still Predominantly Oppose INF Deployment: Some Doubt US Commitment to Negotiations*, Report M–9/19/84 (Washington, D.C., 19 September 1984) Table 4. For a graphical presentation of similar data, see Stockholm International Peace Research Institute, *The Arms Race and Arms Control, 1984* (Philadelphia, Pa:Taylor and Francis, 1985) pp. 16–17.

38. Josef Joffe, "Peace and Populism: Why the European Anti-Nuclear Movement Failed", *International Security*, 11/4 (Spring 1987) p. 39.

39. *Dutch Continuous Surveys* (Amsterdam: Steinmetz Archives Study no. POlll) Waves 9 and 17; and Press and Information Office, Federal Ministry of Defense, *Sicherheit, Verteidigung und Öffentlicher Meinung*

(Bonn, 1979.)

40. Leo Crespi, "West European Public Opinion on Defense–Return to Better Red than Dead?" (Washington, D.C.: United States Information Agency, mimeographed, n.d.); see also Kenneth Adler and Charles Spencer, "European Public Opinion on Nuclear Arms: an Historical View", selected data for presentation to the Convention of the International Studies Association, Washington, D.C., March 1985, Tables 1 and 2.

41. Leon Sigal and John Steinbruner, *Alliance Security: The No-First-Use Question* (Washington, D.C.: Brookings Institution, 1983); Robert McNamara, "The Military Role of Nuclear Weapons", *Foreign Affairs*, 62/1 (Fall 1983) pp. 59–80.

42. Michael Gordon, "Commander of NATO is Opposed to Ridding Europe of All Missiles", *New York Times*, 21 April 1987, p. 6.

43. Elisabeth Noelle-Neumann, "The Art of Putting Ambivalent Questions", *Encounter*, (December 1983) pp. 79–82; and Hans Rattinger, "National Security and the Missile Controversy in the West German Public", paper delivered to the 1986 Convention of the American Political Science Association, Washington, D.C.

44. Office of Research, USIA, *West European Public Opinion on Key Security Issues, 1981–1982*, Table 41.

45. Unpublished surveys by Allensbach (8/1983) for the *Frankfurter Allgemeine Zeitung*; by EMNID (9/1983) for the West German Ministry of Defense; and by Forschungsgruppe Wahlen, E.V. (May, June, July, and September 1983).

46. Harris Poll of October 1983, as cited in Stockholm International Peace Research Institute, *The Arms Race and Arms Control, 1984*, pp. 18–19.

47. This is one line of criticism in James Schlesinger's scathing indictment of President Reagan's handling of the summit. See "Reykjavik and Revelations: a Turning of the Tide?", *Foreign Affairs*, 65/3 (America and the World, 1986) esp. pp. 435–7. Jane Sharp also covers these issues in "After Reykjavik".

48. See, for example, "A Europe of Two Minds", *New York Times*, 3 March 1987, p. 1; "Europeans Troubled by Soviet Arms Proposal", *Boston Globe*, 3 March 1987, p. 5; "NATO Agrees to Study Latest Soviet Offer", *Boston Globe*, 17 April 1987, p. 1; and "Make up Your Mind, Europe", *The Economist*, 2 May 1987, p. 47.

49. For a review of the history of the problem, see Schwartz, *NATO's Nuclear Dilemmas*. For a sample of recent discussions, see "Debate on Ending Missiles in Europe Dividing Experts", *New York Times*, 21 April 1987, p. 1; "Analysts: Soviet Forces in Europe Exaggerated", *Boston Globe*, 26 March 1987; and "A Missile Free Europe Europe: Little Impact on War", *New York Times*, 1 May 1987, p. 1.

50. *Stuttgarter Zeitung*, 3 June 1986, as cited in *The Week in Germany* (New York: German Information Center, 6 June 1986) p. 8.

51. Schlesinger, "Reykjavik and Revelations", pp. 436–7.

52. "A Europe of Two Minds", p. 1.

53. "Bonn Now Seeking US Missiles", *New York Times*, 8 April 1987, p. 18; "Bonn Divided on Missiles", *New York Times*, 28 April 1987, p. 10, "Bonn Coalition Openly Split on Short-Range Arms", *New York Times*,

8 May 1987, p. 9; "Double Zero Missile Question Vexing Kohl", *New York Times*, 19 May 1987, p. 3; and "Bonn's Coalition Agrees to endorse Missiles' Removal", *New York Times*, 2 June 1987, p. 1.

54. Office of Research, USIA, *West European Perceptions of NATO and Mutual Defense Issues*, Report R–7–79 (Washington: December 1979) pp. 28–9. The German poll is from Allensbach, as cited in *Dreissig Jahre NATO*, an unpublished report prepared by the Press and Information Staff of the [West German] Federal Chancellor's Office in 1979.

55. *The Allensbach Report*, no. E–3 (1980) p. 4 and Table 5.

56. Office of Research, USIA, *West European Public Opinion on Key Security Issues, 1981–1982*, Tables 36, 37 and 39; and *Europeans Still Predominantly Oppose INF*, Tables 6 and 7. The 1985 poll is from *World Opinion Update*, 10/1 (January 1986) pp. 6–7.

57. Crewe, "Why the British Don't Like Us Anymore", p. 56

58. In Britain in 1983, 38 per cent considered Reagan "believable" compared to 18 per cent for Gorbachev. In 1987, the figures were 20 per cent Reagan and 44 per cent Gorbachev. These figures were provided by Social Surveys Ltd (British Gallup) in mimeographed form. Similar German surveys are reported in the *New York Times*, 17 May 1987, p. 18.

59. Jeanne Kirkpatrick, "Europe's Drift Away from the United States", *Washington Post*, 25 May 1987, p. 19.

60. Harris survey, as reported in *World Opinion Update*, 9/10 (October 1985) p. 111; and *New York Times*, 1 October 1987, p. D27.

61. American opinion is described in more detail in Chapter 7. See also: Daniel Yankelovich and John Doble, "The Public Mood", *Foreign Affairs*, 63/1 (Fall 1984) pp. 33–47; and William Schneider, "Peace and Strength: American Public Opinion on National Security", in Flynn and Rattinger, *The Public and Atlantic Defense*, pp. 321–4.

62. *The Economist*, 20 June 1987, p. 50; and "Soviet Offer Gets OK From Bonn", *Boston Globe*, 2 June 1987.

63. See "Debate on Ending Missiles in Europe Dividing Experts", and "Analysts: Soviet Forces in Europe Exaggerated"; for the details of the Treaty and the reaction in Europe and Washington, see the *New York Times* of 28 November and 6 December 1987, and the *Boston Globe* of 6 December 1987, especially the "Focus" section on the Treaty and the summit.

64. This is another irony, for the public broadly supports the Agreement that was negotiated. See Office of Research, USIA, *West European Publics Favor Eliminating INF Missiles: Soviets Receive Credit for Progress in Negotiations*, Report M–5/20/87 (Washington, D.C.: May 1987).

65. On this and other points involving the Reykjavik summit, see Michael Mandelbaum and Strobe Talbott, "Reykjavik and Beyond", *Foreign Affairs*, 65/2 (Winter 1986/87) pp. 215–36.

66. Sharp, "Arms Control, Alliance Cohesion, and Extended Deterrence", p. 15.

67. Two comprehensive collections on SDI are Ashton Carter and David Schwartz (eds), *Ballistic Missile Defense* (Washington, D.C.: Brookings Institution, 1984); and Steven Miller and Stephen Van Evera (eds), *The Star Wars Controversy* (Princeton, N.J.: Princeton University Press, 1987).

68. Paul Gallis, Mark Lowenthal, and Marcia Smith, *The Strategic Defense Initiative and US Alliance Strategy* (Washington, D.C.: Congressional Research Service, Library of Congress, 1 February 1985) p. 18.
69. Interview with Mainz Television, 4 March 1984, as cited in Gallis, *et al.*, *US Alliance Strategy*, p. 25.
70. For a review of these European perspectives, see Lord Zuckerman, "The Nuclear Opening", *New York Review of Books*, 34/8 (7 May 1987) pp. 42–5.
71. See *The Economist*, 16 February 1985, p. 45; *New York Times*, 10 February 1985, p. 14; and Gallis, *et al.*, *US Alliance Strategy*.
72. Gallis, *et al.*, *US Alliance Strategy*, p. 72.
73. Office of Research, USIA, *Multi-Issue Survey: March 1986*; and Eymert den Oudsten, "Public Opinion on Peace and War", in Stockholm International Peace Research Institute, *SIPRI Yearbook, 1986* (New York: Oxford University Press, 1987) pp. 28–34.
74. The best example is John Mueller, *War, Presidents and Public Opinion* (New York: Wiley, 1973).
75. For an exception, see George M. Seignious II and J. P. Yates, "Europe's Nuclear Superpowers", *Foreign Policy*, 55 (Summer 1984) pp. 40–53.
76. Poll by the United States Information Agency, as cited in Stephen Szabo, "The West German Security Debate: the Search for Alternative Strategies", paper presented to the Annual Convention of the International Studies Association, Atlanta, Ga, March 1984.
77. See Sharp, "After Reykjavik" for the most recent exposition of the paradox.
78. The entire debate about NFU, as well as proposals for reform short of NFU, are reviewed in the chapters by Steinbruner and by Sigal in Sigal and Steinbruner, *Alliance Security: The No-First-Use Question*.
79. Stanley Hoffmann, "The Crisis in the West", in *Dead Ends: American Foreign Policy in the New Cold War* (Cambridge, Mass.: Ballinger, 1983) p. 181.
80. Lawrence Freedman, "Getting to No", *New Republic*, 15 October, 1984, p. 35.
81. Gallis, *et al., US Alliance Strategy*, pp. 27, 40.
82. Schlesinger, "Reykjavik and Revelations", pp. 435–6.
83. William K. Domke, Richard Eichenberg, and Catherine M. Kelleher, "Consensus Lost? Domestic Politics and the 'Crisis' in NATO", *World Politics*, 39/3 (April 1987) pp. 398–9.

Notes to Chapter 5: The Three Pillars of Western Security

1. Harold Van B. Cleveland, *The Atlantic Idea and Its European Rivals* (New York: McGraw-Hill, 1966).
2. On these elements of stability, see Stanley Hoffmann's Foreword to Alfred Grosser, *The Western Alliance: European–American Relations Since 1945* (New York: Vintage Books, 1982) pp. vii–x.
3. Anton W. DePorte, *Europe Between the Superpowers* (New Haven, Conn.: Yale University Press, 1979) pp. 243–4.

4. Pieter Dankert, "US–European Relations: Defense Policy and the Euro-missiles", in Richard C. Eichenberg (ed.), *Drifting Together or Apart?* (Lanham, Md: University Press of America, 1986) p. 69.
5. See the passage from Schmidt's 1985 article, quoted at the beginning of Chapter 4, and his speech to the Bundestag in June 1984.
6. See especially Hedley Bull, "European Self-Reliance and the Reform of NATO", *Foreign Affairs*, 61/4 (Spring 1983) pp. 874–92; and William Wallace, "European Defence Cooperation: the Reopening Debate", *Survival*, 26/6 (November/December 1984) pp. 251–62.
7. Stanley Hoffmann, "Cries and Whimpers: Thoughts on West European American Relations in the 1980s", *Daedalus*, 113 (Summer 1984) pp. 234–5.
8. De Porte, *Europe Between the Superpowers*, p. 243.
9. Commission of the European Communities, *Public Opinion in the European Community*, 22 (Brussels: December 1984) p. 43. The "neutralist" option, so enthusiastically researched by the pollsters, never exceeded 20 per cent in any country. For complete figures from these latter surveys, see Richard C. Eichenberg, "The Western Alliance: a Three-Legged Stool?" in Eichenberg, *Drifting Together or Apart?*, pp. 14–15.
10. Support for the Community has fluctuated between 60 and 80 per cent in all Community countries except Denmark. In addition, in 1976 overwhelming majorities (except in Britain) favored the creation of a "European army". See Commission of the European Community, *Euro-Barometre: Public Opinion in the European Communities*, no. 25 (Brussels: June 1986) Table 5; and J.-R. Rabier, *et al., Eurobarometer 6: Twenty Years of the Common Market* (Ann Arbor, Mich.: Inter-University Consortium for Political and Social Research, Study no. 7511, 1978) p. 59.
11. Richard Merritt and Donald Puchala (eds), *West European Perspectives on International Affairs* (New York: Praeger, 1968) pp. 328–9.
12. The complete wording of the question is as follows: "The question of the [NATO] Alliance is often debated in the Federal Republic. What is your opinion on this question: should we continue to be a member of the Alliance as it now is [unchanged], should we strive (*anstreben*) for a looser or a tighter Alliance? Or do you think it would be better to leave NATO?" Press and Information Office, Federal Ministry of Defense, *Meinungsbild in der Bundesrepublik Deutschland zur Sicherheitspolitik* (Bonn: 1 October 1984) p. 8, and "Friedenssicherung und Bundeswehr: Ergebnisse einer Meinungsumfrage", *Material für die Presse*, 23/19 (Bonn: 17 November 1986) p. 3.
13. Richard C. Eichenberg, "The Myth of Hollanditis", *International Security*, 8/3 (Fall 1983) p. 156.
14. This seems to be the spirit of Henry Kissinger's "Plan to Reshape NATO", *Time*, 5 March 1984, pp. 20–4.
15. J.-R. Rabier, *et al., Eurobarometer 17: April 1982* (Ann Arbor, Mich.: Inter-University Consortium for Political and Social Research, Study no. 9023, 1983) p. 106.
16. Cited in Grosser, *The Western Alliance*, p. 10.
17. Hoffmann, "Cries and Whimpers", p. 227.

18. William Domke, Richard C. Eichenberg, and Catherine M. Kelleher, "Consensus Lost? Domestic Politics and the 'Crisis' in NATO", *World Politics*, 39/3 (April 1987) pp. 399–400.
19. J.-R. Rabier, *et al.*, *Eurobarometer 11: April 1979* (Ann Arbor, Mich.: Inter-University Consortium for Political and Social Research, Study no. 7752, 1981).
20. Quoted in Eichenberg, *Drifting Together or Apart?*, pp. 144–5.
21. David Aaron's speech to a meeting on Security and Arms Control of the Friedrich Ebert Stiftung, Bonn, West Germany, May 1986, p. 10.
22. Harald Mueller and Thomas Risse-Kappen have documented a generation gap with respect to the American image in West Germany: "Origins of Estrangement: the Peace Movement and the Changed Image of America in West Germany", *International Security*, 12/1 (Summer 1987), pp. 52–88.
23. The 1980 survey is used in this table because later surveys were not available from archives, preventing the tabulation of combined age and partisan differences. However, I have studied the evolution of party differences on the "NATO essential" question between 1978 and 1984. The Dutch and West German data are presented later in this chapter. The British and French data indicate that party polarization on NATO is stable; about 20 percentage points divide the Left and Right in France, and 10 to 15 percentage points in Britain.
24. The empty cells in the French responses are due to the high number of "don't knows" and lesser number of older French with higher education.
25. That is, the table shows the average percentage in each generation that chose "NATO as it now stands", "A European command", and so on, in the surveys displayed in Table 5.2. The two responses involving a "European command" have been combined in this table. Breakdowns by generation for each individual survey were also studied. They confirm the patterns shown here. Surveys for other years are not available for direct analysis, so they are not included in Table 5.5.
26. This pattern of a more "Europeanist" approach on the Left continued, and Gaullists continued to become more "Atlanticist". See: "L'opinion sur l'armée et la défense en 1983", *Armées d'aujourd'hui*, 88 (March 1984) p. 11.
27. Given the very small number of older, educated British respondents, the differences in this generation should be treated with caution.
28. The "dummy variable" for successor generation takes a value of 1 for the young, educated respondents and a value of 0 for all other respondents. In the 1979 survey, the American image is measured using a question on the intentions of American economic policy; it asks if the US seeks to cooperate with Europe, to obtain unfair advantage, or to dominate Europe. In 1980 the American image is measured by asking "how trustworthy are Americans?"; the answers range from "very trustworthy" to "not at all".
29. Consistent with the argument here, USIA reports show that this pattern also characterized opinions of NATO and of the INF deployment in 1984. That is, support for NATO and INF were strongly related to confidence in the US. See Office of Research, USIA, *June 1984 Security*

Survey [Contractor's Reports] (Washington, D.C.: mimeographed); and
West Europeans Still Predominantly Oppose INF: Some Doubt US Commitment to Negotiation, Report M–9/19/84 (Washington, D.C.: September 1984) Table 12.

30. In fact, images of the United States are so closely correlated with ideology that it is difficult to disentangle the two statistically, but this does not change the conclusion drawn in the text.
31. Office of Research, USIA, *Differences in Some Foreign Policy Views Between Supporters of the Major West German Parties*, Report N–11/7/83, (Washington, D.C.: 7 November 1983) Table 9.
32. Josef Joffe, "Europe's American Pacifier", *Foreign Policy*, 54 (Spring 1984) pp. 64–82.
33. For Helmut Schmidt's proposal, see speech to the Bundestag, June 1984. For a French proposal, see Pierre Lellouche, *L'avenir de la guerre* (Paris: éditions Mazarine, 1985). David Yost has reviewed the Lellouche book and raised more general objections to such proposals in "Radical Change in French Defence Policy?", *Survival*, 28/1 (January/February 1986) pp. 53–68.
34. Robbin F. Laird, "The Role of Conventional Forces in French Security Policy", paper delivered to the Symposium on "The Future of Conventional Defense Improvements in NATO", Washington, D.C., National Defense University, 27 March 1987, p. V–5.
35. Stephen Szabo, "European Public Opinion and Conventional Defense", paper delivered to the Symposium on "The Future of Conventional Defense Improvements in NATO", Washington, D.C., National Defense University, 27 March 1987, p. 12.

Notes to Chapter 6: Old Politics and New Politics

1. Werner Feld and John Wildgen, *NATO and the Atlantic Defense* (New York: Praeger, 1982) p. 105.
2. Organization for Economic Cooperation and Development, *National Account Statistics of OECD Member Countries*, (Paris, 1983) vol. II, Table 9.
3. Richard L. Merritt and Donald J. Puchala (eds), *West European Perspectives on International Affairs* (New York: Praeger, 1968) p. 331.
4. The "most important problem" surveys can be found in the following sources. For Britain: Social Surveys Ltd (Gallup), *The Gallup International Public Opinion Polls: Great Britain*, 2 vols (New York: Random House, 1975). Dutch surveys are in Werkgroep nationaal verkiezingsonderzoek, *De Nederlandse Kiezer 1972 [1973]* (Alphen aan den Rijn: Samson Uitgeverij, 1972 [1973]) pp. 44, 71 [113]; G. A. Irwin, *et al., De Nederlandse kiezer '77* (Voorschoten: VAM, 1978) pp. 30–3; and Werkgroep Kontinou-Onderzoek, *Dutch Continuous Survey, 1977–1980* (Amsterdam: Steinmetz Archive, Study no. POlll) Waves 15–23. For West Germany see Hans Klingemann and Charles L. Taylor, "Partisanship, Candidates and Issues: Attitudinal Components of the Vote in West

German Elections", in M. Kaase and K. von Beyme (eds), *Elections and Parties* (Beverly Hills, Calif.: Sage Publications, 1978) p. 129. Finally, French surveys are published in *The Gallup International Public Opinion Polls: France*, 2 vols (New York: Random House, 1975).

5. *British Public Opinion*, 5 (October 1983) p. 7; survey by MORI.

6. Harold and Margaret Sprout, "The Dilemma of Rising Demands and Insufficient Resources", *World Politics*, 20/4 (July 1968) pp. 680–1.

7. Organization for Economic Cooperation and Development, *National Account Statistics of OECD Member Countries*, (Paris, 1984) vol. 2, Tables 5 and 6.

8. Sprout and Sprout, "Dilemma of Rising Demands"; Edward Morse, *Foreign Policy and Interdependence in Gaullist France* (Princeton, N.J.: Princeton University Press, 1974); and Samuel Huntington, "The United States", in Samuel Huntington, *et al., The Crisis of Democracy* (New York: New York University Press, 1975).

9. Peter Flora, "The Welfare State: the Problem or the Solution?", in W. J. Mommsen (ed.), *The Emergence of the Welfare State in Britain and Germany* (London: Croom Helm, 1981); and Hugh Heclo, "Toward a New Welfare State?", in Arnold Heidenheimer and Peter Flora (eds), *The Development of Welfare States in Europe and America* (New Brunswick, N.J.: Transaction Books, 1981).

10. In 1981, 15 per cent of British government revenues were derived from social security taxes; in France, West Germany, and the Netherlands, the figure was over 35 per cent. See OECD, *National Account Statistics* (1983), Table 9.

11. Ronald Inglehart, "Post-Materialism in an Environment of Insecurity", *American Political Science Review*, 75/4 (December 1981) p. 888. Inglehart discusses the tension between the "old" politics and the "new" politics in "The Changing Structure of Political Cleavages in Western Society", in Russell Dalton, *et al.* (eds), *Electoral Change in Advanced Industrial Democracies* (Princeton, N.J.: Princeton University Press, 1984), esp. p. 28.

12. Inglehart, "The Changing Structure of Political Cleavages", p. 39.

13. Ibid., p. 37

14. Ibid., pp. 35, 42.

15. Note that in Inglehart's historical study of value change, "period effects" due to changes in the environment do not result in a closing of the gap between generations: Ronald Inglehart, "Aggregate Stability and Individual-Level Flux in Mass Belief Systems: the Level of Analysis Paradox", *American Political Science Review*, 79/1 (March 1985) pp. 103–5.

16. The conclusion is cautious because of the small size of the sub-samples. In terms of statistical significance, only the British figures in Table 6.6 approach the normal standard (0.08), with the French and German figures less significant in statistical terms. In France 68 per cent of those 65 or older support a trade-off; in Britain it is 84 per cent. In West Germany the percentage is identical to the "over 35" group as a whole.

17. The complete breakdown of this latter question is reproduced in William Domke, Richard C. Eichenberg, and Catherine Kelleher, "Consensus

Lost? Domestic Politics and the 'Crisis' in NATO", *World Politics*, 39/3 (April 1987) p. 392. A similar pattern of a skeptical older (educated) generation also shows up on a question on the use of force "out-of-area" in the USIA's *1980 Multiregional Security Survey*.

18. In addition to the data reviewed in the text and tables, the conclusion is supported by correlation and regression analysis. Partisanship is consistently correlated with views of defense spending. Age and education vary in impact.

19. This argument is reinforced by the fact that responses to the guns–butter trade-off question shown earlier are far more clearly aligned by partisan attachments than by the age and educational groupings that were presented in Table 6.6.

20. For a review of the evidence, see Inglehart, *Silent Revolution*, chs 3 and 11.

21. In West Germany, 14 per cent of the university-educated under thirty-five supported the Greens while only 2 per cent of the same age group without higher education did so. In France, the figures are 28 per cent and 14 per cent for the Ecologists. However, it should also be noted that the Greens and Ecologists also received disproportionate support among those *over* 35 with university education. The figures were computed from J.-R. Rabier, *et al.*, *Eurobarometer 14: Trust in the European Community in October 1980* (Ann Arbor, Mich.: ICPSR, Study no. 7958).

22. For much evidence on these and some of the points raised below, see Andrew Pierre (ed.), *Unemployment and Growth in the Western Economies* (New York: Council on Foreign Relations, 1986).

23. For evidence on these points, see Richard Coughin, *Ideology, Public Opinion and Welfare Policy* (Berkeley, Calif.: Institute for International Studies, 1980) p. 139; *The Economist*, 8 October 1983, p. 49; and Anthony King, "How Ronald Reagan and Margaret Thatcher Have Changed Public Opinion", *Public Opinion*, 8/3 (June/July 1985) p. 58. For opinions in the United States, see David Capitanchik and Richard C. Eichenberg, *Defence and Public Opinion* (Boston, Mass. and London: Routledge and Kegan Paul, 1983) pp. 74–6.

24. Office of Research, USIA, *West European Public Opinion on Key Security Issues, 1981/82*, Report R–10–82 (Washington, D.C.: July 1982) Table 22.

25. Data in the previous paragraph are from the following reports of the Office of Research, USIA: *NATO and Burdensharing*, Report M–9/11/84 Washington, D.C.: 1984) Tables 13 and 14; and *June 1984 Security Issues Survey [Contractor's Reports]* (Washington, D.C.: mimeographed).

26. For a number of viewpoints on the adequacy of NATO's conventional force posture, see the selections in Steven Miller (ed.), *Conventional Forces and American Defense Policy* (Princeton, N.J.: Princeton University Press, 1986), and the contributions by Epstein, Holmes, Mearsheimer, and Posen in *International Security* 12/4 (Spring 1988), pp. 152–202. The nature and cost of proposed reforms in NATO's conventional posture are analyzed in International Institute for Strategic Studies, *Strategic Survey, 1985–1986* (London, 1986) and in Andrew Pierre

(ed.), *The Conventional Defense of Europe: New Technologies and New Strategies* (New York: Council on Foreign Relations, 1986).

Notes to Chapter 7: Two Track

1. For a penetrating analysis along these lines, see Glenn H. Snyder, "The Security Dilemma in Alliance Politics", *World Politics* (July 1984) pp. 461–95.
2. Significantly, it was above all in the United States that there was a reorientation of budgetary priorities, and it was in the United States that there was a negative public reaction to the defense budget. We shall see later in this chapter that American support for defense spending collapsed soon after the large defense increases of 1981/2.
3. Gregory Flynn and Hans Rattinger (eds), *The Public and Atlantic Defense* (Totowa, N.J.: Rowman and Allanheld, 1985) p. 378.
4. Report of the NATO Council on "Future Tasks of the Alliance", reprinted in *Department of State Bulletin*, 8 January 1968, pp. 49–52.
5. I have examined these developments in a review essay: "Familiar Faces: Are the Old Politics the New Politics of German Security?", *German Politics and Society*, 6 (November 1985) pp. 17–22; Schmidt's 1959 proposal is described by Helga Haftendorn, *Security and Détente: Conflicting Priorities in German Foreign Policy* (New York: Praeger, 1985) pp. 56–7.
6. An excellent analysis of Schmidt's strategic thinking will appear in Jeffrey Boutwell, *External and Domestic Determinants of West German Security Policy: Adenauer, Schmidt and Nuclear Weapons* (Ithaca, N.Y.: Cornell University Press, forthcoming).
7. Helmut Schmidt, "Der Doppelbeschluss ist nach wie vor richtig", *Die Zeit*, 10 June 1983, p. 4.
8. The research on this point was cited in Chapter 2 (notes 18 and 19). The most important report remains Ronald Inglehart, "Postmaterialism in an Environment of Insecurity", *American Political Science Review*, 75/4 (December 1981) pp. 880–900.
9. Daniel Yankelovich, "Assertive America", *Foreign Affairs*, 59/3 (America and the World, 1980) pp. 696–713. For a recent review of post-Second World War trends in American opinion, see Robert Y. Shapiro and Benjamin Page, "Foreign Policy and the Rational Public", *Journal of Conflict Resolution*, 32/2 (June 1988) pp. 211–47.
10. William Schneider, "Peace and Strength: American Public Opinion on National Security", in Flynn and Rattinger, *The Public and Atlantic Defense*, p. 340.
11. Miroslav Ninic, "America's Soviet Policy and the Politics of Opposites", unpublished paper, Department of Political Science, New York University, p. 22.
12. These surveys are too numerous to list separately. See the works by Rielly, Holsti and Rosenau, Russett, and Wittkopf in Part II.5 of the Bibliography.
13. Schneider, "Peace and Strength", pp. 359–0.

14. Michael Mandelbaum and William Schneider, "The New Internationalisms: Public Opinion and American Foreign Policy", in Kenneth Oye, Donald Rothchild and Robert Lieber (eds), *Eagle Entangled: US Foreign Policy in a Complex World* (New York: Longman, 1979) pp. 40–4.
15. These studies are too numerous to list separately. See the works of Holsti and Rosenau, Schneider, and Wittkopf listed in Part II.5 of the Bibliography.
16. Schneider, "Peace and Strength", pp. 357–9. For a brilliant analysis of the 1976 American election in these terms, see Mandelbaum and Schneider, "The New Internationalisms".
17. Ole Holsti and James Rosenau, "Consensus Lost, Consensus Regained? Foreign Policy Beliefs of American Leaders", *International Studies Quarterly*, 30/4 (December 1986) pp. 375–410; and Robert Wells, "The Vietnam War and Generational Attitudes in Foreign Policy Attitudes", in Margaret Karns (ed.), *Persistent Patterns and Emergent Structures in a Waning Century* (New York: Praeger, 1986) pp. 99–125.
18. Felix Gilbert, *To the Farewell Address: Ideas of Early American Foreign Policy* (Princeton, N.J.: Princeton University Press, 1961) p. 72.
19. Samuel P. Huntington, *The Soldier and the State* (Cambridge, Mass.: Harvard University Press, 1957) esp. Ch. 6.
20. Flynn and Rattinger, *The Public and Atlantic Defense*, p. 384.
21. Hans Rattinger, "The Federal Republic of Germany: Much Ado About (Almost) Nothing", in Flynn and Rattinger, *The Public and Atlantic Defense*, pp. 172–3.
22. Josef Joffe, "Peace and Populism: Why the European Anti-Nuclear Movement Failed", *International Security*, 11/4 (Spring 1987) pp. 23–34.
23. Ibid., p. 3.
24. The Abravenal–Hughes study is reported in Barry B. Hughes, *The Domestic Context of American Foreign Policy* (San Francisco, Calif.: Free, 1978) p. 109. The other studies mentioned in this paragraph are Russell Dalton and Robert Duval, "The Political Environment and Foreign Policy Opinions: British Attitudes Toward European Integration, 1972–1979", *British Journal of Political Science* 16 (January 1986) pp. 113–34; and Shapiro and Page "Foreign Policy and the Rational Public".
25. This study used a broad definition of "élite" by surveying only affluent respondents who had at least some university education and who reported that they were in higher income or educational categories. See Lloyd Free, *How Others See Us: Report of the Commission on Critical Choices for Americans* (Lexington, Mass.: D. C. Heath, 1976) p. 69.
26. Ibid.
27. Wolf-Dieter Eberwein and Heinrich Siegmann, *Bedrohung oder Selbsgefährdung? Die Einstellungen sicherheitspolitischer Führungsschichten aus Fünf Ländern zur Sichersheitspolitik* (West Berlin: International Institute for Comparative Social Research, Science Center Berlin, 1985).
28. Public opinions on these issues were presented in Tables 4.4 and 4.5.
29. Eberwein and Siegmann, *Bedrohung oder Selbsgefährdung?*, pp. 203–6.

30. Karlheinz Reif and Hermann Schmitt, "West German Party Élite Attitudes Towards European Integration", paper prepared for presentation at the European Consortium for Political Research, Joint Sessions, West Berlin, September 1977, p. 16.

31. Dietmar Schössler and Erich Weede, *West German Élite Views on National Security and Foreign Policy Issues* (Königstein: Athenäum Verlag, 1978) p. 18.

32. Russell Dalton, "Political Parties and Political Representation: Party Supporters and Party Élites in Nine Nations", *Comparative Political Studies* 18/3 (October 1985) p. 294.

33. Russell Dalton, "Generational Change in Élite Political Beliefs: the Growth of Ideological Polarization", *Journal of Politics* (November 1987) p. 985. Dalton observes that this is a particularly good "élite" study because many prominent politicians headed the party lists for this first EC parliamentary election.

34. Ibid., p. 995.

35. Jonathan Dean, for example, begins his recent book on European security with a chapter entitled "The End of the Western Defense Consensus". See his *Watershed in Europe: Dismantling the East–West Military Confrontation* (Lexington, Mass.: Lexington Books, 1987).

36. Leon Sigal, *Nuclear Forces in Europe* (Washington, D.C.: Brookings Institution, 1984) p. 58.

37. Luc Reychler, "The Passive Constrained: Belgian Security Policy in the 1980s", in Gregory Flynn (ed.), *NATO's Northern Allies* (Totowa, N.J.: Rowman and Allanheld, 1985) p. 20.

38. The account in this paragraph is drawn from Joris J. C. Vorhoeve, *Peace, Profits and Principles: A Study of Dutch Foreign Policy* (The Hague: Nijhof, 1979) pp. 124–30.

39. See Jan Siccama, "The Netherlands Depillarized: Security Policy in a New Domestic Context", in Flynn, *NATO's Northern Allies*, pp. 129–43; the resolutions cited in the text are discussed at p. 143.

40. This brief account of Belgian politics is drawn from Lue Reychler, "The Passive Constrained: Belgian Security Policy in the 1980s", in Flynn, *NATO's Northern Allies*, pp. 18–20.

41. The diplomat is cited anonymously in Richard C. Eichenberg (ed.), *Drifting Together or Apart?* (Lanham, Md: University Press of America, 1986) p. 142.

42. Cited in Reychler, "The Passive Constrained", pp. 18, 20.

43. Joffe, "Peace and Populism", p. 25.

44. Ibid., pp. 25–9.

45. Cited in Lothar Wilker, *Die Sicherheitspolitik der SPD, 1956–1966* (Bonn: Verlag Neue Gesellschaft, 1977) p. 57.

46. All quotes in the previous paragraph are from Wilker, *Sicherheitspolitik der SPD*, pp. 187–9.

47. Dean, *Watershed in Europe*, p. 102. I am grateful to Mary Hampton for calling my attention to this reference and for several informative discussions on this point. Ms Hampton analyzes the importance of the Harmel formula for German policy in "The Federal Republic of Germany Between East and West: the Bifurcation of the Western Security Re-

gime", in Hans-Adolph Jacobson and Michael D. Intrilligator (eds), *Élite Perceptions of the East–West Conflict* (Boulder, Col.: Westview Press, forthcoming).

48. Cited in Sigal, *Nuclear Forces in Europe*, p. 82.
49. Joffe, "Peace and Populism", p. 3.
50. For a very thoughtful analysis of these impacts, see Thomas Rochon, *The Politics of the Peace Movements in Western Europe* (Princeton, N.J.: Princeton University Press, 1988).
51. Just before the British election in June 1987, Labour's Neil Kinnock was already hinting about a moderation of Labour's defense policy; see *New York Times*, 10 June 1987, p. 1.
52. On the French defense consensus of the 1980s, see Dominique Moisi, "A European Perspective", in International Institute for Strategic Studies, *Defence and Consensus: the Domestic Aspects of Western Security*, Part III (London: 1983), esp. p. 15; and John Fenske, "The French Socialist Party and the Security of France, 1971–1983", unpublished paper (Cambridge, Mass.: Massachusetts Institute of Technology, 1984).
53. Ronald Inglehart, *The Silent Revolution: Changing Values and Political Styles Among Western Publics* (Princeton, N.J.: Princeton University Press, 1977) p. 260.
54. Dalton, "Political Parties and Political Representation", Table 4.
55. On these points, see Fenske, "The French Socialist Party and the Security of France".
56. Hugh Heclo and Aaron Wildavsky, *The Private Government of Public Money* (Berkeley, Calif.: University of California Press, 1974).

Bibliography of Public Opinion Sources

A. COMPARATIVE OPINION SURVEYS

1. Inter-University Consortium for Political and Social Research (ICPSR)

Rabier, J.-R., *et al.*, *Eurobarometer 11: Year of the Child in Europe, April 1979* (Ann Arbor, Mich.: ICPSR Study 7752, 1981).
——, *Eurobarometer 12: European Parliamentary Elections, October –November 1979* (Ann Arbor, Mich.: ICPSR Study 7778, 1981).
——, *Eurobarometer 13: Regional Development and Integration, April 1980* (Ann Arbor, Mich.: ICPSR Study 7957, 1983).
——, *Eurobarometer 14: Trust in the European Community, October 1980* (Ann Arbor, Mich.: ICPSR Study 7958, 1983).
——, *Eurobarometer 15: Membership in the European Community, April 1981* (Ann Arbor, Mich.: ICPSR Study 7959, 1983).
——, *Eurobarometer 16: Noise and Other Social Problems, October 1981* (Ann Arbor, Mich.: ICPSR Study 9022, 1983).
——, *Eurobarometer 17: Energy and the Future, April 1982* (Ann Arbor, Mich.: ICPSR Study 9023, 1983).
——, *Eurobarometer 18: Ecological Issues, October 1982* (Ann Arbor, Mich.: ICPSR Study 9057, 1983).
——, *Eurobarometer 19: Gender Roles in the European Community* (Ann Arbor, Mich.: ICPSR Study 8152, 1984).
——, *Eurobarometer 20: Aid to Developing Nations, October 1983* (Ann Arbor, Mich.: ICPSR Study 8234, 1985).
——, *Eurobarometer 21: Political Cleavages in the European Community, April 1984* (Ann Arbor, Mich.: ICPSR Study 8263, 1985).
——, *Eurobarometer 22: Energy Problems and the Atlantic Alliance, October 1984* (Ann Arbor, Mich.: ICPSR Study 8364, 1986).
——, *Eurobarometer 23: The European Currency Unit and Working Conditions, April 1985* (Ann Arbor, Mich.: ICPSR Study 8411, 1986).
——, *Eurobarometer 24: Entry of Spain and Portugal, October 1985* (Ann Arbor, Mich.: ICPSR Study 8513, 1986).
——, *Candidates for the European Parliament, April–May 1979* (Ann Arbor, Mich.: ICPSR Study 9033, 1985).

2. Works Based on USIA Surveys

Adler, Kenneth P., "West European Attitudes toward Nuclear Weapons", paper prepared for delivery at the 1986 Conference of the American and

272

World Associations for Public Opinion Research, St Petersburg, Fla, May 1986.

——, "West European Attitudes toward Peace, Defense, and Disarmament", paper prepared for delivery at the 1985 Annual Meeting of the World Association for Public Opinion Research, Wiesbaden, West Germany, September 1985.

——, "Polling the Attentive Public", *Annals of the American Academy of Political and Social Sciences*, 472 (March 1984) pp. 143–54.

——, and Charles S. Spencer Jr, "European Public Opinion on Nuclear Arms: an Historical View", selected data for presentation to a Roundtable on Public Opinion and Nuclear Arms Policy, Convention of the International Studies Association, Washington, D.C., March 1985.

——, and Douglas Wertman, "West European Concerns for the 1980s: Is NATO in Trouble?", Paper presented to the 1981 Annual Meeting of the American Association of Public Opinion Research, Buck Hill Falls, Pa.

——, "Is NATO in Trouble?", *Public Opinion*, 4/4 (August/September 1981) pp. 8–13.

Dalton, Russell, J., *Values in Change: A Panel Study of German Youth, 1976–79* (Tallahassee, Fla: Florida State University, 1980).

Office of Research, USIA, *Western European Public Opinion on Defense – A Return to Better Red Than Dead?* (Washington, D.C.: n.d.). Report by Leo P. Crespi.

——, *West European Perceptions of NATO*, Report M–7–78 (Washington, D.C.: 8 May 1978).

——, *West European Public Perceptions of NATO and Mutual Defense Issues*, Report R–27–79, (Washington, D.C.: 20 December 1979). Report by Helen M. Crossley.

——, *Multi-Regional Security Survey: Questions and Responses* (Washington, D.C.: April 1980).

——, *West German Élite Opinion on European Security and Arms Control*, Report R–7–80 (Washington, D.C.: 14 May 1980). Report by Paul E. Zinner.

——, *Alliance/Security Survey: General Public Opinion Questionnaire and Results* (Washington, D.C., March/April 1981).

——, *A Profile of West European Neutralism*, Report M–10/28/81 (Washington 28 October 1981). Report by Gregory F. T. Winn.

——, *West European Opinion on Security Issues*, Report R–19–81 (Washington, D.C.: October 1981). Report by Robert S. McLellan.

——, *Trends in Perceptions of U.S. Strength and Leadership in Western Europe and Japan*, Report R–16–81 (Washington, D.C.: August 1981). Report by Leo P. Crespi.

——, *Trends in U.S. Standing in West European Public Opinion*, Report R–4–82, (Washington, D.C.: February 1982). Report by Leo P. Crespi.

——, *U.S. Standing in West European Public Opinion: Some Long-Term Trends*, Report R–13–82 (Washington, D.C.: July 1982). Report by Leo P. Crespi.

——, *A Profile of West European "Nuclear Pacifism"* (Washington, D.C.: 7 January 1982).

——, *West European Public Opinion on Key Security Issues, 1981–82*, Report R–10–82 (Washington, D.C.: June 1982). Report Stephen M. Shaffer.

——, *Differences in Some Foreign Policy Views Between Supporters of the Major West German Parties*, Report N–11/7/83 (Washington, D.C.: 7 November 1983). Report by Stephen M. Shaffer.

——, *British Public Widely Supports NATO and Narrowly Approves INF Deployment*, Report N–9/11/84–B (Washington, D.C.: 11 September 1984). Report by Charles S. Spencer Jr.

——, *Most West Germans Support NATO, But Many Lack Confidence in the U.S. Defense Commitment*, Report N–9/11/84–c (Washington, D.C.: 11 September 1984). Report by Kenneth P. Adler.

——, *NATO and Burden-Sharing: NATO Membership Widely Supported, But Increased Defense Efforts Broadly Opposed*, Report M–9/11/84 (Washington, D.C.: 11 September 1984). Report by Douglas A. Wertman.

——, *June 1984 Security Issues Survey: Contractor's Reports [Britain, West Germany, Netherlands]* (Washington, D.C.: mimeographed).

——, *West Europeans Still Predominantly Oppose INF Deployment*, Report M–9/19/84 (Washington, D.C.: 19 September, 1984). Report by Charles S. Spencer.

——, *March 1986 Multi-Issue Survey: Contractor's Reports [Britain, France, West Germany]* (Washington, D.C.: mimeographed).

——, *West European Publics Favor Eliminating INF Missiles*, Report M–5/20/87 (Washington: 20 May 1987). Report by Dennis N. Gombert.

Merritt, Richard, and Donald Puchala (eds), *Western European Perspectives on International Affairs* (New York: Praeger, 1968).

Richman, Alvin, "Trends and Structure of Foreign Attitudes Toward the United States and the USSR", paper prepared for delivery at the Annual Meeting of the American Political Science Association, New Orleans, Louisana, September 1973.

US Advisory Commission on Information, *The 28th Report* (Washington, D.C.: Government Printing Office, 1977).

Winn, Gregory F. T., "Westpolitik: Germany and the Atlantic Alliance", *Atlantic Community Quarterly*, 21/2 (Summer 1983) pp. 140–50.

3. USIA: Machine-Readable Files

Machine-Readable Branch, US National Archives and Records Service, *1976 International Attitudes Survey: Germany* (Washington, D.C.: n.d.) Study no. 7601.

——, *1976 International Attitudes Survey: France* (Washington, D.C.: n.d.) Study no. I7601.

——, *1976 International Attitudes Survey: Great Britain* (Washington, D.C.: n.d.) Study no. 7601.

——, *1977 Military Security Trends Survey: Germany* (Washington, D.C.: n.d.) Study no. I7703.

——, *1977 Military Security Trends Survey: Great Britain* (Washington, D.C.: n.d.) Study no. I7703.

——, *1977 NATO Security Rider: Germany* (Washington, D.C.: n.d.) Study no. 7702.

——, *1977 NATO Security Rider: France* (Washington, D.C.: n.d.) Study no. 7702.

——, *1977 NATO Security Rider: Great Britain* (Washington, D.C.: n.d.) Study no. 7702.

——, *1977 NATO Security Rider: Netherlands* (Washington, D.C.: n.d.) Study no. 7702.

——, *1978 NATO Summit Rider: West Germany* (Washington, D.C.: n.d.) Study no. 7806.

——, *1978 NATO Summit Rider: France* (Washington, D.C.: n.d.) Study no. 7805.

——, *1978 NATO Summit Rider: Great Britain* (Washington, D.C.: n.d.) Study no. 7802.

——, *1978 NATO Summit Rider: Netherlands* (Washington, D.C.: n.d.) Study no. 7801.

——, *1979 German SALT August Poll* (Washington, D.C.: n.d.) Study no. 7913.511.

——, *Perceptions of SALT II and Security: West Germany* (Washington, D.C.: n.d.) Study no. I7906.RM260511.

——, *Public Attitudes Toward SALT II and Security: France* (Washington, D.C.: n.d.) Study no. I7906.RS220511.

——, *Britain SALT II* (Washington, D.C.: n.d.) Study no. I7906.RM200511.

——, *Perceptions of the Soviet Military Threat: West Germany* (Washington, D.C.: n.d.) Study no. I7904.RS260511.

——, *Perceptions of the Soviet Military Threat: France* (Washington, D.C.: n.d.) Study no. I7904.RS220511.

——, *Multi-Regional Security Survey: West Germany* (Washington, D.C.: n.d.) Study no. I8007.RM260512.

——, *Multi-Regional Security Survey: France* (Washington, D.C.: n.d.) Study no. I8010.RS220512.

——, *Multi-Regional Security Survey: Great Britain* (Washington, D.C.: n.d.) Study no. I8005.RS200512.

——, *Perceptions of Iran and Afghanistan: West Germany* (Washington, D.C.: n.d.) Study no. I8014.RM260512.

——, *Perceptions of Iran and Afghanistan: France* (Washington, D.C.: n.d.) Study no. I8022.RM220512.

——, *Britain: Iran/Afghanistan* (Washington, D.C., n.d.) Study no. I8013.RM200512.

——, *July 1982 NATO Summit Follow-up: France* (Washington, D.C.: n.d.) Study no. I8235.

——, *July 1982 NATO Summit Follow-up: West Germany* (Washington, D.C., n.d.) Study no. I8229.

——, *July 1982 NATO Summit Follow-up: Great Britain* (Washington, D.C., n.d.) Study no. I8230.

——, *July 1982 NATO Summit Follow-up: Netherlands* (Washington, D.C., n.d.) Study no. I8234.

——, *1982 Economic Summit: France* (Washington, D.C., n.d.) Study no. I8224.

——, *1982 Economic Summit: Great Britain* (Washington, D.C., n.d.) Study no. I8218.

——, *1982 Economic Summit: West Germany* (Washington, D.C., n.d.) Study no. I8223.

——, *1982 Rowne Arms Control Issues: France* (Washington, D.C., n.d.) Study no. I8245.

——, *1982 Rowne Arms Control Issues: Great Britain* (Washington, D.C., n.d.) Study no. I8244.

——, *1982 Rowne Arms Control Issues: West Germany* (Washington, D.C., n.d.) Study no. I8264.

——, *1982 Rowne Arms Control Issues: Netherlands* (Washington, D.C.: n.d.) Study no. I8243.

4. Other Comparative Sources

Abramson, Paul R., and Ronald Inglehart, "Generational Replacement and Value Change Among the West European Public: 1970–1984; 1984–2000", paper prepared for delivery at the Annual Meeting of the Midwest Political Science Association, Chicago, Illinois, April 1985.

Armbruster, Frank E., and Doris Yokelson, *The Environment of the Long-range Theater Nuclear Force Program, Its Opponents and the Effects of Specifics of the Program on Opposition*, (Croton-on-Hudson, N.Y.: Hudson Institute, 1983).

Atlantic Institute – Harris Poll, "Industrial Democracies and World Economic Tensions" (Paris: Atlantic Institute for International Affairs, 16 May 1983).

——, "Security and Industrial Democracies" (Paris: Atlantic Institute for International Affairs, 1983).

Atlantic Institute–International Herald Tribune–Louis Harris Poll, "Europe and the U.S.: Diverging Perceptions" (Paris: Atlantic Institute for International Affairs, 20 October 1982).

Böltken, Ferdinand, and Wolfgang Jagodzinski, "In an Environment of Insecurity: Postmaterialism in the European Community", *Comparative Political Studies*, 17/4 (January 1985) pp. 453–84.

Capitanchik, David, and Richard C, Eichenberg, *Defence and Public Opinion*, Chatham House Papers in Foreign Policy, no. 20 (Boston, Mass. and London: Routledge and Kegan Paul, 1983).

Coffey, J. I., and Jerome Laulicht, *The Implications for Arms Control of Perceptions of Strategic Weapons Systems*, vols 1–6, report prepared for the US Arms Control and Disarmament Agency (Pittsburgh, Pa: University of Pittsburgh, 1971).

Coughin, Richard, *Ideology, Public Opinion and Welfare Policy* (Berkeley, Calif.: Institute for International Studies, 1980).

Dalton, Russell, "Generational Change in Élite Political Beliefs: the Growth of Ideological Polarization", *Journal of Politics*, (Fall 1987) pp. 976–97.

——, "Political Parties and Political Representation: Party Supporters and Party Élites in Nine Nations", *Comparative Political Studies*, 18/3 (October 1985) pp. 267–99.

——, Scott Flanagan and Paul A. Beck (eds), *Electoral Change in Advanced Industrial Democracies* (Princeton, N.J.: Princeton University Press, 1984).

Daniel, Donald C. (ed.), *International Perceptions of the Superpower Military Balance* (New York: Praeger Publishers, 1978).

De Boer, Connie, "The Polls: Our Commitment to World War III", *Public Opinion Quarterly*, 45 (1981) pp. 126–34.

——, "The Polls: the European Peace Movement and Deployment of Nuclear Missiles", *Public Opinion Quarterly*, 49 (Spring 1985) pp. 119–32.

Deutsch, Karl, *et al.*, *France, Germany and the Western Alliance* (New York: Scribner's, 1967).

——, and Lewis J. Edinger, *Germany Rejoins the Powers* (Stanford, Conn.: Stanford University Press, 1959).

——, *Arms Control and the Atlantic Alliance* (New York: Wiley, 1967).

Domke, William, Richard Eichenberg and Catherine Kelleher, "Consensus Lost? Domestic Politics and the 'Crisis' in NATO", *World Politics*, 39/3 (April 1987) pp. 382–407.

Eberwein, Wolf-Dieter, and Heinrich Siegmann, *Bedrohung oder Selbstgefährdung? Die Einstellungen sicherheitspolitischer Führungsschichten aus Fünf Ländern zur Sicherheitspolitik* (West Berlin: International Institute for Comparative Social Research, Science Center Berlin, 1985).

——, *Sicherheitspolitik in der Krise?*, Discussion Paper no. 83–107, (Berlin: International Institute for Comparative Social Research, 1983).

Eichenberg, Richard, "Public Opinion and National Security in Europe and the United States", in Linda Brady and Joyce Kaufmann (eds), *NATO in the 1980s* (New York: Praeger, 1985) pp. 226–48.

Feld, Werner J., and John K. Wildgen, *NATO and the Atlantic Defense* (New York: Praeger, 1982).

Flynn, Gregory, and Hans Rattinger (eds), *The Public and Atlantic Defense* (Totowa, N.J.: Rowman and Allanheld, 1985).

Flynn, Gregory, *et al.*, *Public Images of Western Security* (Paris: Atlantic Institute for International Affairs, 1985).

Free, Lloyd, *How Others See Us: Report of the Commission on Critical Choices for Americans*, vol. 3 (Lexington, Mass. D. C. Heath, 1976).

Inglehart, Ronald, "New Perspectives on Value Change: Response to Lafferty and Knutsen, Savage, and Böltken and Jagodzinski", *Comparative Political Studies*, 17/4 (January 1985) pp. 485–532.

——, "Aggregate Stability and Individual-Level Flux in Mass Belief Systems: the Level of Analysis Paradox", *American Political Science Review*, 79/1 (March 1985) pp. 97–116.

——, "The Changing Structure of Political Cleavages in Western Society", in Russell Dalton, Scott Flanagan and Paul Beck (eds), *Electoral Change in Advanced Industrial Democracies* (Princeton, N.J.: Princeton University Press, 1984) pp. 25–69.

——, "Generational Change and the Future of the Atlantic Alliance", *PS*, 17/3 (Summer 1984) pp. 525–35.

——, "Postmaterialism in an Environment of Insecurity", *American Political Science Review*, 75/4 (December 1981) pp. 880–900.

——, *The Silent Revolution: Changing Values and Political Styles Among Western Publics* (Princeton, N.J.: Princeton University Press, 1977).

Institut International de Géopolitique, "Guerres et Paix: Quelles Guerres, Quelle Paix?" (Paris 1983).

Joffe, Josef, "Peace and Populism: Why the European Anti-Nuclear Movement Failed", *International Security*, 11/4 (Spring 1987) pp. 3–40.

Lerner, Daniel, and Morten Gordon, *Euratlantica* (Cambridge, Mass.: MIT Press, 1966).

Mahoney, Robert B. Jr, "Public Opinion and Military Policy in the United Kingdom, France and the Federal Republic of Germany" (Washington, D.C.: CACI, December 1977).

Mundy, Alicia, and Robert B. Mahoney, Jr, "Western European Perceptions of Arms Control/National Security Issues", paper prepared for presentation at the Annual Meeting of the International Studies Association, Philadelphia, Pa, March 1981.

Rochon, Thomas, R., *The Politics of the Peace Movement in Western Europe* (Princeton, N.J.: Princeton University Press, 1988).

Russett, Bruce, and Donald R. Deluca, "Theater Nuclear Forces: Public Opinion in Western Europe", *Political Science Quarterly*, 98/2 (Summer 1983) pp. 179–96.

Stockholm International Peace Research Institute, *The Arms Race and Arms Control* (London and Philadelphia, Pa: Taylor and Francis, annually, 1983–7).

Szabo, Stephen, "European Public Opinion and Conventional Defense", paper delivered to the NATO Symposium on The Future of Conventional Defense Improvements in NATO, Washington, D.C., National Defense University, 27 March 1987.

——, "European Opinion after the Missiles", *Survival*, (November/December 1985) pp. 265–73.

—— (ed.), *The Successor Generation: International Perspectives of Postwar Europeans* (London: Butterworths, 1983).

Taylor, H., "Nine Nations Assess Economic and Security Issues", *Public Opinion*, 6/4 (August/September 1983) pp. 16–17.

Wattenberg, Benjamin, "Bad Marx: How the World Sees the Soviets", *Public Opinion*, 9/6 (March/April 1987) pp. 9–11.

Ziegler, Andrew, "The Structure of West European Attitudes Toward Atlantic Cooperation: Implications for the Western Alliance", *British Journal of Political Science*, (July 1987) pp. 457–77.

——, "Public Attitudes in Europe Toward Atlantic Cooperation: a Comparative Analysis", paper prepared for presentation at the Convention of the International Studies Association, Washington, D.C., March 1987.

B. NATIONAL OPINION SURVEYS

1. West Germany

Baker, Kendall, Russell Dalton and Kai Hildebrandt, *Germany Transformed* (Cambridge, Mass.: Harvard University Press, 1981).

Bundesminister for Labor and Social Affairs, *Forschungsbericht: Bürger und Sozialstaat* (Bonn: 1980).

Dalton, Russell J., "The Persistence of Values and Life Cycle Changes", in

Hans D. Klingemann and Max Kaase (eds), *Contributions to Political Psychology* (Weinheim/Basel: Beltz Verlag, 1981) pp. 189–207.

——, "The West German Party System Between Two Ages", in Russell J. Dalton *et al.* (eds), *Electoral Change in Advanced Industrial Democracies* (Princeton, N.J.: Princeton University Press, 1984) pp. 104–33.

——, "The Contours of West German Opinion", in P. Wallach and G. Romoser (eds), *West German Politics in the Eighties* (New York: Praeger, 1985).

Faiss, Jürgen Hartmut, and Berthold Meyer, "Die Armee in der Grauzone: Entsprechen Bundeswehr und NATO Strategie dem Sicherheitsbedürfnis der Bundesbürger?", in Studiengruppe Militärpolitik, *Aufrüsten, um Abzurüsten?* (Reinbek bei Hamburg: Rowohlt Verlag, 1980) pp. 194–216.

Forschungsgruppe Wahlen, E.V., "Politik in der Bundesrepublik, Februar 1983" (Mannheim: 1983).

——, "Politik in der Bundesrepublik, Marz 1983" (Mannheim: 1983).

Friedrich Ebert Stiftung, *America and the Germans* (Washington, D.C.: 1987). Survey by SINUS.

Greiffenhagen, Martin, and Sylvia Greiffenhagen, *Ein Schwierges Vaterland* (Munich: List Verlag, 1979).

Institut für Soziologie, Freie Universität Berlin, *Bundesweite Untersuchung zum Thema "Nachrüstung"* (Berlin: October 1983).

Kaltefleiter, Werner, "The American Shield: How Others See it Today", *Public Opinion*, 2/2 (March/April 1979) pp. 10–12.

Merritt, Richard, "Public Opinion and Foreign Policy in the Federal Republic of Germany", in Patrick McGowan (ed.), *Sage Yearbook of Foreign Policy Studies* (Beverly Hills, Calif.: Sage Publications, 1973).

Mueller, Harald, and Thomas Risse-Kappen, "Origins of Estrangement: the Peace Movement and the Changed Image of America in West Germany", *International Security*, 12/1 (Summer 1987) pp. 52–88.

Neumann, E. P., *Die Deutschen und die NATO* (Allensbach: Verlag für Demoskopie, 1969).

——, and Elisabeth Noelle-Neumann, *Jahrbuch der Öffentlichen Meinung*, vol. 2 [1957] (Allensbach: Verlag für Demoskopie, 1957).

——, *Jahrbuch der Öffentlichen Meinung*, vol. 3 [1958–64] (Allensbach: Verlag für Demoskopie, 1964).

——, *Jahrbuch der Öffentlichen Meinung*, vol. 4 [1965–7] (Allensbach: Verlag für Demoskopie, 1967).

——, *Jahrbuch der Öffentlichen Meinung*, vol. 5 [1968–73] (Munich: Verlag Fritz Molden, 1976).

Noelle-Neumann, Elisabeth (ed.), *Allensbacher Jahrbuch der Demoskopie*, vol. 6 [1974–6] (Munich: Verlag Fritz Molden, 1976).

——, *Allensbacher Jahrbuch der Demoskopie*, vol. 7 [1976–7] (Munich: Verlag Fritz Molden, 1977).

——, and Edgar Piel, *Allensbacher Jahrbuch der Demoskopie*, vol. 8 [1978–83] (Munich: X-G Saur, 1983).

——, "The Missile Gap: the German Press and Public Opinion", *Public Opinion*, 6/5 (October/November 1983) pp. 45–9.

——, "The Art of Putting Ambivalent Questions", *Encounter* (December 1983) pp. 79–82.

Office of the Federal Chancellor, Press and Information Staff, "Dreissig Jahre NATO", report of surveys conducted on the occasion of NATO's thirtieth anniversary (Bonn: 29 October 1979). Surveys by Allensbach.

Press and Information Office, Federal Ministry of Defense, *Meinungsbild zur Wehrpolitischen Lage [Sicherheitspolitik]* (Bonn: 1969–87). Surveys by EMNID.

——, "Die Legitimität der Verteidigungspolitik: Sondertabellenband" (Bonn: July 1975). Survey by INFAS.

——, "Verteidigungsklima, 1976" (Bonn: November 1976). Survey by INFAS.

——, *Sicherheit, Verteidigung, und Bundeswehr in der Öffentlichen Meinung* (Bonn: 1978). Survey by INFAS.

——, *Hinweise für Öffentlichkeitsarbeit*, Nr. 7/79 (Bonn: 14 September 1979).

——, *Meinungs und Haltungslage der Bevolkerung zu Fragen der Sicherheitspolitik und der Bundeswehr* (Bonn: February 1984).

——, *Meinungsbild in der Bundesrepublik Deutschland zur Sicherheitspolitik* (Bonn: 1 October 1984).

——, "Friedenssicherung und Bundeswehr: Ergebnisse einer Meinungsumfrage", *Material für die Presse*, 23/19 (Bonn: 17 November 1986).

Rattinger, Hans "Change versus Continuity in West German Public Attitudes on National Security and Nuclear Weapons in the Early 1980s", *Public Opinion Quarterly*, 51 (December 1987) pp. 495–521.

——, "National Security and the Missile Controversy in the West German Public", paper presented to the Annual Meeting of the American Political Science Association, Washington, D.C., 1986.

——, "The Federal Republic: Much Ado About (Almost) Nothing", in Gregory Flynn and Hans Rattinger (eds), *The Public and Atlantic Defense* (Totowa, N.J.: Rowman and Allanheld, 1985).

Schmidt, Peter, "Public Opinion and Security Policy in the Federal Republic of Germany", *Orbis*, (Winter 1985) pp. 719–42.

Schmitt, Rudiger, "From Old Politics to New Politics: Three Decades of Peace Protest in West Germany", in John R. Gibbon (ed.) *Politics and Contemporary Culture* (London: Sage Publications, 1988).

Schössler, Dietmar, *Militär und Politik* (Koblenz: Bernard and Graefe Verlag, 1983).

——, and Erich Weede, *West German Élite Views on National Security and Foreign Policy Issues* (Königstein: Athenäum, 1978).

Schweigler, Gebhard, *Grundlagen der aussenpolitischen Orientierung der Bundesrepublik Deutschland* (Baden-Baden: Nomos Verlagsgesellschaft, 1985).

——, *West German Foreign Policy: The Domestic Consensus* (Beverly Hills, Calif.: Sage Publications, 1983).

——, "Anti-Americanism in West German Public Opinion" (Washington, D.C.: Friedrich Ebert Foundation, 31 March 1985).

SINUS [Sozialwissenschaftliches Institut Nowak und Sorgel], *Rückwirkungen weltpolitischer und weltwirtschaftlicher Ereignisse auf die politische Lage unseres Landes* (Munich: October 1982).

——, *Sicherheitspolitik, Bundnispolitik, Friedensbewegung* (Munich: October 1983).

Szabo, Stephen, "The Federal Republic of Germany: Public Opinion and Defense", in Catherine M. Kelleher and Gail Mattox (eds), *Evolving European Defense Policies*, (Lexington, Mass.: D.C. Heath, 1987) pp. 185–202.

——, "Brandt's Children: the West German Successor Generation", *Washington Quarterly*, 7/1 (Winter 1984) pp. 50–9.

——, "The West German Security Debate: the Search for Alternative Strategies", paper presented to the Annual Meeting of the International Studies Association, Atlanta, Ga, March 1984.

——, "West Germany: Generations and Changing Security Perspectives" in Stephen Szabo (ed.), "The Successor Generation: International Perspectives of Postwar Europeans (London: Butterworth, 1983).

——, "The Successor Generation in Europe", *Public Opinion*, 6/1 (February/March 1983) pp. 9–12.

Zoll, Ralf, "Public Opinion and Security Policy: the West German Experience", paper presented to the Research Committee on Armed Forces and Society, 9th World Congress of Sociology, Uppsala, Sweden, 14–19 August 1978.

——, "Public Opinion on Security Policy and Armed Forces in the USA and the FRG: a Comparative Study", paper presented at the 20th Anniversary Conference of the Inter-University Seminar on Armed Forces and Society, Chicago, Ill. 23–25 October 1980.

——, "Sicherheitspolitik und Öffentliche Meinung in der Bundesrepublik", in Ralf Zoll (ed.), *Wie Integriert ist die Bundeswehr?* (Munich: Piper Verlag, 1979) pp. 166–82.

——, "Militär und Gesellschaft in der Bundesrepublik – Zum Problem der Legimität von Streitkräften", in Ralf Zoll (ed.), *Wie Integriert ist die Bundeswehr?* (Munich: Piper Verlag, 1979) pp. 41–76.

2. Britain

Alt, James E., "Dealignment and the Dynamics of Partisanship in Britain", in Russell J. Dalton, Scott C. Flanagan and Paul Allen Beck (eds), *Electoral Change in Advanced Industrial Democracies: Realignment or Dealignment?* (Princeton, N.J.: Princeton University Press, 1984) pp. 298–329.

"A British Finger on the Trigger", *The Economist*, 29 January 1983, p. 51.

Crewe, Ivor, "Why the British Don't Like Us Anymore", *Public Opinion*, 9/6 (March/April 1987) pp. 51–6.

——, "Britain: Two and a Half Cheers for the Atlantic Alliance", in Gregory Flynn and Hans Rattinger (eds), *The Public and Atlantic Defense* (Totowa, N.J.: Rowman and Allanheld, 1985) pp. 11–68.

——, "Britain Evaluates Ronald Reagan", *Public Opinion* (October/November 1984) pp. 44–9.

"Cruise Missile Debate", *British Public Opinion*, 5/9 (November/December 1983) pp. 3–6.

Dackiw, Oksana, *Defense Policy and Public Opinion: The Campaign for Nuclear Disarmament, 1945–1985*, unpublished doctoral dissertation, Columbia University, 1986.

Gallup, George H. (ed.), *The Gallup International Public Opinion Polls: Great Britain* (New York: Random House, 1975) 2 vols.

Gallup Poll (Social Surveys Ltd), "British Thoughts on Reagan's 'Star Wars'", *World Opinion Update*, 9/3 (March 1985) pp. 28–9.

——, "U.S.–British Relations", *World Opinion Update*, 8/6 (June 1984) pp. 89–91.

Market and Opinion Research International, "Great Britain – Cruise Missiles: Deployed or Not?", *World Opinion Update*, 8/2 (February 1984) pp. 24–5.

"Missiles Are Fine, If They Are British", *The Economist*, 29 October 1983, p. 56.

"Nuclear Arms", *Political, Social and Economic Review*, 42 (June 1983) pp. 15–18.

"Nuclear War", *Political, Social and Economic Review*, 34 (December 1981) pp. 20–7.

"Nuclear Weapons", *Political, Social and Economic Review*, 45 (December 1983) pp. 10–16.

Parkin, Frank, *Middle-Class Radicalism: The Social Bases of the British Campaign for Nuclear Disarmament* (Manchester: Manchester University Press, 1968).

Sabin, Philip, *The Third World Scare in Britain* (London: Macmillan, 1986).

3. France

"La Défense Militaire de la France", *Sondages* (1969) pp. 41–3.

Fritsch-Bournazel, Renata, "France: Attachment to a Nonbinding Relationship", in Gregory Flynn and Hans Rattinger (eds), *The Public and Atlantic Defense* (London: Croom Helm, 1985).

. Harrison, Michael, "The Successor Generation, Social Change and New Domestic Sources of Foreign Policy in France", in Stephen Szabo (ed.), *The Successor Generation* (London: Butterworth, 1983) pp. 17–42.

Lech, Jean-Marc, "L'Évolution de l'opinion des Français sur la défense à travers les sondages de 1972 à 1976", *Défense nationale*, 33 (August/September 1977) pp. 47–71.

Lewis-Beck, Michael S., "France: the Stalled Electorate", in Russell J. Dalton, Scott C. Flanagan and Paul Allen Beck (eds), *Electoral Change in Advanced Industrial Democracies: Realignment or Dealignment?* (Princeton, N.J.: Princeton University Press, 1984) pp. 425–48.

"Opinion et défense en 1985", *Armées d'aujourd'hui*, 104 (October 1985) pp. 15–17.

"Opinion sur l'armée et la défense en 1983", *Armée d' aujourd'hui*, 88 (March 1984) pp. 8–11.

"La Paix à tout prix", *Le Point*, 403 (9 June 1980) pp. 51–3.

"Les Relations est/ouest et les rapports de forces USA/URSS vus par les Français" (Montrouge: SOFRES, November 1985).

4. Netherlands

Ehren, A. M. A., and G. Teitler, "On the Relationship Between the Dutch and their Armed Forces", *Netherlands Journal of Sociology*, 15 (1979) pp. 27–45.
Eichenberg, Richard, "The Myth of Hollanditis", *International Security*, 8/2 (Fall 1983) pp. 143–58.
Everts, Philip P., "The Impact of the Peace Movement on Public Opinion: the Case of the Netherlands", paper prepared for the 21st European Conference of the Peace Science Society International, Amsterdam, September 1986.
——, "Ontwikkelingen in de publieke opinie", in *Jaarboek vrede en veiligheid 1985/1986* (Alphen aan den Rijn: Samson, 1986).
——, "Ontwikkelingen in de publieke opinie", in *Jaarboek vrede en veiligheid 1984/1985* (Alphen aan den Rijn: Samson, 1985).
——, "Ontwikkelingen in de publieke opinie", in *Jaarboek vrede en veiligheid 1983/1984* (Alphen aan den Rijn: Samson,1984).
——, "Public Opinion on Nuclear Weapons, Defense and Security: the Case of the Netherlands", in Gregory Flynn and Hans Rattinger (eds), *The Public and Atlantic Defense* (London: Croom Helm, 1985).
——, "The Mood of the Country: New Data on Public Opinion in the Netherlands on Nuclear Weapons and Other Problems of Peace and Security", *Acta Politica*, 17/4 (1982) pp. 497–553.
——, "Wat Vinden de Mensen in het land?", *Acta Politica*, 16/3 (July 1981) pp. 305–54.
Inter-University Consortium for Political and Social Research, *Dutch Election Study 1970* (Ann Arbor, Mich.: 1973) ICPSR Study no. 7261.
——, *Dutch Election Study 1971* (Ann Arbor, Mich.: 1975) ICPSR Study no. 7261.
——, *Dutch Election Study 1971* (Ann Arbor, Mich.: 1975) ICPSR Study no. 7311.
——, *Dutch Election Study 1970–1973* (Ann Arbor, Mich.: 1977) ICPSR Study no. 7261.
Infomart (Hilversum), *NAVO enquête* [NATO Study] (Amsterdam: Steinmetz Archive, 1967) Steinmetz Study no. P0064.
Irwin, Galen, and Karl Dittrich, "And the Walls Came Tumbling Down: Party Dealignment in the Netherlands", in Russell J. Dalton, Scott C. Flanagan and Paul Allen Beck (eds), *Electoral Change in Advanced Industrial Democracies: Realignment or Dealignment?* (Princeton, N.J.: Princeton University Press, 1984) pp. 267–97.
Irwin, G. A., *et al.*, *De Nederlandse Kiezer '77* (Voorschoten: Vam, 1978).
Nederlands Instituut voor de Publieke Opinie (NIPO), *Zo zign wij* (Amsterdam: Elsevier, 1970).
Nederlands Instituut voor de Publieke Opinie (NIPO), *NIPO Berichten*, Report no. A–407/42 (Amsterdam: NIPO, 1979).
Rebel, Hendrik, J. C., "Public Attitudes in the Netherlands Toward NATO, Peace and Security Affairs" (The Hague: Ministrie van Defensie, n.d.).
Sociaal-Wetenschappelijk Instituut van de Vrije Universiteit, *De Nederlandse Kiezers in 1967* (Amsterdam: Elsevier, 1967).

Stapel, Jan, *De Nederlander en het Kruisluchtwapen* (The Hague: Netherlands Institute of International Relations, 1986).

Stichting Krijsmacht en Maatschappij, *De publieke opinie over Krijsmacht en defensie* (The Hague: January 1982).

Vervoort Martkonderzoek (Amsterdam), *Politiek Onderzoek* (Amsterdam: Steinmetz Archive, 1968) Study no. P0056.

Voorheve, J. C., *Peace, Profits, Principles* (The Hague: Martinus Nijhoff, 1979).

Werkgroep Kontinu-Onderzoek FSW-A, *Dutch Continuous Survey* (Amsterdam: Steinmetz Archive, annually) Study no. P0111.

Werkgroep nationaal verkiezingsonderzoek, *De Nederlandse Kiezer, 1967* (Alpen aan den Rijn: Samson Uitgeverij, 1967).

Werkgroep nationaal verkiezingsonderzoek 1971, *De Nederlandse Kiezer '71* (Alpen aan den Rijn: Samson Uitgeverij, 1971).

Werkgroep nationaal verkiezingsonderzoek 1972, *De Nederlandse Kiezer '72* (Alpen aan den Rijn: Samson Uitgeverij, 1973).

Werkgroep nationaal verkiezingsonderzoek 1973, *De Nederlandse Kiezer '73* (Alpen aan den Rijn: Samson Uitgeverij, 1973).

Werkgroep nationaal verkiezingsonderzoek 1977, *De Nederlandse Kiezer '77* (Alpen aan den Rijn: Samson Uitgeverij, 1977).

Werkgroep nationaal verkiezingsonderzoek 1981, *De Nederlandse Kiezer '81* (Amsterdam: Steinmetz Archive, 1981) Study no. P0350.

5. United States

Graham, Thomas, *Future Fission? Extended Deterrence and American Public Opinion* (Cambridge, Mass.: Center for Science and International Affairs, Harvard University, 1987).

——, and Bernard M. Kramer, "The Polls: ABM and Star Wars: Attitudes Toward Nuclear Defense, 1945–1985", *Public Opinion Quarterly*, 50/1 (Spring 1986) pp. 125–34.

Holsti, Ole R., "Public Opinion and Containment", in Terry L. Deibel and John Lewis Gaddis, *Containment: Concept and Policy* (Washington, D.C.: National Defense University Press, 1986) pp. 67–115.

——, and James N. Rosenau, "Consensus Lost, Consensus Regained? Foreign Policy Beliefs of American Leaders", *International Studies Quarterly*, 30/4 (December 1986) pp. 375–410.

——, *American Leadership in World Affairs:Vietnam and the Breakdown of Consensus* (Boston, Mass. and London: Allen and Unwin, 1984).

——, "The Three-Headed Eagle: the United States and System Change", *International Studies Quarterly*, 23/3 (September 1979) pp. 339–59.

Hughes, Barry, *The Domestic Context of American Foreign Policy* (San Francisco, Calif.: Freeman, 1979).

Jennings, Kent, "Residues of a Movement: the Aging of the American Protest Generation", *American Political Science Review*, 81/2 (June 1987) pp. 367–82.

Mandelbaum, Michael, and William Schneider, "The New Internationalisms: Public Opinion and American Foreign Policy", in Kenneth Oye,

Donald Rothchild and Robert Lieber (eds), *Eagle Entangled: U.S. Foreign Policy in a Complex World* (New York: Longman, 1979) pp. 34–90.

Mueller, John, *War, Presidents and Public Opinion* (New York: Wiley, 1973).

Nincic, Miroslav, "America's Soviet Policy and the 'Politics of Opposites'" (New York: Department of Political Science, New York University, 1987).

Page, Benjamin I., Robert Y. Shapiro, and Glenn Dempsey, "What Moves Public Opinions?", *American Political Science Review*, 81/1 (March 1987) pp. 23–43.

——, and Robert Y. Shapiro, "Effects of Public Opinion on Policy", *American Political Science Review*, 77/1 (March 1983) pp. 175–90.

Richman, Alvin, "Public Attitudes on Military Power", *Public Opinion*, 4/6 (December/January 1982) pp. 44–6.

Rielly, John E., *American Public Opinion and U.S. Foreign Policy, 1987* (Chicago, Ill.: Chicago Council on Foreign Relations, 1987).

——, *American Public Opinion and U.S. Foreign Policy, 1983* (Chicago, Ill.: Chicago Council on Foreign Relations, 1983).

——, *American Public Opinion and U.S. Foreign Policy, 1979* (Chicago Ill.: Chicago Council on Foreign Relations, 1979).

——, *American Public Opinion and U.S. Foreign Policy, 1975* (Chicago Ill.: Chicago Council on Foreign Relations, 1975).

Russett, Bruce, and Elizabeth C. Hanson, *Interest and Ideology: The Foreign Policy Beliefs of American Businessmen* (San Francisco, Calif.: Freeman 1975).

Schneider, William, " 'Rambo' and Reality: Having It Both Ways", in Kenneth Oye, Robert Lieber and Donald Rothchild (eds), *Eagle Resurgent? The Reagan Era in American Foreign Policy* (Boston, Mass: Little, Brown, 1986).

——, "Peace and Strength: American Public Opinion on National Security", in Gregory Flynn and Hans Rattinger (eds), *The Public and Atlantic Defense* (Totowa, N.J.: Rowman and Allanheld, 1985).

Shapiro, Robert Y., and Benjamin I. Page, "Foreign Policy and the Rational Public", *Journal of Conflict Resolution*, 32/2 (June 1988) pp. 211–67.

Wittkopf, Eugene, "Élites and Masses: Another Look at Attitudes Towards America's World Role", *International Studies Quarterly*, 31/2 (June 1987) pp. 131–60.

——, "On the Foreign Policy Beliefs of the American People", *International Studies Quarterly*, 30/4 (December 1986) pp. 425–46.

Index